This book is to be

WOMEN AND INDUSTRIALIZATION

Feminist Perspectives

Series Editor: Michelle Stanworth

Published

Forthcoming

Women and Industrialization

GENDER AT WORK IN NINETEENTH-CENTURY ENGLAND

Judy Lown

Polity Press

First published 1990 by Polity Press in association with Basil Blackwell

Editorial office:
Polity Press, 65 Bridge Street, Cambridge
CB2 1UR, UK

Marketing and production:
Basil Blackwell Ltd
108 Cowley Road, Oxford OX4 1JF, UK

ISBN 0 7456 0202 9

British Library Cataloguing in Publication Data
A CIP catalogue record for this book is available from the British Library.

Typeset in 10½ on 12pt. Times
by Photo·graphics, Honiton, Devon.
Printed in Great Britain by T. J. Press, Padstow

*For my mother and father, Joan and William
Norman, and my daughter, Kate Lown*

The writing of history is impossible, and so is an action based on true knowledge. We only know what we believe about ourselves, about others, and about our mutual destiny.

Nicola Chiaramonte, The Paradox of History

CONTENTS

LIST OF PLATES

ACKNOWLEDGEMENTS

This book grew out of a long-standing involvement in the Women's Liberation Movement and feminist networks of historians and sociologists. I learned many things from many women over the years and am grateful to them all.

I would like to thank Leonore Davidoff for first encouraging me to undertake this project and for her continuous support and inspiration throughout the period of research. I am also indebted to many other feminist scholars in Britain, France and the United States for helpful insights and discussions. Earlier on, members of the London Feminist History Group and *History Workshop Journal*, and participants of the Sexual Divisions group of the British Sociological Association, the Patriarchy Study Group and the Conference for Women Postgraduates Doing Feminist Research, provided invaluable support. In addition, members of the Sociology Department at the University of Essex provided important feedback and I would especially like to thank members of my research committee, Mary McIntosh and Paul Thompson, and my examining committee, Margaret Stacey and Gordon Marshall, for their comments. Cynthia Enloe and Sylvia Mann also gave enormous support. I am grateful to them and to Catherine Hall, Ludmilla Jordanova and Jane Lewis for reading various early drafts. I would never have completed the research, either, without consistent help from Linda George, Brenda Corti, Carole Allington and Mary Girling in the Sociology Department office at the University of Essex. I also owe thanks for the time and trouble taken by archive and library staff at the Essex Record Office, Halstead Public Library, Colchester Public Library, the Fawcett Library and the University of Essex Library, especially Nancy Briggs, Janet Smith, Jane Brooks, Terry Tostevin and Austin Baines. Members of the Halstead and District Local History Society were extremely generous with their time and taught me a lot about the history of the locality. Special thanks to Albert Cross, Carole Bagshaw and Percy Bamberger and to Gus Wicker, Ivy and May Mead and Fred Brown, former Halstead mill workers, who spent hours talking to me about their experiences of mill life and explaining many of the processes involved in the production of silk. Other huge sources of inspiration and enthusiasm have been provided by the many students with whom I have worked over the years at Grey Friars Adult Education Centre in Colchester, the University of Essex, Hillcroft College, the Open University and the ILEA Adult Education Training Unit.

For help in getting me through the last few years of work, I am particularly grateful to Pam Cox for typing various drafts of the book, to Eve Hostettler and Katherine Clarricoates for reading them and giving encouragement, to Gwen Andrews and Tricia Smoothy for additional typing, to Eileen Aird for constant support and invaluable help with editing, to Kate Lown for endless patience and interest, and last, but by no means least, to Michelle Stanworth for being such a sympathetic and painstaking editor.

Judy Lown

Plates 1, 11, 20 and 22 are reproduced by courtesy of the Essex Record Office. Thanks are due to Courtauld PLC for permission to reproduce plates 3, 4, 6, 7, 8, 9, 10, 13, 17, 18, 19 and 21. Plates 5 and 16 appear by courtesy of Carol Adams and plate 26 is reproduced by permission of the Mansell Collection.

INTRODUCTION

> Oh did we but all know our proper stations and could but be
> content with acting properly in them, what a world of pain it
> would save us.
>
> Ruth Courtauld, *The Courtauld Family Letters, 1782–1900*

At the beginning of the nineteenth century when Ruth
Courtauld expressed her confusion about where she belonged
and how she should behave, women's place was becoming one
of the most hotly debated controversies of the day. Married
to a silkthrowster who had failed in the business, in 1819 Ruth
Courtauld watched anxiously as her oldest son, Samuel,
attempted the same enterprise. Women who were a generation
older than she had been craftsworkers in their own right.
Although she was a source of money and advice, Ruth could
find no clear part to play in her son's establishment. The
workers in his first mill were girls and young women from the
workhouses of Essex. His sisters were brought in to supervise
them. Samuel managed the business. Her plea was a response
to the shifting positions of women in the economy and the
increasingly uncertain social expectations surrounding such
shifts.

These uncertainties found expression in an increasing
preoccupation with what became popularly known as the
'Woman Question'. At the heart of the 'Woman Question'
was the place of women in relation to men in a society
undergoing rapid economic transformation which undermined
traditional expectations and definitions. Women had worked

for centuries but now their employment was becoming a major contested issue. The key question was, should women do paid work? If so, which women and what types of work? If not, what should they do? Different people asked such questions in different ways and came up with different answers, producing a range of consequences for both women and men.

Exploring the forms and outcomes of these contests is not easy. This book concentrates mainly on one particular case study. It looks at the early development of the silk industry in England and the establishment of one mechanized mill in Halstead by Samuel Courtauld in the nineteenth century. This is not to claim any typicality but to enable an analysis of a sphere of activity in which both women and men have played a significant part. Chapter 1 examines the organization of the trade and the sexual division of labour in three main periods of the industry's history: the fourteenth century, when silk production took the form of a precapitalist urban trade within a predominantly peasant economy; the eighteenth century, which saw the burgeoning of a 'proto-industrial'[1] form of capitalistic production combined with a domestic putting-out system; and the nineteenth century, when silk was predominantly produced in mechanized factories. Although silk manufacture was among the last of the textile trades to undergo mechanization it shared with other branches an early experience of capitalization. The processes involved in capitalization and subsequent industrialization, together with the consequences of both, are of crucial importance. Inter-connections between economic and familial relationships, traced in the earlier periods, require close examination in circumstances where workplace and household became physically separated. Chapters 2 and 3 attempt to cut across the conceptual divide between 'work' and 'family' by the examination of intersecting historical records. One set relates to employment patterns and practices within the Halstead mill (chapter 2) while the other sheds light on the household structure and living arrangements of millworkers (chapter 3). Combining these sources allows a reconstruction of the links between workplace and household.

This reconstruction distinguishes between 'households' as forms of living arrangement and 'families' as particular constellations of ideals and attitudes.[2] 'Household' and 'family' were not coterminous structurally and ideologically in past times as they are assumed to be in present day industrial society. Both had, and continue to have, changing and fluid boundaries. Familial relations in the past were not restricted to kin. The head of the household production unit in the centuries preceding industrialization was not the biological father of all over whom he had authority. Young apprentices, stepchildren, lodgers and servants of both sexes, as well as the wife and immediate offspring, could come under the familial authority of the male father/master.[3] The relationship between the male head and the rest of the household was both economic *and* familial. All those who came under the authority of the paterfamilias were in a relationship of dependency to him. This relationship was a separate and distinctive category deriving from a traditional form of authority.

Power hierarchies based on this form of authority required strategies for their maintenance on the part of those benefiting from them. One such strategy present in both precapitalist and industrial capitalist contexts is that of paternalism. Originally associated with a social hierarchy shaped out of relationships to the land,[4] paternalistic dominance is based on mutual rights and duties connected to unequal relationships of authority, property and social rank. In the nineteenth century it emerged as a major means among many 'captains of industry' of rationalizing the social order.[5] Paternalism relies heavily on an appeal to personal ties of dependency interpreted in familial terms.[6] For industrialists it acted as a means of reconstituting traditional authority relations, hitherto located in the household/workshop, within the factory and its environment.

Familial relationships served not just as a system of accommodation into the factory system[7] but as a central organizing principle of workplace relations. They enabled traditional authority to be carried over into market relationships and provided a means of legitimizing the emerging economic and social arrangements.[8] A distinctive feature of Courtauld's paternalism was not only its appeal to ties of dependency, based on the special combination of industrial property holding and rural cultural bonds, but also its strong association with the new domestic ideology connected with the 'separation of spheres'.[9] The ways in which this complex web of ideals and motives manifested itself in the Courtauld mill in Halstead and in the locality as a whole are explored in chapters 4 and 5.

The predominance of women and children in the early factories was highlighted by government investigations in the 1830s. These tapped into and reinforced a range of male anxieties which were channelled into increasing attempts to regulate women's employment by 'protective' legislation. Courtauld was always opposed to such legislation since he depended upon female labour and regarded it as *his* duty, not that of the state, to protect his workforce. Throughout the nineteenth century, women's participation in various trades and industries fluctuated according to the deskilling, diluting and excluding strategies followed by both employers and male workers. Debates concerning 'protective' legislation continued with varying results in parliament. The only areas of employment to be actively promoted for women became those considered compatible with the 'domestic ideal' which emphasized women's 'natural' caring and nurturing capacities. The numbers of women in teaching, nursing and clerical work increased. Domestic service also expanded as a female occupation since it involved activities 'connected with other existences which they embellish, facilitate and serve'.[10] All these developments took place in the midst of a moral panic about 'surplus women'.[11] Chapter 6 traces some of the changes in women's employment throughout the period of expansion of Courtauld's mill in the nineteenth century and examines some of the major responses among different groups of women and men to such changes.

As with most historical inquiries, the issues explored in these pages were stimulated partly by modern concerns with their own theoretical, practical and political implications. The present position of women in the labour market has been well documented as one of segregation into predominantly secondary, low paid and low status occupations,[12] with racism acting to direct black women into the poorest jobs of all.[13] This is accompanied by an ideological emphasis on women's domesticity and its practical translation into many women's lives. In seeking the sources and remedies of this situation, both historical and contemporary research has been hindered by the inadequacy of concepts and language needed to reconstruct relationships obscured by the ideology of 'separate spheres'. At a theoretical level, this has led some writers into a search for determining factors either in the labour market or in 'the family'.[14] Other approaches are developing a new conceptual framework out of the need for a 'double vision' which allows us to 'see not two spheres of social reality (home and work, private and public), but two (or three) sets of social relations',[15] or 'two worlds in one'.[16] By using a single lens through which to view the 'public' and the 'private' realms a whole web of intersecting connections shaped by capitalist and patriarchal relations is revealed.

The precise nature of the relationship between capitalism and patriarchy is as contested an issue as women's employment.[17] The conclusion of this book elaborates further the analytic and explanatory framework used throughout to elucidate the links between capitalist and patriarchal relations in shaping the changes in women's employment patterns in the nineteenth century. Power relations between women and men are given the same theoretical importance as power relations between social groups occupying different positions in the economic hierarchy. The form taken by these power relations changes in different historical contexts. Patriarchy, as an institutionalized system of male dominance, is not a transhistorical concept,[18] but one which enables us to examine these different forms.[19] In such an approach, gender and class emerge not as two separate systems but as a complex matrix of shifting definitions, fluid alliances and continuously contested boundaries.

Not only were the identities and experiences of women and men growing up in the nineteenth century shaped by the language of class formation but the very formation of those classes was itself a highly gendered process.[20] Far from being fixed and rigid categories, gender and class were simultaneously constructed and reconstructed, negotiated and renegotiated both within and across generations, stages in the life cycle and geographical location.

NOTES

1 See, for example, H. Medick, 'The proto-industrial family economy', *Social History*, October, 1976; and F. Mendels, 'Proto-industrialisation: the first phase of the process of industrialisation', *Journal of Economic History*, xxxii, 1972.

2 See P. Laslett and R. Wall (eds), *Household and Family in Past Time*, Cambridge University Press, 1972; R. Rapp et al., 'Examining family history', *Feminist Studies* 5 (1), 1979; M. S. Rosaldo, 'The use and abuse of anthropology: reflections on feminism and cross-cultural understanding', *Signs*, 5 (3), 1980; M. Chaytor, 'Household and kinship: Ryton in the late sixteenth and early seventeenth centuries', *History Workshop Journal*, no. 10, 1980; B. Thorn and M. Yalom (eds), *Rethinking the Family: Some Feminist Questions*, Longman, 1982.

3 J. L. Flandrin, *Families in Former Times: Kinship, Household and Sexuality*, Cambridge University Press, 1979; M. Chaytor and J. Lewis, Introduction to A. Clarke, *Working Life of Women in the Seventeenth Century*, Routledge and Kegan Paul, 1982; A. Kussmaul, *Servants in Husbandry in Early Modern England*, Cambridge University Press, 1978.

4 See D. Roberts, *Paternalism in Early Victorian England*, Croom Helm, 1979, Introduction.

5 Roberts, *Paternalism*, and P. Joyce, *Work, Society and Politics: The Culture of the Factory in Late Victorian England*, Harvester Press, 1980. For a range of articles exploring the role of paternalism, past and present, in a variety of countries, see *Le Mouvement Sociale*, 'Paternalisme d'hier et aujourd'hui', 144, July–September, 1988.

6 As Roberts puts it, 'to be a paternalist was to act towards dependents as a father does to his wife, his children and his servants', *Paternalism*, p. 8.

7 See T. Hareven, *Family Time and Industrial Time*, Cambridge University Press, 1982.

8 In this respect, paternalism is the *outcome* of the stratification system rather than the source of it, see H. Newby, 'The deferential dialectic', *Comparative Studies in Sociology and History*, 17 (2), April 1975.

9 The processes shaping the 'separation of spheres' are documented very fully in L. Davidoff and C. Hall, *Family Fortunes: Men and Women of the English Middle Class 1780–1850*, Hutchinson, 1987.

10 W. R. Greg, 'Why are women redundant?', *National Review*, 14, 1862, pp. 434–60.

11 The 1851 Census gives figures of 1,767,194 spinsters and 795,194 widows. Greg's solution (ibid.) was the mass emigration of such women to find husbands in the 'New World'.

12 See, for example, F. Hunt (ed.), *Women and Paid Work*, Macmillan, 1987; J. Jenson et al., *Feminization of the Labour Force*, Polity Press, 1988; Veronica Beechey, *Unequal Work*, Verso, 1987.

13 See, for example, A. Wilson, *Finding a Voice: Asian Women in Britain*, Virago, 1979; B. Bryan et al., *The Heart of the Race: Black Women's Lives in Britain*, Virago, 1985; A. Phizacklea, *One Way Ticket: Migration and Female Labour*, Routledge and Kegan Paul, 1983.

14 For a summary of these see S. Walby, *Patriarchy at Work: Patriarchal and Capitalist Relations in Employment*, Polity Press, 1987, chapter 4, 'Theories of Women and Paid Work', p. 70.

15 Joan Kelly, 'The doubled vision of feminist theory: a postscript to the "Women and Power" Conference', *Feminist Studies*, 5 (1), Spring 1979, pp. 221–2.

16 E. Pleck in 'Two worlds in one: work and family', *Journal of Social History*, 10 (2), Winter 1976.

17 See, for example, L. Sargent (ed.), *The Unhappy Marriage of Marxism and Feminism: A Debate on Class and Patriarchy*, Pluto Press, 1981. For an overview of the various perspectives see Walby, *Patriarchy at Work*, especially chapter 2, 'Theories of gender inequality: a critique', p. 5, and chapter 3, 'Towards a new theory of patriarchy', p. 50.

18 For an overview of the debate surrounding this interpretation of the concept see Beechey, 'On patriarchy' in *Unequal Work*; see also S. Friedman, 'The Marxist paradigm; radical feminist theorists compared', BSA Conference paper, 1982.

19 See K. Millett, *Sexual Politics*, Abacus, 1970; G. Lerner, *The Creation of Patriarchy*, Oxford University Press, 1986, pp. 238–9.

20 One of the difficulties involved in the process of deconstructing existing theory and of constructing new paradigms is the lack of appropriate language. This problem occurs throughout this study in relation to traditional concepts of stratification. For clarity, I have tended to use the terms 'middle class' and 'working class' in relation to the nineteenth century but in the context of data and concepts which suggest these terms are not unproblematic.

1

THE THREAD OF
PATRIARCHY

Victorian industrialists dependent upon female labour were
inevitably caught up in the 'Woman Question'. Most were
compelled to state their views on the issue. The Courtauld
firm, now a large multi-national concern and one of the ten
biggest corporations in the UK, began as a small family
business in the north-east corner of Essex at the beginning of
the nineteenth century. One of the Courtauld men expressed
a view in 1846 symbolizing the dilemma running through the
'Woman Question' for men in his position. Commenting upon
female employment in the family's mills George Courtauld II
wrote that:

> among the girls and young women the various evils of
> ignorance are not only much aggravated by their being
> brought together in large numbers and to some extent
> compelled to associate – but the nature of their employment
> takes from them even the poor preparation they might have
> received at their *homes* for the duties of wives and mothers.[1]

Having deliberately recruited cheap female labour in the
early years, Courtauld and his brother Samuel were by mid-
century increasingly trying to reconcile their dependency on
female labour with their espousal of the 'domestic ideal'. They
did this primarily by adopting a pervasive paternalism which
recreated 'the family' in the mill and served to reinforce the
division of labour upon which the industry was constructed.

In doing so they reformulated the patriarchal relationships which represented the central organizing principle in the silk trade throughout its history.

'MISTERY AND CRAFT': THE EARLY SILK INDUSTRY IN ENGLAND

In the fourteenth century, English silk production was mainly confined to narrow ribbon weaving.[2] It was a highly organized craft operated almost entirely by female hands. Based predominantly in London, it occupied more than a thousand women. It is a measure of the degree of organization among these women that in 1368 they presented a petition to the mayor proclaiming that

> many a worshipful woman within the said committee have lyved full honourably, and therewith many good households kept, and many gentilwymmen and other in grete noumbre like as nowe be mou than a thousand, have be drawen under theym in learning the same craftes and occupation.[3]

They were successful in their plea for government protection but lacked the same kind of craft status accorded to men at that time. An Act in 1363 restricted men to one trade but allowed women, 'that is to say, Brewers, Bakers, Carders and Spinners, and Workers as well of wool, as of Linen Cloth, and of Silk, Brawdesters, and Breakers of Wool, and all others that do use and work all handy works'[4] to pursue their work freely in as many trades as they chose. Most women in medieval London were engaged in work of a casual or irregular nature, connected to the production of textiles, food and drink.[5] They mainly assisted in a man's trade as wife, daughter or maidservant and contributed additional services to the household economy via their numerous casual activities. The silkwomen, although occupied in a protected and prestigious trade serving a luxury market mostly consisting of the aristocracy, were no exception. Their status and rights were shaped, as were those of all women, by the guild system and the rules of coverture governing this system. The guilds enforced strict rules of apprenticeship forbidding the use of female labour in many crafts unless it was the labour of wives and daughters.[6] Female kin were accorded only a peripheral status and could never train to become a master in the trade. The rules of coverture subjected women legally and socially completely to their husbands.[7] There were no guilds of women – not even among the silk workers who took apprentices and registered their indentures in the usual way.

Female silk workers could not reach the same craft status as men. Apprenticeship for them was part and parcel of the period of maintenance and general training before marriage expected of all girls.[8] Conversely apprenticeship for boys meant a systematic technical training and entrance into a network of fraternal bonds bolstering their journey towards master status.[9] Through the male hegemony of the guilds men's activities were increasingly regulated and legitimated. Most women workers were involved in throwing[10] and weaving alongside a multitude of other activities. Of those occupied in trading, the majority were married, mostly to mercers (silk merchants), and were controlled in their dealings by the rules of coverture. The few operating independently did so by virtue of a loophole in the laws governing urban trading allowing women to act as 'femmes soles' in order to protect their husbands.[11] Under this system marriage and kin ties intertwined with economic activity to produce a structure in which the roles of father and master were inseparable. 'The family' in this context meant not those related by blood ties but all who lived and worked in one household. The father/master was at the head of this household with a hierarchy of women and boys and girls beneath him.[12] It was this structure – based on the supremacy of the male and the exploitation of women and children – which laid the foundations for future hierarchical divisions in the industry.

THE DOMESTIC ECONOMY OF THE SPITALFIELDS SILK WORKERS

By the beginning of the eighteenth century the British silk industry had become a flourishing trade. So large was the market that in 1728 Dean Swift wrote:

> Now to another scene give place;
> Enter the folk with silks and lace;
> 'Observe this pattern; there's a stuff;
> I can have customers enough'.[13]

Although it never assumed the same significance as the woollen industry, silk stood at the forefront of British manufacture with estimates placing it as the fifth most profitable trade in the late eighteenth century.[14] Despite its supremacy in the market, however, the silk industry by this time was wracked by widespread hardship and resentment among its workers. These changes mainly resulted from early restructuring along capitalistic lines. Commercial production combined with a domestic putting-out system (the system often referred to as 'proto-industrialism' whereby work organized for the market was carried out in the homes of the workers) led to a sharply defined hierarchy of specialized functions. This accentuated the pre-existing age and gender divisions so that women were demarcated into a readily identifiable category of cheap labour.

Broadloom weaving superseded the narrow variety in the sixteenth and seventeenth centuries mainly because of the arrival of Huguenot refugees from the Netherlands bringing their broad looms and skills with them.[15] A main area in which the refugees began to establish their silk producing communities was Spitalfields in London's East End. As early as 1621, thirty-six years after the Sack of Antwerp, it is estimated that about twelve Flemish throwsters and hundreds of Flemish weavers were settled in the East End.[16] An estimate of the numbers arriving in the two years after the repeal of the Edict of Nantes in 1685 put the total figure at more than 100,000.[17] Money from Parliament and private subsidies helped to establish the Huguenot communities. By the end of the seventeenth century many houses had been built with specially large windows on the first floor, where the looms were kept, for the accommodation of the Spitalfields silk workers. Looms were used mainly for hand production of velvets, lustrings, brocades, damasks and satins.

At the top of the hierarchy now emerging were silk importers or merchants, followed by silkmen who brought the raw silk from the importers, had it thrown and passed it on to the master weavers. There were some brokers and factors acting as go-betweens between the silkmen and the master weavers. Before the silk reached the master weavers it frequently underwent a separate dyeing process. All the functions described so far were fulfilled by men. When the master weavers finally bought the silk they put it out to weavers including both journeymen and journeywomen. There were far more journeymen than women: the majority of women and children were concentrated in the low status and low paid throwing and preparatory branches. The finished piece was sold to male mercers.

Sex ratios were first officially documented in 1765 when a House of Commons Committee reported, in response to a series of petitions concerning the silk trade, 'that in the Throwsters Trade there are a great many children employed at seven years old, and that in 1,500 [Mr John Sharrard, a Silk Thrower], thinks the proportion is 1,400 women and children, and 100 men'.[18]

The major features of the industry at this time, therefore, were: extensive use of low paid female and child labour and the existence of two main groups of men – those engaged in marketing functions and those occupied at weaving. Most women and children worked in their own homes using simple wooden throwing equipment. The hands engaged in this process were the lowest paid in a trade that became increasingly subject to poor wages at all levels of production.

Apart from throwing, women and children also wound the silk yarn on to bobbins and quills in preparation for the weaver. This work, similarly carried out in the home, was also extremely low paid. Mostly, this task was undertaken by the wives and daughters of weavers or by a woman or child employed in the weaver's home. Alternatively, weavers could obtain wound silk from many of the London workhouses which, after 1732, put inhabitants to work at winding.

The difference between male and female weavers was that women predominantly undertook plain or narrow silk weaving whilst men produced the more 'fancy' work such as brocades, velvets and satins. 'Fancy' work was paid at approximately twice the rate of plain work and was usually carried out on the more elaborate Jacquard loom. Contemporaries considered ribbon weaving to be 'a pretty light trade and fit for lads of a slender make, or even girls'.[19]

So, a household might reflect a division of labour based firmly upon a hierarchy with the husband/father heading the domestic economy as a weaver, the wife/mother engaging in various preparatory processes and the male and female children's labour being distributed among age- and gender-specific subsidiary activities. A contemporary observer described a Spitalfields household as follows:

> The father, assisted by one of his sons, was occupied with a [Jacquard] machine . . ., punching card slips from figures which another son, a fine intelligent lad about thirteen years of age, was 'reading on'. Two other lads, somewhat older, were in another apartment, casting, drawing, punching and attaching to cords the leaden plummets or lingos, which form part of the harness for a Jacquard loom. The mother was engaged in warping silk with a [warping] machine . . . One of the daughters was similarly employed at another machine, and three other girls were in separate looms . . .[20]

The authority structure would not differ if some of the male weaver's assistants were not related to him by blood. 'The family' in this patriarchal network included non-kin who were economically part of the household. The male head was 'father' to all those in the household including servants. His position as patriarchal head was both familial and economic.

Increasing specialization and differentiation was accompanied by an escalation of political battles among the various participants in the silk industry. In 1769 an injunction against female labour in weaving processes was pressed by London journeymen weavers. It urged that:

> No woman or girl to be employed in making any kind of work except such works as are herein fixed and settled at $5\frac{1}{2}$d per ell or $5\frac{1}{2}$d per yard or under for the making and those not to exceed half an ell in width . . . And no woman or girl is to be employed in making any sort of handkerchief

of above the usual or settled price of 4s.6d per dozen for
the making thereof . . .[21]

This attempt to restrict women's activities was integral to
the struggle being fought between the two major groups of
men involved in the silk industry. Journeymen weavers were
desperately fighting to retain their patriarchal status in
conditions which were increasingly driving a wedge between
them and the master weavers who put out the work. Earlier
on, masters and journeymen were united in their guild
organizations while their wives and daughters were assigned a
peripheral and subordinate position.

Journeymen worked for the masters in the confidence that
they would become masters themselves. This likelihood receded
with the increasing commercialization of the silk trade in the
eighteenth century. Silk workers struggled for the survival of
their households but, in so doing, were trapped into individual
competition for wages. Dealers and merchants were then at a
considerable advantage in being able to pay low prices. Fewer
journeymen became masters, and masters became more
prosperous as they paid wages which were among the lowest
of the London trades. In struggling to ensure the familial and
economic authority of their patriarchal position, male silk
workers increasingly expressed hostility towards women weavers. In the 1760s there were outbreaks of rioting among
Spitalfields weavers fighting to raise the level of wages and
protect their livelihoods. The Spitalfields Acts, which resulted,
sought to improve conditions concerning the fixing of prices,
terms of apprenticeship and the limiting of numbers within
silk weaving.[22] These Acts expressly protected only male
weavers until a labour shortage due to the Napoleonic Wars
led to the inclusion of women weavers in 1812.

Meanwhile, women and children engaged in throwing and
preparatory processes, the most subordinate and lowest paid
positions in the trade, were not seen as a threat. It was only
women *weavers* who posed a direct threat to the patriarchal
power of male silk workers. Weavers had to buy or hire looms
and pay for winding and warping unless the labour of wife
and/or children was used in which case one payment from the
master had to cover all the labour which contributed to the

production of the piece. Inherent in this system was the payment of wages to the journeyman weaver – who was also head of the household – who then procured subsidiary labour or acquired the free services of his wife and children.

As this system developed women were increasingly seen as a threat to the livelihoods of male weavers. Various societies and organizations replaced the former guilds and companies providing sources of mutual aid and combination in opposition to the masters. These organizations excluded women and strengthened the identity of male weavers as specialized craftsmen needing to control the size and membership of their craft.

During this period a process was under way whereby the patriarchal structure of the former urban trading households and the fraternalism of the guilds were transferred to the domestically based silk producing households and societies of the commercially organized trade of eighteenth century Spitalfields. Kinship provided the basis for such developments to take place. Wives and daughters continued in their subsidiary role of providing free services to their husbands and fathers but in the context of the wage nexus and market conditions of an increasingly commercial society. The political battles between journeymen and masters restricted women to the low paid, low status activities of winding, warping and throwing.

THE DECLINE OF THE SPITALFIELDS SILK TRADE

Men's interests in the guild system had united in the overall promotion of their trade, even to the extent of ratifying the widespread use of female kin so long as they were excluded from the jural rights of their husbands and fathers. The descendants of these men became increasingly divided in the seventeenth and eighteenth centuries. Those at the top got wealthier while those beneath them were increasingly vulnerable to the fluctuations of boom and slump trading. The tendency toward greater capitalization during the eighteenth century widened the gap between the top and bottom ends of the pyramid. In particular, a whole group predominantly of

women – the macklers, or small-scale dealers who sold weavers'
goods to shopkeepers (the last surviving group to bear any
resemblance at all to the medieval silkwomen of London) –
were fast disappearing by the last quarter of the eighteenth
century.[23] Two extremes now existed. One consisted of wealthy
merchants far removed from the actual weaving and throwing
of the silk who occupied large houses in Spital Square and
other wealthy neighbourhoods. The other was made up of
thousands of hands labouring at manufacturing. The merchants
were entirely composed of men. The vast majority of those at
the bottom end of the pyramid were women.

Apart from considerable fluctuations in wages,[24] conditions
became notoriously hazardous to the health and welfare of
those working in 'small, crowded rooms in horribly insanitary
dwellings, and the air was carefully excluded by paper pasted
over the cracks of the windows, to prevent the silk from losing
weight and so making the weaver liable to deductions from
his earnings'.[25] Conditions worsened in the years leading up
to and following the repeal of the Spitalfields Acts in the
1820s. A description by Knight in his book of London, written
in 1842, starts off:

> In my visits to the districts inhabited by the weavers with
> an endeavour to view the processes of the manufacture, our
> enquiries were too often met by the sad reply – 'I have no
> work at present', but at one house we mounted a dark
> staircase to the upper floor occupied by an elderly weaver
> and his wife. The room formed the entire upper storey and
> was approached, not by a door, but by a trap in the floor
> opening a communication with the stairs beneath.[26]

He goes on to provide a detailed picture of the inside of this
weaver's dwelling:

> At each end of the room, front and back, were windows of
> that peculiar form so characteristic of the district, which are
> made very wide in order to admit light to all parts of the
> loom adjacent to them. At each window was a loom, the
> husband being at work at one, and the wife at the other.
> Near the looms were two quill wheels used for winding the
> weft onshoot on to the quills for filling the shuttles. In the

middle of the room was a stump bedstead, covered with its patchwork quilt, and near it – some on the floor, some on shelves and some hanging onto the walls of the room – were various miscellaneous articles of domestic furniture, for the room served as a parlour, kitchen, bedroom, workshop and all. A few pictures, a few plants, and two or three singing birds, formed the poetical furniture of the room. The man was weaving a piece of black satin, and the woman a piece of blue. In reply to enquiries on the subject, we learned that they were to be paid for their labour at the rate of sixpence and fourpence halfpenny per yard respectively. This at close work would yield about 7 or 8 shillings per week each.[27]

Where women wove alongside men they frequently received lower wages for the same work. The issue of cheap labour intensified acrimony towards women workers in the early decades of the nineteenth century. Addressing himself specifically to the conditions in Spitalfields in the 1820s, Francis Place commented that:

It is the ease with which women and children can be set to work, that keeps these weavers in poverty and rags and filth and ignorance. There are certain employments which to a small extent married women might follow, but in these cases in which the woman and her children can generally find employment in her husband's business, the very worst consequences must follow.[28]

Other contemporary commentators, too, were quick to link the lowering of male wage rates and the increasing hardship of the Spitalfields population to the employment of women and children in the trade.[29] Their views represent a reversal of the attitude towards kin labour prevalent in earlier centuries. What was advantageous to tradesmen when the guild system and domestic organization ensured male control of female labour was now becoming a threat. In the social and economic conditions of early industrialism male workers felt increasingly undermined by the competition of female wage labour.

THE SPREAD OF MECHANIZATION

Early capitalization of the textile industry accelerated intense wage competition underpinned by the spread of the factory system. It was no neutral march of technology, however, that determined the labour hierarchy of industrial capitalism. The continuation of patriarchal interests, which had dominated the process of economic survival for centuries, shaped the occupational structure.

The first stages of silk manufacture organized on a factory basis were throwing, winding and warping – activities in which women and children predominated and which were already imbued with subordinate status in the period of domestically organized production. By the end of the eighteenth century enough throwing machinery was installed in some mills to occupy more than a hundred hands.[30] Initially, millworkers were vastly outnumbered by workers still operating hand-throwing equipment in their homes. By the early decades of the nineteenth century throwing mills appeared more rapidly outside London, beginning significantly to replace hand production.

The first experiment in power-driven textile machinery took place in Thomas Lombe's silk mill near Derby in the 1720s.[31] The use of such machinery enabled 200 or 300 bobbins to be wound at once, replacing the much slower methods used in the home.[32] Once again, women and children were mainly engaged to work the machinery. Low wages and definitions of skill defined these tasks just as in hand production. When other silk manufacturers followed Lombe's example they often looked to the agricultural areas in places like Essex with its close proximity to the London market. Contemporary histories of Essex refer to three silk throwing mills in Little Hallingbury in the first half of the eighteenth century. A mill at Sewardstone, in Waltham Abbey, was established at about the same time.[34]

Important centres of silk production developed in large urban locations such as Coventry and Macclesfield.[35] Wherever silk mills appeared, especially in rural areas, women and children predominated in the workforce. By the beginning of the nineteenth century, weaving, as well as throwing, appeared in a number of towns in Essex from Stratford and East Ham in the south to Saffron Walden, Halstead, Coggeshall, Bocking and Braintree in the north.[36] In handloom production men formed the majority of weavers, but with the introduction of power-driven looms and factory organization manufacturers recruited women. Handloom silk weaving survived alongside factory methods for most of the nineteenth century with men working the handlooms. The association of women with cheap labour fostered deliberate policies of female recruitment among silk manufacturers.

The influx of women into mills created moral panic among many members of the local aristocracy. On the closure of the Saffron Walden mill in 1834, Lord Braybrooke commented that

> Some years ago a manufactory for Norwich crape was introduced into the parish, which employed many hands, principally young females, but the high wages obtained led to idle and extravagant habits, so that the discontinuance of the work cannot be a matter of regret.[37]

Wages in Essex silk mills were, contrary to Braybrooke's claim, extremely low. Lying beyond the control of the Spitalfields Acts of the early decades of the century, wages were frequently set at two-thirds of the Spitalfields rate and continued at this level after the repeal of the legislation in the 1820s. Braybrooke reacted to the fact that women in the mills were earning more than it was possible for them to earn otherwise in an area of high unemployment and severe poverty. He joined a chorus of voices expressing a common fear that women coming together visibly into paid employment in the public sphere would gain access to an independence and control that they had hitherto been denied.

No doubt observers like Braybrooke welcomed the difficulties experienced by many English silk manufacturers faced by increasing free trade legislation. The flooding of the market with predominantly French goods accompanying such legislation led to the demise of many English silk firms. The final blow came in 1860 with the Cobden Treaty. Until 1860 Essex manufacturers fared better than their counterparts in the North of England and Midlands. In 1836 106 power looms were

TABLE 1 Female occupations in England and Wales in 1851

Occupations	Total females
Outdoor agricultural labourers and indoor farm servants	199,150
Domestic servants	905,165
Milliners, dressmakers, seamstresses and shirt-makers	340,365
Washerwomen, manglers, laundry keepers and charwomen	200,796
Cotton factory workers	160,052
Woollen and worsted factory workers	77,135
Silk factory workers	29,190

Compiled from 1851 Census, G. B. Command Papers, Ages, Civil Condition etc., vol. I, 1852–3, and 1850 Returns on Factories, Board of Trade Accounts and Papers, 10, 1850, XLII.

reported to be operating in Essex.[38] Nationally and locally women outnumbered men in the workforce, the proportion being particularly pronounced in the Essex mills. By 1850, 272 silk mills were recorded in England, containing 6,092 power looms and employing a total of 29,190 women and 12,513 men.[39] In 1847 the total number engaged in silk mills in Essex was 2,227, constituting the fourth largest silk workforce in the country. Of this number, 1,818 were female and 409 male.[40]

The process of mechanization in the silk industry reflected the spread of industrialization in the textile trades in general, although silk was slower to mechanize and remained less mechanized than cotton and wool throughout the century. The proportion of hand to power looms in the silk industry remained high well into the third quarter of the nineteenth century.[41] This repeats the pattern of unevenness characterizing the spread of the factory system during this period.[42] This feature of occupational development makes the outcry against women's employment in factories particularly ironic. Of all the women and girls in paid employment at mid-century, a relatively small number were engaged in textile factories compared to those involved in farm work, domestic services, garment-making and other kinds of household-based activities (table 1).

The discrepancy between domestic service and factory work is particularly marked. It becomes even more marked when we include the 128,251 women and girls in the agricultural category who worked as indoor farm servants. The vast majority of women workers, engaged in either their own households or those of others, received far less negative attention than the minority within the factory system. Indeed, the former tended to attract the enthusiastic approval of contemporary observers like Greg.[43] Women in factories were caught in the ideological crossfire of those who purposefully sought cheap labour and those who were offended and frightened by the prospect of women working outside the home. Employers like the Courtaulds found ways of combining elements of both.

ESSEX AT THE TURN OF THE EIGHTEENTH CENTURY

Until the late eighteenth century Essex shared the prosperity which woollen cloth-making brought to East Anglia.[44] Arriving with Flemish refugees in the latter part of the sixteenth century, the 'New Draperies' acquired a distinctive status for inhabitants of the wool-producing areas of Essex, Suffolk and Norfolk.[45] The association with immigrant refugees was one similarity between the wool trade of the Eastern counties and the silk trade of London's East End. The two industries also shared a structure in which female labour predominated and was concentrated into the lowest levels of the hierarchy. Just as women and girls were marginalized by the male hegemony of the silk guilds so too was their position in the wool industry increasingly jeopardized by male fears concerning apprenticeship and earnings. The major difference was that women and girls had been long identified with the spinning and other preparatory processes in wool manufacture while men had been established as weavers. Insecurity in the seventeenth and eighteenth centuries strengthened and sharpened these divisions.

Apprenticeship to wool weaving became so tightly controlled that very few girls attained such positions by the end of the

PLATE 1 Contemporary print of Halstead, published in 1833, shortly after the arrival of the Courtauld silk mill. The portrayal emphasizes the agricultural character of the town; the mill, situated to the right of the picture, is not visible.

eighteenth century.[46] Even unofficial assistance by wives and daughters of male weavers came under much closer scrutiny. Gaps in earnings between male weavers and female spinners also became much wider. In 1796 Arthur Young observed during his travels in the region that

> By all the accounts I could gain of the weavers, I found that they earned on average about 9 shillings a week; woolcombers about 12 shillings; stout girls, 15 or 16 years old, 4d or 5d a day at spinning; and girls of 7 or 8, 1 shilling a week for rolling the weavers quills; all these prices are lower than the Sudbury ones. They further informed me that in summer they did whatever husbandry work they were able; being better paid for it, such as hoeing turnips and wheat, making hay and harvesting.[47]

The wages of men working on the land were higher than those of women engaged in a combination of 'husbandry work' and spinning wool.[48]

This widening gulf between 'men's work' and 'women's work' (and 'men's wages' and 'women's wages') taking place in the Essex countryside paralleled developments shaping the silk industry's diversification into mechanized production. Shifting economic arrangements accompanying the reorganization of agriculture and industry intensified class antagonisms among those whose livelihoods depended upon the land and manufacture. Central to these antagonisms were conflicts over gender relations. The new hierarchies emerging from the increasing gap between journeymen and masters in the textile trades posed a threat to the patriarchal basis of household organization.

This process encouraged a sharper distinction between different sections within the labouring class. In particular, a definable division was occurring between those regarding themselves as skilled artisans, with traditional apprenticeships governing access to such a status, and those working manually without serving an apprenticeship. Such a distinction was noted by William Dodd, who in 1847 identified eight classes in English society. His fifth class was 'The higher order of Mechanics known as "skilled labourers", (from their being obliged to pay large fees, and to serve an apprenticeship of seven years to the trade which they follow), shopkeepers, etc.'[49] This class was also characterized by accompanying familial ideals and expectations for Dodd adds that 'they are an industrious and intelligent class, and are sufficiently remunerated for their services to enable them to bring up their families in a respectable manner, and to lay by something for the comforts of old age'.[50]

As a contrast, the sixth class

> comprehends a great number of individuals who get their living by the 'sweat of their brow', but who are not required to serve seven years at their trade or calling. Manufacturing, agricultural, and many other kinds of labourers, come under this head. This class is a hard-working, ill-paid and ill-used set of human beings; frequently dying with every symptom of premature decay at from 35 to 50 years of age.[51]

The efforts of 'skilled labourers' throughout the period of industrialization to protect and maintain their privileged position worked systematically to the detriment of women workers. Fraternal organizations such as Friendly Societies and trade clubs flourishing during this period not only safeguarded the bargaining powers of their members, but assured the maintenance of male domination in household arrangements.[52]

The constellation of social and economic factors affecting agricultural and industrial production in Essex at the end of the eighteenth century encouraged the development of male-dominated elites. The decline of the woollen trade was accompanied by extensive 'improvements' in agriculture. Land was mostly arable, being used primarily to produce wheat, hops, vegetables, fruit, seeds, caraway, coriander and teazel. Enclosure was completed by 1700 and the following century witnessed the burgeoning of the 'substantial farmer'. Many former woollen clothiers were quick to see the main chance and transferred their assets to farming. They merged with the local aristocracy to form a ruling elite of capitalist landowners. With the withdrawal of farmers' wives from the business enterprise[53] economic power became more closely consolidated in the hands of the men of this stratum. At the same time, political and social power was similarly concentrated via the operation of predominantly male vestry meetings and clubs. Associations for protecting property and prosecuting horse thieves were established and run by male property owners. Meeting in public houses they established another set of links – this time between landowners and shopkeepers.

Meanwhile, the labouring households of the area were spiralling down into deeper poverty. The combined effects of the collapse of woollen manufacturing and the capitalization of agriculture brought a devastation to towns like Halstead which William Pitt, who was Prime Minister in the final decade of the eighteenth century, deplored. A biography of Pitt describes a visit he made at the time:

> Towards the end of 1795 Pitt went down to stay with a friend in Essex and, after talking one evening of the good fortune which an industrious and virtuous labourer could enjoy in Britain, was taken by his host to view the dwellings of the poor in the town of Halstead. The [Prime] Minister surveyed it in silent wonder, and declared he had no conception that any part of England could present such a spectacle of misery.[54]

As men, women and children among the poor competed for work, occupational and gender distinctions became more apparent. Agricultural employment, such as it was, mainly absorbed male labourers, and living-in farm service was diminishing, so farmwork became more clearly identified as male waged day labour. Since wool spinning was no longer required by the 1790s, vast numbers of women and girls became dependent on fragmented and casual occupations mainly associated with seasonal activities such as dibbling wheat, weeding, gleaning, cutting and sorting. The situation was so dire that the Marquis and Marchionness of Gosfield Hall introduced strawplaiting. Schools of industry were set up to teach girls how to plait straw for the hat- and bonnet-making trades of Luton and Dunstable. The activity spread to become a major cottage industry in the area until the late nineteenth century. Like spinning, plaiting could be done in the home and combined with other chores. For example, 'the mother could also rock the cradle with her foot, whilst using both hands at the plaiting'.[55] In contrast to some contemporary observers who extolled the virtues of roaming the streets, laughing and talking while plaiting straws,[56] a parliamentary report of the 1860s revealed that 'the head is bent forward each time a new straw is required, which recurs constantly . . . [and there is] . . . constant bending of the head and cramped position of the left arm, to say nothing of the injury done by the constant habit of holding dyed straws in the mouth'.[57]

Wages for strawplaiting varied according to the quantity produced but were not much higher than the rate at which spinning was paid shortly before its disappearance. According to Arthur Young,[58] though, girls earned more at plaiting than in the only other alternative form of employment, domestic service.

While poverty was experienced by men, women and children it was women and girls who bore the main burden and it was their labour which increasingly became marginalized and devalued. The Napoleonic Wars widened the gap between the status of men's and women's work by depleting the male labour force through enlistment and leading to wage increases for the remaining male agricultural workers. At the same time, new industries, such as foundries and ironmongeries, connected to changing agricultural technology, recruited boys and men not girls and women. The Wars also offered employment to former wool weavers in making army blankets – again, it was male, not female, hands who were engaged.

The results for women's lives were both material and ideological. Signs of economic hardship had long been present in the textile producing areas of East Anglia. Most inmates of parish workhouses, where so much spinning had been carried out during the heyday of the wool trade, were women and girls. More than half of the 120 workhouses started in Essex between 1720 and 1776 were in the wool producing towns of Braintree, Halstead, Colchester and Coggeshall.[59] With the accelerating decline of the cloth trade after the 1770s many workhouses had to close down. Poor relief rose steeply and was directed mostly towards women deprived of their former main means of livelihood. At the same time, the strengthening of customs surrounding notions of appropriate work for women, buttressed by the occupational strategies of many labouring men, served to identify women and girls with casual, intermittent and low status labour.

Another advantage favouring male workers in the cloth industry was the fact that many weavers had the vote, providing them with a platform for formal political alliances with men further up the social scale. Throughout the eighteenth century the wealthy elite in Essex saw no great cause for concern over the stability of the local social order. With a solid structure of paternalism, rooted in the 'natural' rights and obligations of relationships based on property, authority and social rank,[60] the wealthy had long relied on the loyalty and deference of their 'inferiors'. Expressions of unrest and discontent among both textile workers and agricultural labourers certainly occurred. But, in the cloth trade, opposition to machinery was short-lived and disputes over earnings soon settled, conflicts of both kinds mostly being resolved in the long-term interests of the male as opposed to female workers. Farmworkers, including women, organized riots against food prices in 1740, 1772 and 1795, but these were usually accompanied by the return of the proceeds of the sale of seized goods to the owners. Male farm labourers had no vote with which to bargain and lacked the organizational framework of male craftsworkers.

Religion also played a significant part in the changing context of economic and social relations in Essex during this period. A major heritage of the textile trade in the region was the prevalence of Nonconformist religions. Their chief centres were in Colchester, Bocking, Braintree, Halstead, Coggeshall, Thaxted and Saffron Waldon, and in satellite villages like Great Maplestead, Pebmarsh and Stebbing. Significantly, Nonconformity was also strong in non-textile towns like Chelmsford drawing support from farmers, agricultural workers, clothiers and textile workers. From 1750, Nonconformism declined in some of the former textile villages but chapels and membership continued to flourish in the towns. Ministers in the Nonconformist religions occupied a similar social standing to professional groups such as doctors, lawyers and surveyors, whose numbers were growing with the enhancement of urban trade accompanying the expansion of capitalist agricultural interests. They were not, however, integral to the local power elite as were members of the Anglican clergy. The system of tithe-gathering and glebe farming had enriched many clergymen who frequently invested their gains into modernizing their parsonages and living well. The alliance of political interests between the Church of England and the state did not extend to the Nonconformist religions. Members of the Nonconformist congregations were often in the forefront of dissent concerning political as well as religious matters.

THE ARRIVAL OF THE COURTAULDS IN ESSEX

It was into this region, characterized by the domination of merged industrial and agricultural interests over an impoverished and fragmented labouring population, that members of the Courtauld family came in the early nineteenth century. Coming from a tradition of Nonconformism themselves, their absorption into the local elite was by no means straightforward and unproblematic. Building the Courtauld empire involved complex negotiations and conflicts concerning gender and class relationships at all levels of the Victorian social order.

George Courtauld I, the descendant of a Huguenot family of silversmiths arriving in England during the purges of Calvinists from France in the late sixteenth century, first broke with family tradition by entering the silk industry. He also strayed from the orthodox Calvinistic Nonconformity of the Huguenot community by becoming a Unitarian and bringing his children up in this faith. Unitarianism was built on a rationalistic Christianity which predisposed its followers to radical political opinions and active reforming zeal.[61]

George Courtauld I was an apprentice silk throwster in Spitalfields in the 1770s and set up on his own account in 1782. Motivated by the failure of his enterprise and a strong sympathy for the revolutionary cause in North America, he sold his silk mills in 1785 and bought land in New York State. By the 1790s he was back in England with Ruth Minton, whom he had married in 1789, and their first two children, Louisa and Samuel III. Emulating London silk throwsters, George set up and managed a water-powered silk throwing mill for the London firm of Witts and Company in Pebmarsh, a few miles outside Halstead. Like all the other mills,

Courtauld's plant relied on the use of plentiful female labour made available by the demise of the woollen trade and the lack of other employment in the area. He deliberately sought to recruit hands from among the poorest sections of the female population, initially by employing young women and girls from the remaining workhouses. He continued to pursue this policy when he set up a silk throwing mill in Braintree in partnership with Joseph Wilson of Cheapside in 1809. With a customary sense of social mission he viewed the employment of impoverished girls as a worthy preparation for life, commenting that: 'my establishment of apprentices will prove a nursery of respectable young women fitted for any of the humble walks of life'.[62] However, the minimization of labour costs must also have been a primary consideration. Silk throwing, even when it was organized in mills, was extremely labour-intensive with costs accounting for up to half the total cost of production. George Courtauld kept these down by engaging female workhouse inmates who came with a £5 fee to bind them until they were twenty-one, whereupon they earned between 6 and 8 shillings per week. In addition, he expected them from the age of seventeen 'to attend to their own expenses and in a great measure support themselves by suitable agreements with them respecting the product of their employment'.[63]

Another strategy which Courtauld considered to be of immense importance was the adequate training and supervision of the workforce. By this time, he had four daughters to whom he turned for assistance in maintaining order and ensuring quality. They prescribed 'perfect silence except the singing of hymns which we find a useful relaxation and a help to industry, attention and orderly conduct'.[64] At this stage in the development of business enterprises it was considered appropriate to make use of daughters in 'the middle ranks of life' on the business premises in this way. Less than fifty years later it became totally unacceptable.[65] Discipline and quality control continued to be a source of contention for a long time; one observer recalled that after Courtauld had left the firm:

When young girls were taken on, they were given a shilling which bound them for twelve months. They were subjected to very harsh treatment. If they made too much waste, one form of punishment was that they were made to wear a 'fool's cap' with the waste silk on it all day.[66]

By 1816 legal battles ensued between Courtauld and his partner, Wilson. Although Courtauld won the case he left the silk trade for the last time, returning to North America. Meanwhile, his eldest son, Samuel III, worked in the Pebmarsh mill from 1807 until about 1812 and in the Braintree mill from 1814 to 1815. In 1816, after a period of illness, Samuel set up as a silk throwster on his own account in Panfield Lane, Bocking. A year later he persuaded his cousin, Peter Alfred Taylor I, to enter a joint venture with him. Peter Taylor was the son of William Taylor, who had originally served a silk apprenticeship alongside Samuel's father and who married George's sister, Catherine Courtauld I. Such family inter-connections were a central characteristic of early business enterprises.

The first partnership of Courtauld and Taylor bought land in Braintree and built a mill, known as 'New Mills', suitable for horse power. At the same time, Courtauld bought the former cloth-fulling mill belonging to John Savill in Bocking intending to use it for water-powered silk throwing. During the next few years, the fortunes of the enterprise reflected the fluctuations of the silk trade nationally. In 1819, during an ebb in the industry, 'New Mills' in Braintree and the Panfield Lane establishment were relinquished. Peter Taylor married Samuel's sister, Catherine II, withdrawing from active partner-ship in the silk firm. Business became concentrated at the Bocking mill. The next three years were difficult and Samuel tried to sell the whole business. By 1823, a year after Samuel's marriage to Ellen Taylor, the younger sister of his sleeping partner in the firm, the silk industry nationally was booming and profits in the Courtauld enterprise began to rise again. In the eyes of some Essex newspaper reporters, this development signalled a lamentable change in the social status of women in the trade. Foreshadowing Lord Braybrooke's judgements a decade later, the *Chelmsford Gazette* commented in 1823:

Means are afforded by this lucrative employment for the young women to dress in the greatest extravagance, so much so that on a Sunday those who formerly moved in the most

PLATE 2 The eighteenth-century wooden weather-boarded corn mill, known as Town Mill, on the River Colne, purchased by Samuel Courtauld in 1825 and converted into a steam-powered silk weaving mill. In the foreground, to the right, is the Lodge House where the lodge keeper checked the time of arrival of the silk workers as they entered the mill.

humble social sphere and appeared in woollens and stuffs have lately been so disguised as to be mistaken for persons of distinction.[67]

In January 1825 Courtauld expanded his venture into Halstead, purchasing and converting a water-powered corn mill, Town Mill, on the River Colne in the centre of Halstead. By this time, Samuel's father had died and his brothers and sisters had returned from North America to Essex. Samuel's younger brother, George II, was established at Bocking helping to prepare the machinery. His sisters were again brought in to supervise the young women whom Samuel continued to recruit. A specific kind of labour discipline adapted to the perceived needs of a female workforce developed as a crucial linchpin for Courtauld's successful business. When setting up the first mill in Bocking he explicitly spelt out the type of labour he was seeking. In a contemporary letter he writes that,

> The kind of machinery I am now making requires the accuracy of Clockwork, but my finances will not admit of my employing *really superior* workmen and I have found it more practicable to obtain assistance from mere workhouse children than from what are called *good* workmen, who with little available ingenuity of their own are far less teachable and indeed far less expert when taught than children, but of course these require all the various tools to be continued and made for them as to render their work as simple as possible.[68]

Industrial technology, far from being neutral, was shaped according to the preferred gender and age of those hired to operate it. The reason behind the selection of young female workers was not only that they were cheaper but that they lacked the sociopolitical power of '*really superior*' workmen. By '*good* workmen' Courtauld meant those who had achieved protection and a high status for their craft. Their level of 'skill' was gained through political manipulation rather than any innate or learned repository of abilities. Courtauld was only too aware of this in his assumption that young hands would learn their tasks more readily than older 'skilled' ones.

Not only did he need to adapt technology but he also faced the problem confronting his father of maintaining control over a young female workforce. In the early days he made extensive use of higher status women, significantly his own sisters. As time went on, though, Samuel and his sisters disagreed about the 'proper' activities of men and women of the 'middle ranks'. Definitions of gentility were both important and negotiable during this period. One of Samuel's sisters, Louisa, eventually departed for Edinburgh to establish a school as this was considered a good deal more 'genteel' than factory work, even in a supervisory capacity. Incipient ideals of gentility, closely tied to notions of domesticity, were already being formulated by this time. Although mainly forged by clergymen, such ideals gained currency among early industrialists of all religious persuasions and were also espoused by women of the 'middle ranks'. Those born in the 1780s or 1790s, like Samuel

Courtauld's generation, were very active in proselytizing ideals of gentility and domesticity for their own womenfolk early in the nineteenth century even if they were not yet in a position to live fully according to such principles themselves. Samuel's mother, Ruth, represents a transitional lifestyle between that of her mother-in-law, who was a craftswoman in the silversmithing trade, and her daughter-in-law, Ellen, who by the mid-nineteenth century adopted the fully fledged philanthropic mode of the 'angel of the house'. It was at this juncture that she expressed a longing to know 'our proper stations' and how to act in them.[69]

Even after the introduction of greater mechanization and expansion from throwing into power loom weaving, women and girls formed the majority of Courtauld's workforce. In the early years, as Coleman has pointed out, 'it can hardly be doubted that so long as protection lasted, low wages and an adequate supply of young women and children helped to slow down the adoption of improved techniques and make it worthwhile to keep slow, manually operated plants in existence'.[70]

With the great move towards Free Trade in 1824, silk prices began to fall and there was increasing pressure on manufacturers to improve their machinery and sources of power to remain competitive. There were two other silk mills in Halstead, Cape Mills and the mill belonging to Jones and Foster of Parsons Lane.[71] In nearby Coggeshall, John Hall set up a mill in 1818, and the Norwich firm of Grout, Baylis and Company employed more than 3,500 people by the 1820s in towns and villages all over East Anglia.[72] Walters and Sons moved out from Spitalfields in 1820 and set up in Braintree, whilst in Colchester, Stephen Brown opened a mill in St Peters Street in 1826.[73] To remain competitive Samuel Courtauld used his Halstead mill to expand into large-scale weaving of black mourning crape and asked his brother George to design the simplest and lightest of steam-powered looms to suit his preconceived notion of female weavers' strengths and abilities.

By the mid 1830s, steam-powered looms were a matter of local controversy. In 1836 one Essex newspaper reported that,

A great outcry is made against Messrs. Courtauld and Taylor for having introduced into their manufactories additional

PLATE 3   Close-up view of the black mourning crape in which the Courtauld mills specialized for most of the nineteenth century. The crape was marketed with an emphasis upon the spotted and crimped effect seen here. Crimping was a secret process preserved for male workers.

machinery, which may throw out of employment some of the weavers. We sympathise with those who may thus lose their employment, but it must be recollected that it is by the perfection of our machinery alone that England can expect to maintain the proud position which she occupies.[74]

The view expressed in the latter half of the extract was particularly pronounced among employers and the urban middle class following a depression in the silk trade in the early 1830s.[75] Despite this depression, and the one in the mid 1820s, Courtauld's enterprise flourished and prospered. Apart from the six-horse power engine installed at Halstead in 1828, a smaller four-horse power engine had been set up a few years earlier. Peter Taylor re-entered a more active partnership and Samuel appointed Joseph Ash, his brother-in-law, as manager of the Halstead mill. A special machine shop for George II's

PLATE 4 A mid-nineteenth-century print showing middle-class women wearing black mourning dress. Such attire was very popular at this time, particularly after the death of Prince Albert in 1860.

TABLE 2 Male and female workers in the Halstead mill, 1838

		No. employees
Females		
	13 and under	15
	14–18	98
	19 and over	212
	Total	325
Males		
	13 and under	28
	14–18	17
	19 and over	20
	Total	65

Compiled from figures in Reports from Commissioners . . . on the State of the Handloom Weavers: 1839, XLIII, extracted from D. C. Coleman, *Courtaulds: an Economic and Social History*, vol. 1.

surveillance, know as 'Steam Factory', was built next to the Bocking Mill in 1826. While Spitalfields experienced severe depression[76] and unemployment in Halstead soared, the Courtauld business continued to grow. Despite fears of labour displacement by machinery, the workforce increased, with the numbers at Halstead alone reaching 390 by 1838.[77] Over three-quarters of the workers were female. Sex ratios and age breakdowns are shown in table 2 .

The age, as well as the gender, divisions reveal important aspects of the employers' recruitment strategies. Young males were directed into winding whilst most of the hands engaged on the weaving looms were women aged nineteen and over. The older men formed a core of highly paid 'skilled' mechanics and overseers, for while men were not regarded as suitable for the mass of weaving jobs they were considered appropriate for the smaller number of tasks connected to repairing and maintaining machinery and supervising the lower paid women and young people. It was unheard of now for Courtauld's sisters to have any physical contact with the mill, even in a supervisory role. This job was now filled by men.

By the 1830s, the Courtauld mill in Halstead, supplemented by a small pool of predominantly male handloom weavers

PLATE 5 The manager's house directly adjoining Town Mill in Halstead. The first manager, Joseph Ash, lived here with his family and had immediate access to the mill by way of an internal connecting door. By the early 1830s managers took over the close surveillance of the workforce in each of Samuel Courtauld's mills, which he and members of his family had previously carried out. By this stage, Samuel and his wife, Ellen, had moved to the countryside, a few miles away from any of the mill premises.

working in their homes subject to the demand for their labour, was already the biggest single employer in both the town and the surrounding area. While other silk mills gave up the struggle, Courtauld's grew from strength to strength.[79] This rise in fortunes was reflected by Samuel and Ellen Courtauld's move in the early 1830s from the house they had inhabited in Bocking Church Street, close to the Bocking mill, to Folly House, a large sprawling building situated in the countryside at High Garrett, midway between Bocking and Halstead. Joseph Ash, as manager of the Halstead plant, was installed with his family in the house adjoining Town Mill next to the River Colne. The contours were being drawn for how succeeding generations of men, women and children in the locality would live their lives under the shadow of the 'family' firm of Courtauld's.

NOTES

1 George Courtauld, in *Courtauld Family Letters, 1782–1900*, ed. by S. L. Courtauld, vol. vii, Bowes and Bowes, 1916, p. 3193, quoted in D. C. Coleman, *Courtaulds: An Economic and Social History*, Clarendon Press, 1969, vol. I, p. 248, emphasis in original. The two volumes of this book provide a full description of the development of the Courtauld industry from its early inception up until the late 1960s.

2 The kinds of goods being produced were mainly ribbons, laces, small luxury items and corses (ribbons serving as bases for ornamentation with metalwork or embroidery for use as garters and girdles).

3 Rotuli Parliamentorum V, 325, 1368, quoted in A. Abram, *Social England in the Fifteenth Century*, Routledge, 1909.

4 Liber Albus, pp. 205–6, quoted in M. Dale, *Women in the Textile Industry and Trade of Fifteenth Century England*, London, 1928, p. 27. See also A. Abram, 'Women traders in medieval London', *Economic Journal*, XXVI, 1916, p. 276.

5 Abram, 'Women traders'; E. Power, *Medieval Women*, Cambridge University Press, 1975, pp. 59–60.

6 Abram, 'Women traders'; Power, *Medieval Women*; G. Unwin, *The Guilds and Companies of London*, 4th edn, Cass, 1963.

7 These rules included, for example, the sole administration by the husband of all the wife's property, the prohibition on a wife making contracts, suing or being sued, being held responsible for criminal actions or having any legal rights over her own children.

8 J. Dunlop and R. D. Denman, *English Apprenticeship and Child Labour*, London, 1912.

9 M. A. Clawson, 'Early modern fraternalism and the patriarchal family', *Feminist Studies*, 6(2), Summer 1980.

10 Throwing is a process in the preparation of nett silk yarn for weaving similar to the process of spinning in cotton and wool production.

11 This loophole was an exemption in the rules of coverture protecting a man from his wife's debts.

12 It can be seen that the kind of patriarchal relations being identified here include relationships of age as well as gender: older men have power over younger men who will, however, assume a position of dominance over those younger than themselves.

13 Dean Swift, *The Journal of a Modern Lady*, 1728, quoted in M.

Phillips and W. S. Tomkinson, *English Women in Life and Letters*, Oxford University Press, 1926, p. 101.

14 Macpherson's *Annals of Commerce*, cited in J. Bischoff, *A Comprehensive History of the Woollen and Worsted Manufactures*, vol. I, 1842, Smith, Elder and Co., p. 233.

15 F. Warner, *The Silk Industry of the United Kingdom*, Dranes, 1921, ch. 3.

16 Ibid.

17 G. B. Hertz, 'The English silk industry in the eighteenth century', *English Historical Review*, XXIV, 1909, p. 710l

18 *Journals of the House of Commons*, vol. XXX, 10 January 1765 to 16 September 1766, p. 212.

19 Collyer, *Parents' Directory*, 1761.

20 L. Porter, *Silk: Treatise on the Origin, Progressive Improvement and Present State of the Silk Manufacture*, London, 1831, p. 328.

21 Anon., *A List of Prices in those Branches of the Weaving Manufactory called the Black Branch, and the Fancy Branch, together with the Persians, Sarsnets, Drugget Modes, Fringed and Italian Handkerchiefs, Cyprus and Draught Gauzes and Plain and Laced Nets*, 'printed in the year 1769 at the expense of those manufacturers' journeymen who were subscribers for carrying on the work', p. 27.

22 J. H. Clapham, 'The Spitalfields Acts 1773–1824', *Economic Journal*, vol. XXVI, 1916.

23 M. D. George, *London Life in the Eighteenth Century*, Kegan Paul and Co., 1925, p. 178.

24 *Two Reports of the Select Committee on Petitions of Ribbon Weavers*, House of Commons Reports, 1818; *Report of the Select Committee on the Present State of the Silk Trade*, vol. XIX, House of Commons Reports, 1831–2.

25 George, *London Life*, p. 194. See also, *Report on Handloom Weavers*, vol. XXIII, House of Commons Reports, 1840; *Report of the Select Committee on the Present State of the Silk Trade*, House of Commons Reports, 1831–2.

26 Knight, 1842, ch. XLIX, quoted in Warner, *Silk Industry of the UK*, ch. 5. See also *Report on Handloom Weavers*, and *Report from the Select Committee on the Silk Trade*.

27 Knight, 1842, ibid.

28 Francis Place, Letter to Hume, 9 February 1824, quoted in George, *London Life*, p. 195.

29 See, for example, R. Badnall, *A View of the Silk Trade*, John Miller, 1828; 'Tracts on the Poor Laws 1821–1846', *Mechanics Magazine*, vol. I, 1823–4, 30 August 1823, pp. 83–104.

30 Porter, *Treatise*, p. 211.

31 W. Hutton, *The History of Derby, from the remote ages of antiquity to the year* MDLLXCI, 1791, J. Nichols; D. P. Davies, *A new*

historical and descriptive view of Derbyshire, from the remotest period to the present time, S. Mason, 1811; W. English, *The Textile Industry. An Account of the Early Invention of Spinning, Weaving and Knitting Machines*, Longmans, 1969, ch. 3.

32 *Encyclopaedia Britannica*, 1771, p. 356; W. Fairbairn, *Treatise on Mills and Millwork*, Longmans, vol. II, 1865, p. 212.

33 Holman's *History of Essex*, 1720 and Salmon's *History of Essex*, 1740, both quoted in *Victoria County History of Essex*, vol. II, 1907, p. 462.

34 *Victoria County History of Essex*, p. 463.

35 Warner, *The Silk Industry of the United Kingdom*, Book II; Fairbairn, *Treatise on Mills and Millwork*, p. 212.

36 *Victoria County History*, p. 462.

37 Quoted in Warner, *The Silk Industry of the United Kingdom*, ch. XXVII.

38 A return of the Number of Power Looms used in Factories in the Manufacture of Woollen, Cotton, Silk and Linen respectively, House of Commons Acts and Papers, 1836, XLV, p. 152.

39 Returns of Factories, Board of Trade Accounts and Papers, 10, 1850, XLII.

40 Return of Total Number of Persons Employed in Silk Factories, 1847, XLVI, p. 609.

41 For example, in 1870, it is estimated that only 22 per cent of all silk looms were power looms, see Honegger, 'Looms for the silk and rayon industries: with reference to their structure and performance', *Journal of the Textile Institute*, vol. 25, 1934, p. 116.

42 R. Samuel, 'The workshop of the world: steam power and hand technology in mid-Victorian Britain', *History Workshop Journal*, no. 3, Spring 1977; M. Berg (ed.), *Technology and Toil in Nineteenth Century Britain*, CSE Books, 1979.

43 W. R. Greg, 'Why are women redundant?', *National Review*, 14, 1862, pp. 434–60.

44 See, for example, Nigel Heard, *Wool: East Anglia's Golden Fleece*, Lavenham Press, 1970;

45 J. E. Pilgrim, 'The rise of the "new draperies" in Essex', *University of Birmingham Historical Journal*, no. 7, 1959.

46 ERO T/Z 27. See Heard, *Wool* and Pilgrim, 'The rise of the "new draperies"' for a fuller discussion of the woollen industry in East Anglia.

47 Arthur Young, *Six Weeks Tour of England*, 1769.

48 A. F. J. Brown, *Essex at Work 1700–1815*, ERO Publications, 1969, p. 136.

49 An Englishman (William Dodd), *The Labouring Classes of England, especially those concerned in agriculture and manufactures; in a series of letters*, J. Putnam, 1848, p. 9.

50 Ibid., p. 10.
51 Ibid.
52 See Clawson, 'Early modern fraternalism'.
53 See Alice Clarke, *Working Life of Women in the Seventeenth Century*, Routledge and Kegan Paul, 1982, ch. 3; Ivy Pinchbeck, *Women Workers and the Industrial Revolution 1750–1850*, Virago, 1981, ch. 2.
54 Lord Archibald Rosebery, *Pitt*, Macmillan, 1891.
55 Edwin Grey, *Cottage Life in a Hertfordshire Village; 'How the agricultural labourer lived and fared in the late sixties and the seventies'*, Fisher, Knight and Co. Ltd., 1935.
56 Anonymous, *Essex Review*, XLVII, 1840.
57 First Report of the Commissioners on the Employment of Children, Young Persons and Women in Agriculture, 1867–8 (4068.1), XVII, p. 753, Appendix Part II (f).
58 A. Young, *A General View of the Agriculture of Essex*, 1807.
59 ERO D/P 219/13/33.
60 D. Roberts, *Paternalism in Early Victorian England*, Croom Helm, 1979, Introduction.
61 See R. V. Holt, *The Unitarian Contribution to Social Progress in England*, G. Allen and Unwin Ltd., 1938; I. Sellers, *Nineteenth Century Non-conformity*, Holmes and Meier, 1977.
62 Letter from George Courtauld I to Mr Mann, 11 December 1813, ERO D/F 3/3/94.
63 Courtauld Mss: George Courtauld I to R. W. Oldham, 8 February 1816, cited in D. C. Coleman, *Courtaulds: An Economic and Social History*, vol. 1, Clarendon Press, 1969, p. 43.
64 ERO D/F 3/2/94 George Courtauld I to Joseph Wilson, 24 September 1814.
65 See L. Davidoff with C. Hall, 'Marriage and enterprise: the English middle class in town and countryside 1780–1850', *Anglo American Historical Association* paper, July 1982.
66 John Williams, writing in 1895, cited in C. H. Ward-Jackson, *A History of Courtaulds*, Curwen Press, 1941.
67 *Chelmsford Gazette*, 12 September 1823.
68 Letter from Samuel Courtauld III to John Minton, 31 August 1816, in S. L. Courtauld, *The Huguenot Family of Courtauld*, vol. 3, privately published, 1967, p. 5; emphasis in original.
69 S. L. Courtauld (ed.), *The Courtauld Family Letters*, vol. (ii), p. 561, quoted in Coleman, Courtaulds, vol. I, p. 214.
70 Coleman, *Courtaulds*, vol. I, p. 64.
71 Pigot and Company, *Essex Directory*, 1827.
72 Report of the Select Committee on the Present State of the Silk Trade, 1831–32, vol. XIX, p. 691.
73 Ibid., XIX, p. 1.

74 *Essex Independent*, 12 November 1836, Colchester Public Library, Local History Room.
75 Report from the Select Committee on the Silk Trade, 1832.
77 Ibid.
78 Reports from Commissioners . . . on the State of the Handloom Weavers, 1839, vol. XLIII, extracted from Coleman, *Courtaulds*, vol. 1, 1969, table 28, p. 231.
79 The only other silk firm in the area to survive and prosper after the Cobden Free Trade Treaty of 1860 was Walters and Sons of Braintree, which was taken over by Warners in 1895.

2

COURTAULD'S:
A 'FAMILY' FIRM

The venture which had started out from such uncertain
beginnings had by the middle of the nineteenth century
established its owner as one of the richest and largest employers
in East Anglia. The workforce in the Halstead mill alone had
increased by 1857 to 1,089, of whom 900 were women and
girls. At the same time, the population of Halstead had
expanded rapidly. Between 1811 and 1851 it had more than
doubled from 3,279 to 6,982.[1] Nearly 4,000 of these were
women and girls. As in other parts of the country, it was the
women and girls who worked in the mills who were singled
out as representing a new-found independence and freedom
for womankind.

On the occasion of a Courtauld public dinner held in 1846,
a *Daily News* reporter describes the arrival of 'the factory
girls, too, in long rank, with free and graceful step, that told
some not unwarranted consciousness of their appearance,
blended with the sense of independence so often denied to
the sex and an honest pride in the business of the day'.[2] This
image echoes Elizabeth Gaskell's portrayal of Northern mill
girls in *North and South* in which an anxiety about unruliness
and lack of manners is combined with a scarcely concealed
admiration for their free-spirited bravado:

> They came rushing along, with bold, fearless faces, and loud
> laughs and jests, particularly aimed at all those who appeared
> to be above them in rank or station. The tones of their

PLATE 6 A group of women workers, flanked by two men, from the Halstead mill in the 1850s. The occasion for and purpose of the photograph are not clear, but it seems apparent that the women are not wearing their everyday working clothes. Of particular interest is the contrast between the stance of the women and that of the men, especially that of the man on the right who is possibly the mill manager or a senior overseer.

unrestrained voices and their carelessness of all common rules of street politeness, frightened Margaret a little at first. The girls with their rough but not unfriendly freedom, would comment on her dress; even touch her shawl or gown to ascertain the exact material; nay, once or twice she was asked questions relative to some article which they particularly admired.[3]

There was much ambivalence among observers of this very visible new section of the industrial workforce. The emerging stereotype of the female millworker had her poised precariously between a dangerous and degenerate evil and a praiseworthy and upright vanguard of the 'lower orders'. The reality of women's lives in the mills suggests neither of these extremes.

WOMEN'S WORK IN THE HALSTEAD MILL

With the arrival of mechanized silk work women and girls continued to be recruited into winding and other jobs connected to the preparation of the yarn. As Courtauld introduced ever increasing numbers of power looms women and girls were also put to work as weavers. By 1861 over half the entire workforce of more than a thousand hands in the Halstead mill were female weavers. No men at all were employed at the looms inside the mill. The only remaining male weavers in the town were those engaged on soft silk handloom weaving in their own homes.

At six o'clock every morning for six days a week, hundreds of local women and girls poured through the lodgekeeper's gate to spend up to twelve hours[4] in the mill. Female wages were all paid on a piece rate basis which made them very susceptible to fluctuation owing to breakages and productivity slow-downs. Average earnings for weavers in 1861 varied between 5/6d and 8 shillings per week. No woman could start weaving until she was seventeen years old. Once on the weaving she usually stayed on it after she married, usually in her early to mid twenties, and continued on it for many years. Younger women and girls working in the winding sheds, earned between 2 shillings and 4/6d per week. Some women

PLATE 7 A steam-powered silk loom used in the production of black mourning crape. This type of loom was designed and built in the Bocking premises in the 1830s and 1840s for use in the mills which were still owned by the partnership of Courtauld, Taylor and Courtauld up until 1849 – hence the names embossed at the top of the machine. Women weavers mostly operated two of these looms at a time.

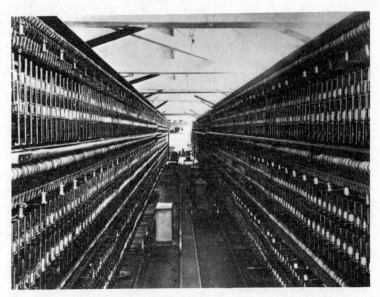

PLATE 8 The wooden-framed crape throwing mills designed and manufactured by Samuel Courtauld and used throughout the nineteenth century. This photograph was taken in the 1890s and shows the bobbins on to which the silk thread was wound as part of the preparatory processes prior to weaving. Women – mainly young women – predominated in the jobs associated with these preparatory processes.

engaged on warping and twisting could average up to 10 shillings per week but there were very few women in these positions. There were even fewer women in quality control posts earning the highest female weekly rates in the mill of between 10 and 11 shillings.

The wages of Courtauld's female workers compared unfavourably with those of their counterparts in other branches of the textile industry in the North of England. Women power loom weavers in the Yorkshire woollen industry earned around 12 shillings per week in 1857 while women cotton weavers in Manchester earned about the same amount in 1860.[5] Even the female cotton weavers of Preston in Anderson's study were paid wages starting at around 8 shillings per week.[6] The women and girls working in Courtauld's mill also earned less than those occupied in the silk industry in other regions of the country.[7] Their earnings fell far below Levi's estimate for the national average weekly pay of men, women and children, which was just over 15 shillings in 1866.[8]

The main alternative employment for women and girls in north-east Essex at this time was still strawplaiting, a craft at which earnings remained at less than 3 shillings per week.[9] As a cottage-based industry strawplaiting was an occupation at which men, women and children were intermittently engaged as a means of supplementing the household income.[10] It was mainly associated with female labour and all those local inhabitants who were defined as strawplaiters in the Census Reports of 1851 and 1861 were women and girls. Over 90 per cent of Essex strawplaiters lived in and around Halstead.[11] Between 1851 and 1871 the total number of strawplaiters in Essex increased from 1,569 to 2,889.[12] By the 1880s the situation reversed dramatically. A sudden drop in demand reduced the level of earnings even further, causing one contemporary newspaper reporter to comment that in the area around Toppesfield near Halstead

> A few of the women may be seated on the cottage steps or leaning against the doors or garden gates, busily twisting the straws, but they told me it was starving work, and the price per score was getting worse and worse. They said they only did a little at odd times because they could get nothing else to do. They are not bringing their daughters up to it.[13]

While strawplaiting declined, domestic service steadily grew, offering another major alternative for women and girls, particularly from the 1870s onwards. The only other activities for women and girls were a range of casual occupations such as taking in washing, doing cleaning and charring and taking in lodgers and boarders. The demand for female labour in agriculture, on the decline since the eighteenth century, was practically non-existent in the area by this time. There were only very sporadic opportunities helping with the harvest or doing some stone picking.[14]

In an area so lacking in female employment opportunities Courtauld's strategy of labour-intensive recruitment mostly of women and girls found a secure foothold for much of the nineteenth century. Whilst they were lower than wages in other parts of the country, female earnings in the mill were higher than any outside it within the locality. One consequence of this was that once inside the mill, women remained in its employment for many years. Over half of the female workers present in 1861 spent between ten and thirty years altogether in the mill. Mill work was not a supplementary activity for these women. It was a central and significant part of their everyday lives and formed an essential contribution to the survival of their households. Throughout their employment most women occupied similar 'routine' machine-tending jobs with very few reaching a high rank in the job hierarchy.

There were two distinct job hierarchies within the mill – one female and one male – with very little interchange between the two. The majority of women present in 1861 had just two jobs during their entire career. These were usually winding and weaving. Few women even had the opportunity of working at one of the preparatory processes other than winding. For those who were removed from the winding sheds there was further segregation between operations connected to winding and those connected to weaving. The main type of mobility for women was rigidly circumscribed inside these two areas of work and took a predominantly horizontal form (see figure 1).

MEN'S WORK IN THE HALSTEAD MILL

Men's jobs in the mill marked a sharp contrast to those occupied by women. In the male hierarchy the predominant jobs were overseeing, clerical work and maintaining and repairing the machinery where earnings were at least twice as high as any of the women's. Male wages were paid at a basic flat rate which increased progressively with age and experience. In 1861, overseers and clerks were on weekly wages varying between 15 shillings and 32/6d. In the same year attendants engaged on maintaining and repairing the power looms earned between 14 and 15 shillings per week while those attending to

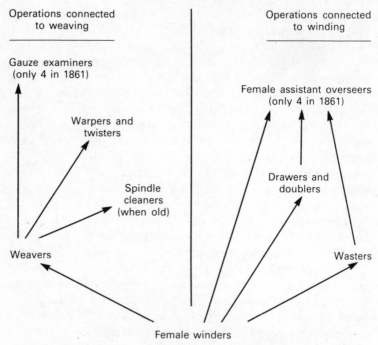

FIGURE 1   Female mobility in the Halstead mill

the winding machinery earned between 10 and 15 shillings per week.

Unlike the wages of women in the mill those of male machinery attendants compared well with the earnings of male textile workers elsewhere. Automatic mule operators in the Manchester district earned around 16 shillings per week in 1860[15] and male cotton workers in Preston averaged 15 shillings per week in the 1850s.[16] These kinds of wages were, of course, considered to be near poverty level. Above this category of male workers in the Courtauld mill were the mechanics and engine drivers who collectively formed a 'labour aristocracy' within the mill and the surrounding community and to whose ranks other men in the mill aspired. These men might not have attained the degree of power and autonomy which has been attributed to the millwrights and mechanics of Oldham,[17] but they represented a local working-class elite whose interests

PLATE 9 Male mechanics employed by Samuel Courtauld, photographed in 1859. Again the purpose of the photograph is uncertain, but the men appear not to be dressed in working clothes and it is interesting to compare their poses with those of the women pictured in plate 6.

most closely cohered with those of their middle-class male employers. It was these men who corresponded to Dodd's fifth class of 'skilled labourers'[18] and who were central pillars of the local Co-operative Society, the Halstead Working Men's Club and various benefit and provident societies, roles which tended to enhance their intermediary function between the paternalistic employers and the rest of the labouring community.

James Hunt and Thomas Ready, two of the initial founders of the Halstead Industrial Co-operative Society, established in 1860, were clerks in the Courtauld mill. In the 1830s and 40s they had been active supporters of the Charter and later had become officials in Joseph Arch's Agricultural Labourers' Union. The decline of Chartism and male working-class radicalism has often been associated with the presence of Nonconformist paternalist employers like Courtauld who forged political alliances with radical labouring men over issues like the anti-corn Law movement.[19] This kind of unity laid the basis for an increasing commonality of purpose between male middle-class industrialists and the upper echelons of the male section of the working class.

These labouring men were ranked above other men in the locality by both status and earnings. The majority of male labour in the area was tied to agriculture. During the second half of the nineteenth century agriculture in Essex went through a series of fluctuations. The period between 1850 and 1875 was one of relative recovery but even during these years average weekly wages on the land rose no higher than about 11 shillings.[20] By the late 1870s and early 1880s depression hit Essex agriculture so badly that some of the land was reduced to total dereliction. By this time, many Essex labourers had already left the county seeking employment in the North of England. Many had supported Joseph Arch's Union in the 1870s in the midst of unrest at both the introduction of machinery and the low rate of wages. Agricultural depression continued right through the 1890s and did not really ebb until the second decade of the twentieth century.

Other occupations for men and boys in the locality were mainly labouring jobs in the coalyards, tanyards and brickworks and work in trades such as grocery, butchery, milling, baking, building and the maltworks. Later in the century more jobs appeared with the growth of iron foundries and agricultural machinery plants.[21] Wages in all these spheres were low in comparison to similar male occupations in other parts of the country as well as being lower than the rates operating in the Courtauld mill. None of them sufficiently offset the decline in agricultural employment.

Another contrast between the male and female labour hierarchies within the mill was the different type of mobility experienced by the men. Apart from higher wages, their jobs were characterized by greater security and rapid mobility to higher status and authority. Upward mobility for male workers was fairly automatic: of the thirty-nine men in the machinery attending and cleaning categories in 1861, twenty-eight went on to experience promotion into the highest ranks of the male hierarchy. Because of this stable ladder of opportunities, a large number of men who remained beyond the age of fifteen proceeded to spend more than forty years in the mill. Those who reached the pinnacle and became mill managers tended to stay in that one job for many years. William Davidson, who succeeded Joseph Ash, occupied the position for more than twenty years and his successor, Carey Clements, remained in post for about thirty years. With this position came the residency of the house adjoining the mill which lent further symbolic authority and actual means of control to its occupants. As in other mills of this period, a connecting door led directly from the second floor of this house into the mill.

Once beyond the winding stage, proportionately more men than women had at least three different jobs during their employment at the mill. While women's position remained static, much greater speed and fluidity marked the progress of men through the mill (see figure 2).

MALE AND FEMALE MOBILITY PATTERNS

There were only two jobs in the whole mill which were performed by both male and female workers. Significantly, both jobs were related to age. The first was winding, at which girls up to seventeen years old and boys up to fifteen years

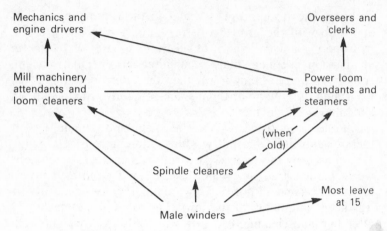

FIGURE 2 Male mobility in the Halstead mill.

old were engaged. In 1861 this job accounted for the second largest group of female workers in the mill, employing 188 in all. In the same year, the largest single group of male hands, amounting to thirty-eight altogether, were working in this capacity. The second job shared by men and women was spindle cleaning, a task allocated either to boys under fifteen years old or elderly workers of either sex who were considered too infirm to do anything else. The wages attached to both these jobs, occupying either the youngest or the oldest workers, were the lowest in the mill.

Although winding was performed by both male and female workers the job had different meanings in terms of mobility patterns within the mill. By 1861, legislation determined that no child under twelve years old could be employed in a mill. Both girls and boys were recruited at this age into Courtauld's mill.[22] But from the time they entered the mill boys and girls were subjected to a policy of deliberate and self-conscious gender segregation. Such a policy is highlighted by a warning issued by Samuel Courtauld in September 1859. In it he informed 'little boys' that they would have to leave the mill at fifteen years of age to seek other employment since 'there is not in the mills fitting employment for any considerable number of grown-up Men, and because it therefore would not be for the ultimate advantage of boys to be allowed to remain

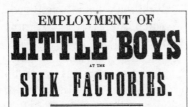

EMPLOYMENT OF

LITTLE BOYS

AT THE

SILK FACTORIES.

BOYS will now be taken to the Silk-winding, at the Bocking Factory, between the ages of Twelve and Thirteen-and-a-half.

BUT at Fifteen years of age, these boys will have to leave the Silk mills, and seek other employment.

BECAUSE there is not in the Mills fitting employment for any considerable number of grown-up Men, and because it therefore would not be for the ultimate advantage of Boys to be allowed to remain at such work as Silk-winding after Fifteen years of age.

SAMUEL COURTAULD & Co.

Sept. 13th, 1859.

A. CARTER, PRINTER AND BINDER, HALSTEAD.

PLATE 10   Notice posted in the Courtauld silk mills in 1859 warning boys that there would be very few opportunities for their continued employment beyond the age of fifteen. Most boys left the winding sheds by that age while a small minority were retained to form a 'skilled' elite within the mills.

at such work as Silk-Winding after fifteen years of age' (see plate 10). A small proportion of boys helped to compensate for any shortfall in the recruitment of girls and also provided a pool of male labour from which individuals could be selected for training into the higher paid jobs in the male hierarchy. Boys who were kept on at the mill started their training at fifteen years old whereas girls had to wait until they were seventeen to be moved from the winding.

For boys aged between twelve and fifteen, winding and spindle cleaning formed stepping stones in the promotion process attached to the male hierarchy. Out of the thirty-eight boys who were occupied as winders in 1861, nearly thirty left the mill when they reached the age of fifteen. But of those who remained in the mill, two were trained as mechanics and engine drivers, one went on to become a carpenter, one became a power loom attendant and three were also trained as attendants after short periods on spindle cleaning. This job, along with tasks like taking messages and sweeping, formed a stop-gap for boys when there were no immediate vacancies for training in a more 'skilled' job. They usually proceeded from these jobs to the higher positions in the male hierarchy. William Amey, for example, who was promoted to the position of gauze examiner overseer in May 1861, had started his career at the mill as a winder in the late 1830s. During the 1840s he occupied various cleaning and attending positions until 1854 when he commenced 'duties analogous to that of an overseer' at a wage of 15 shillings per week. By May 1862 Amey's wages reached 25 shillings.[23]

For women, winding was a low paid preamble to long-term occupation of another low paid job in either the winding department or the weaving sheds. Mary Ann Rayner, for example, was a winder for four years before she was put on the weaving in May 1862. She remained a weaver until her departure in August 1873. The longer periods spent at winding by girls also prolonged the time when they were receiving the lowest wages in the mill.

Another more detailed comparison of any two employment profiles – one female and one male – illustrates the sharp discrepancies between the two labour hierarchies within the mill. A girl called Marianne Jarvis of Tan Yard in Halstead started work as a winder in September 1859 at the age of thirteen. Four years later she started to train on the power looms. In December 1879 she left work owing to illness. She returned again in June 1880 to be sent to the twisting department where she stayed until February 1881. She was ill and died in April of the same year. Throughout her working life in the mill her wages rarely rose above 8 shillings per week.

A boy called John Disney also started work in the mill as a winder. By his early twenties he had progressed to the position of an oiler attending the mill machinery, earning 12 shillings per week by 1857 and 14 shillings by 1860. In November 1871 he became an 'overseer of men in the mills and collector of money [wages from bank]' at a wage of 16 shillings per week. By the 1880s he was receiving 21 shillings per week. In 1898 he became increasingly incapacitated through advancing years and ill health so he left the mill but was "placed on the allowance list at 3/6d weekly to commence January 1899".

The payment of allowances to men retiring from the mill marked another inequality between the conditions of employment in the male and female hierarchies. Such payments were frequent for male workers but a very rare occurrence for women who had also spent a lifetime in the mill. Most of the men retired from a highly paid job within a position of authority whereas the majority of women left low paid, low status jobs. There were very few positions of authority open to women. In 1861 there were only four women occupied as assistant overseers. Two of the women held these positions for over twenty years after lengthy periods in other jobs. One, Mary Chaplyn, was a winder for many years before becoming an assistant overseer in 1860. She remained in this post until 1886 when, owing to old age and infirmity, she was demoted once more to winding. Unlike her male counterparts she was not put on an allowance list. The four women who were gauze examiners in 1861 had similar experiences. Anne Prentice spent seventeen years as a weaver before she was promoted to gauze examining in December 1856 at a wage of 9/6d per week. She remained in this post until the 1870s but there is no record of her name on any allowance list after that time.

The experiences of these women were very different from those of men with similar service records. Frederick Hawkes, for example, spent the same length of time in the mill as Anne Prentice. He was put in charge of the winding floor in 1855 at a wage of 16 shillings per week. In 1872 he was still in an overseeing post and his wages had increased to 27/6d per week. Women could never become part of the male labour elite to which Frederick Hawkes belonged. What excluded them was not only the level of their wages but, more crucially, their lack of authority.

Women in overseeing positions were assistants to male overseers in the winding department. This was a section of the mill occupied by the lowest paid workers who were also defined as having the lowest status and least skill in the whole workforce. They were, in addition, the *youngest* workers in the mill. The female gauze examiners in the weaving sheds did not share the authority which male overseers had over the weavers. Their tasks were solely connected to quality control. Such a patriarchal set of authority relationships was not far removed from those characterizing the domestically based units common to both silk workers and woollen cloth workers a century earlier. Men had ultimate authority and occupied key positions of control. Those few women who reached the top female positions either assisted men in their supervision of children and young people or monitored the quality of goods being produced. All women came under the authority of men while children had the lowest status of all. In constructing such relationships Courtauld effectively took over from the sociopolitical triumphs of the male handloom weavers in the previous century. These had worked to ensure a form of occupational segregation which kept women and children in a subordinate position. The concrete results of Courtauld's policies by the mid nineteenth century are illustrated in table 3.

CONTINUITY AND CHANGE IN THE MILL WORKFORCE

The absence of trade union organization until the 1890s, together with Courtauld's persistent opposition to restrictive legislation, strengthened the employers' control over recruitment and labour policies for many years. By the second half of the nineteenth century the whole enterprise relied on a large fluid pool of women workers many of whom were not the young single females common to the stereotype. In 1861 more than a third of the women in the mill were married and more than twenty years old. As the firm expanded from the 1830s onwards Courtauld had to look beyond the workhouse for hands to operate his looms. During the boom which was to last until the 1880s more and more power looms were introduced.[24] In order to keep the looms running further hands were needed.[25] It was to the women of the poor labouring households in and around Halstead to whom Courtauld turned.

So urgent was Courtauld's need for a ready supply of cheap workers that he adopted a deliberately flexible stance towards marriage and childbirth among his female workforce. The

TABLE 3 Courtauld employees at Halstead in 1861

	No.	Approximate weekly wages	Age	Marital Status
Total males and females: 1,015[a]			Most frequent	
MALES				
Mill manager	1	£1,000 p.a. (+ 3% profits)	Over 30	Married
Overseers and clerks	26	15/- to 32/6	Over 30	Married
Mechanics and Engine Drivers	6	17/- to 25/6	Over 30	Married
Carpenters and blacksmiths	3	14/- to 21/-	Over 30	Married
Lodgekeeper	1	15/- + hand loom produce	Over 40	Married
Power loom machinery attendants (in weaving sheds) and Steamers	16	14/- to 15/-	Over 20	Married
Mill machinery attendants (in winding dept) and loom cleaners	18	10/- to 15/-	Over 20	Married
Spindle cleaners, bobbin stampers and packers, messengers and sweepers	5	5/- to 12/-	Between 14 and 25 and over 40	Single and married
Watchmen	NA[b]	7/- to 10/-	NA	NA
Coachmen, grooms and van driver	NA	5/- to 10/-	NA	NA
Winders	38	2/- to 4/6	Between 12 and 15	Single
Total males	114			
FEMALES				
Gauze examiners	4	10/- to 11/-	Over 30	Married
Female assistant overseers	4	9/- to 10/-	Over 30	Married
Warpers	16	7/6 to 10/-	Over 20	Married
Twisters	9	7/- to 10/-	Over 20	Married
Wasters	4	6/6 to 9/-	Over 20	Married
Weavers	589	5/8 to 8/-	Over 17	Single and married
Plugwinders	2	6/- to 7/6	Over 20	Married
Drawers and doublers	83	4/6 to 6/6	Over 17	Married
Winders	188	2/- to 4/6	Between 12 and 17	Single
Housekeeper	1	NA	NA	NA
Schoolteacher	1	NA	NA	NA
Total females	901			

Source: Constructed from the Courtauld Register of Employees, 1830–1919 (ERO D/F 3/3/1 to 3/3/10), Wages Book, 1852–1876 (ERO D/F 3/3/27); Letters Book of Mill Manager, 1873–1890 (ERO D/F 3/3/22/, Memo Book, 1873–1896 (ERO D/F 3/3/24).
[a]The actual total figure of 1,089 is given in the Wages Book, ERO D/F 3/3/27, for the year 1857. The figure of 1,015 refers to the total number of employees recorded in the Register of Employees as present in the year 1861 for whom I could construct reliable employment profiles.
[b]NA=not available.

common pattern for young women entering the mill in their early teens was to remain millworkers for the rest of their lives with marriage and childbirth representing short and temporary absences from work. Of all the women workers present in the mill in 1861 only 25 per cent were recorded as having absences during their careers of more than one month's duration. For men the proportion was only 10 per cent. This discrepancy highlights the additional burden of family responsibilities falling upon the women. It was not only childbirth which accounted for the longer and more frequent absences among female workers but also 'looking after relatives', particularly fathers.

No male worker ever left the mill to look after a relative. For those who did spend periods of time away from the mill the absences were usually prolonged, often for more than ten years, and were spent in other forms of employment. Many of the women weavers, on the other hand, were away for a total of less than one year. They were usually trying to piece together the demands of domestic and family life with those of paid work. Sometimes the pull of domestic service accounted for short periods of absence followed frequently by a return to mill employment. It was not uncommon for young women to try both factory work and domestic service. These were the only two forms of regular employment for women for many years until the extension of shop work and clerical jobs at the turn of the twentieth century. A very small number of women had temporary spells at dressmaking and a few occasionally turned to soft silk weaving in their homes up until the 1880s when this activity declined. A small handful of women were dismissed from their mill jobs for behaviour that was regarded by their employers as 'immoral', for breaking company rules, for bad standards of work or for illegal activity.

An indication of Courtauld's reliance on the labour of women lies in the fact that all of those who left the mill temporarily, including those who were dismissed, were taken back again. This held true for male workers too, underlining the way in which Courtauld made use of a workforce that was not only plentiful and fluid but which was also being imbued with characteristics of continuity and stability. The control which Courtauld had over labour supply was only seriously threatened after the 1870s when his own increasing labour needs were accompanied by rising competition for female hands from domestic service and for male hands from the new 'heavy' industries in iron and agricultural machinery.

By the end of the century, domestic service figured as an increasing reason for not only temporary absences among women but for leaving mill employment altogether. By this time, marriage also became a more likely reason than in earlier decades for leaving mill employment, although the numbers disappearing from the mill altogether to marry were still not high. Similarly, other forms of employment like nursing, shopwork and clerical work attracted women away from mill employment permanently in a way that was not possible earlier on.

One cause of termination of mill work which remained significant for both women and men throughout the century was ill health. Many more women than men left through bad eyesight which was brought about from concentrating in poor light on the fine silk filaments. Women were also more prone to lung conditions from breathing in the waste from the silk threads but men too suffered from a variety of respiratory diseases related to the working conditions. Such illnesses were aggravated for both women and men by the common diseases of consumption, typhoid, dysentery and cholera which swept through towns like Halstead owing to the insanitary conditions of their housing which persisted long after the passage of public health legislation in the 1840s.

The circumstances of poverty, hardship and the 'double burden' of employment and family responsibilities characterizing the lives of Halstead's female millworkers do little to support a stereotype of newly found freedom and independence accompanied by either moral uprightness or evil profligacy. On the contrary, it seems likely that the transcendant image of the graceful and proud mill girl, particularly prevalent in the local media, was created principally in order to *prevent* her conforming to the alternative stereotype of the evil and abandoned woman so feared in the national consciousness at this time. This fear was part of a wider – and deeper – anxiety surrounding the possibility of severing the economic and familial dependence which formed the central characteristic of traditional relationships between the sexes. Courtauld's response to this anxiety was the reconstruction of patriarchal relationships within which both workplace and household patterns of authority and status could be shaped. The hierarchical structure of the workforce ensured that women's experience of mill life was tightly circumscribed by low wages, narrow promotion opportunities and low status and authority definitions. This is not to deny that women working in the mill took pride in their work and realized strengths and powers of their own.[26] It simply highlights the way in which any 'freedom' attaching to female mill work was perceived only in relation to the even greater poverty and insecurity of women and girls not employed in the mill. It was the distance between women and men's positions and experience which suggests little credence for any notion of freedom and independence for mill women in nineteenth-century Halstead – a distance which is underlined by the household situations of Courtauld's workers at this time.

NOTES

1 1851 Census, G. B. Command Papers, Population Tables, vol. I, p. 20.
2 *Daily News*, 2 July 1846.
3 Elizabeth Gaskell, *North and South*, Penguin edition, 1970, p. 110.
4 By the 1860s, after the gradual extension of 'protective' legislation, women and young people worked on weekdays from six o'clock in the morning till six o'clock in the evening, with an hour's break for breakfast and dinner, and from six o'clock in the morning, till two o'clock in the afternoon on Saturdays.
5 A. Bowley, *Wages in the United Kingdom in the Nineteenth Century*, Cambridge University Press, 1900, p. 13 and Weekly Wage Tables. These figures are estimates but are corroborated for 'The Woolen Trade of Yorkshire' in T. Baines, *Yorkshire Past and Present: a history and description for the three ridings of the great county of York from the earliest ages to the year 1870*, W. Mackenzie, 1871–77, in E. Baines and J. H. Clapham, *The Woollen and Worsted Industries*, Methuen, 1907.
6 M. Anderson, *Family Structure in Nineteenth Century Lancashire*, Cambridge University Press, 1971.
7 D. C. Coleman *Courtaulds: An Economic and Social History*, Clarendon Press, 1969, vol. 1, ch. 2.

8 Calculated from Weekly Wage Tables in Bowley, *Wages in the UK*. These are based on collapsing male and female earnings which produces an over-estimate of the majority of female wages.

9 R. W. Rose, 'The Art of Strawplaiting in Essex', *Essex Countryside*, April 1965.

10 *Victoria County History of Essex*, vol. II, 1907, p. 375.

11 1851 and 1861 Census Reports. G.B. Command Papers.

12 1871 Census Report, G.B. Command Papers.

13 *Chelmsford Chronicle*, 28 January 1881.

14 *First Report of the Commissioners on the Employment of Children, Young Persons and Women in Agriculture*, 1867.

15 J. Foster, *Class Struggle and the Industrial Revolution*, Weidenfeld and Nicolson, 1974, p. 82.

16 Anderson, *Family Structure*, p. 32.

17 Foster, *Class Struggle*, p. 225.

18 W. Dodd, *The Labouring Classes of England*, J. Putnam, 1848, see chapter 1 above, 'The thread of patriarchy', pp. 23–4.

19 WEA Eastern District, *Chartism in East Anglia*, WEA publication, 1951.

20 Bowley, *Wages in the UK*.

21 J. Booker, *Essex and the Industrial Revolution*. ERO, 1974.

22 Many children of both sexes gained access to the mill before their twelfth birthday by lying about their age. (Personal communication from Carole Bagshaw, of the Halstead and District Local History Society, who has produced a family history relating to generations of Courtauld workers commencing with Emma Cresswell who entered the mill as a weaver in 1873. I am very grateful to Carole Bagshaw for sharing this family history with me).

23 All examples of individual workers in this chapter and the rest of the book are taken from the following business records: Courtauld Register of Employees, 1830–1919 (ERO D/F 3/3/1 to 3/3/10); Wages Book, 1852–1876 (ERO D/F 3/3/27); Letters Book of Mill Manager, 1873–1890 (ERO D/F 3/3/22); Memo Book, 1873–1896 (ERO D/F 3/3/24). Unacknowledged quotations come from the Register of Employees.

24 Between 1836 and 1873 the number of power looms in the Halstead mill increased from 106 to 740, ERO D/F 3/1/8, 3/1/9 and 3/3/22.

25 The total workforce increased from 1,089 in 1857 to 1,229 by 1878 and 1,577 by 1886, ERO D/F 3/3/24.

26 The forms these took are explored later, see chapters 4 and 5 below.

3

THE THRESHOLD
BETWEEN HOME AND
WORKPLACE

By 1861 the Courtauld mill was the central landmark in a burgeoning township. The expansion in population was accompanied by a number of 'improvements' common to many industrializing towns in nineteenth-century England. A gasworks, owned by Robert Greenwood, arrived in 1835. A Town Hall was erected on Market Hill in 1850. A new Union House, estimated to be able to house up to 500 paupers, was built in 1838 to replace the former parish workhouse. In 1860 the first portion of the Halstead and District Railway was opened with stations connecting Halstead, Earls Colne, Chappel, Marks Tey and Castle Hedingham and extending in 1870 to Haverhill and Cambridge. By the 1850s a police station had been built in Chapel Street and two banks, a Savings Bank and a Stamp Office had arrived. Churches and chapels increased too: St Andrew's Church at the top of the High Street was rebuilt in the 1850s and a new church, Holy Trinity, erected in Chapel Street in 1844. In nearby Greenstead Green, the Church of St James was a new addition in the 1850s. In 1866 there were two chapels for Independents, two for Baptists and a meeting house for the Society of Friends.[1]

Samuel and Ellen Courtauld had moved from Folly House in High Garrett by this time. In 1854 Samuel had bought Gosfield Hall, the huge manor house formerly owned by the

PLATE 11 Local Board of Health map of Halstead, 1855, showing the Courtauld silk mill situated at the bottom of the High Street next to the River Colne, the gasworks to the west of the High Street and the Union Workhouse to the north on Hedingham Lane. Most of the Halstead millworkers lived in the streets shown on the map but many walked into town from surrounding villages.

PLATE 12   Gosfield Hall near the village of Gosfield. Samuel Courtauld bought this former manor house, together with 2,000 acres of farmland, in 1854. This move symbolized his attempt to identify with the local landowning aristocracy.

Marquis and Marchionness of Gosfield, along with 2,000 acres of farm land.[2] This represented another step up in the Courtauld fortunes and an attempt by Samuel to enter the ranks of the local landed aristocracy. He was never quite accepted by the local Tory landowners who regarded him with suspicion as a self-made magnate and radical dissenter. The magnitude of his capital and the influence it gave him, however, made it unnecessary for him to be completely absorbed into the local elite. His access to control lay in his ability to govern the lives of so many local inhabitants through his massive industrial enterprise.

The mill contributed significantly to the rise in the local population. Mary Merryweather, an evening school mistress appointed by Courtauld in 1847, attributes the rise directly to the presence of the mill:

PLATE 13   Samuel Courtauld.

The labouring men, excepting those employed in the silk
trade and other mechanical trades usually found in a small
town, are agricultural labourers, drawn here in greater
number on account of the employment given to the women
and girls of their families: often to their own serious
inconvenience, having to walk miles to their work.[3]

THE HOUSING CONDITIONS OF MILLWORKERS

Not all the millworkers lived in Halstead. Nearly one-fifth of
the women working there in 1861 lived out of town, many of
them over a mile away, some of them even as far as 12 miles
away in Finchingfield and 14 miles away in Glemsford, Suffolk.
So they also had to walk miles to their work. Most of those
from further afield walked to Halstead early on a Monday
morning and lodged in the town during the week, returning
home again on a Saturday afternoon. This was not necessary
for any of the male workers, as they all lived in Halstead.
The mill formed the nucleus of a community whose everyday
life was dominated by the rhythms of the silk industry. It
was situated at the bottom of the High Street, its tall white
weather-boarded walls straddling the River Colne where it
dissects High Street to the north and Bridge Street to the
south.

Many of Courtauld's silk workers lived in the streets and
courtyards surrounding the mill. For the most part the hierarchy
of status distinctions characterizing the labour force inside the
mill was replicated in the location and condition of the housing.
The principle mechanic and millwright, who in 1861 was John
Arnold Senior, lived in Factory House, a large house in
Factory Row immediately adjacent to the mill on the opposite
side of the river from the manager's house. This house was
built specially for him by the employers. Cottages for other
ranks of workers were also especially commissioned but
although they were of a high standard for the day, and even
had gas and running water, they were very small in number
compared to the total size of the workforce. The stock was
increased in the 1870s by the addition of twelve mechanics'
dwellings along the Causeway, the approach drive to the lodge

PLATE 14 Houses built in the 1870s for male mechanics and their households. The houses were provided by Samuel Courtauld and were built on the Causeway, a road directly adjacent to the Halstead mill. There were twelve of these dwellings available. The Lodge can be seen to the left at the end of the Causeway.

house and mill entrance, and sixteen three-storey terraced dwellings for weavers in Factory Terrace on the opposite side of the river to the Causeway.

Relatively few of the millworkers benefited from this provision. Those who did, although undoubtedly better off than many other Halstead inhabitants, were segregated physically and socially. The houses in the Causeway and Factory Terrace were not only separated by the Colne but were also markedly different in style, appearance and size (see plates 14 and 15). While the mechanics' houses were expected to house just one household, the houses in Factory Terrace were intended to include up to six lodgers, with two in each bedroom, as well as the tenant household.[4] The terms of tenancy stated that if only one bedroom was required by the tenant, leaving three bedrooms to accommodate six lodgers, the tenant was paid 3 shillings per week by Courtaulds. If two

PLATE 15   Factory Terrace, built in the 1870s by Samuel Courtauld
for weavers and their households. Factory Terrace is directly opposite
the Causeway, on the other side of the River Colne, also adjacent to
the Halstead mill. There are sixteen houses in the terrace.

bedrooms were required, leaving two available for four lodgers,
there was no rent charged. If three bedrooms were required,
leaving only one for two lodgers, the tenant paid a rent of 3
shillings per week.[5]

Most of the remaining cottages in the town were owned by
other wealthy locals, particularly R. E. Greenwood, the
gasworks proprietor. Courtauld workers renting these cottages
paid between 1/6d and 2/6d per week in the 1860s. Their
conditions were deplored by local health officials who described
the inhabitants as 'living together in crowded courts many
without back doors to their cottages, without water and
altogether without drainage'.[6] The courtyards were served by
inadequate cess pools, and typhus struck the town every
autumn. Owing to increasing complaints over the 'frightful
cases of fever'[7] a Local Board of Health was finally established
in 1852. Rates were levied for cleansing, draining, paving and
lighting the streets. Local landowners periodically objected to

the amount of rates levied on them and to the use of their land for some of the drainage and sewerage schemes.[8] Despite this kind of opposition, by the 1860s a waterworks was under construction and the sewage scheme was eventually implemented.

Samuel Courtauld and his brother, George, were in favour of 'improvements'.[9] Their cottages were praised in comparison to the majority of other habitations in the town:

> The cottages belonging to Mr. Courtauld are, many of them, newly erected and in good condition and have three bedrooms with separate entrances, and two of the three with fireplaces. Other conditions are indifferent and some miserable bad, 'not fit for human habitation' and in the opinion of Doctor Borham, who is acquainted with them, a prolific source of rheumatism followed in many cases by consumption.[10]

Dwellings to the south of the river, in streets like Tidings Hill, Mount Pleasant, Trinity Street and Chapel Hill, tended to be the largest with small gardens attached in which animals and poultry could be kept and vegetables grown.[11] They were also not as susceptible to the bad drainage conditions of the cottages closer to the mill and High Street. Most of the male overseers and clerks lived in this part of town. Some silk workers lower down the labour hierarchy lived in these streets too, but they were mainly distributed throughout the streets closer into town. Some male workers lived in the eighteenth century handloom weavers' cottages in Parsonage Street and Weavers Row. It was quite likely that some of them were descendants of longstanding handloom weaving families. James Cable, a mill machinery attendant living in Parsonage Street in 1861, for example, was the son of a handloom weaver.

The dwelling places of the female workers depended partly on their own occupational designation and on that of their husband. The few women at the top of the female job hierarchy lived in some of the larger terraced houses in streets towards the edge of town. Anne Prentice, a gauze examiner for many years, was married to James Prentice, an assistant overseer in the Store Room at the mill. In 1861 they lived in a house in Sudbury Road, to the south-west of the town. Anne had

PLATE 16　Eighteenth-century weavers' cottages in Parsonage Street, Halstead. These cottages had large windows on the first floor to allow plenty of light in for the work of the handloom weavers. Some handloom weavers continued to work at home after the arrival of the Courtauld mill. As the nineteenth century progressed handloom weavers diminished in numbers and either depended increasingly upon the labour of other members of their households or contributed to the household income through transferring to mill work.

started employment in the mill in 1839 as a young single woman in the winding department, living in one of the poorer courtyards off the High Street. Many weavers lived in these small cramped courtyards near the mill. Hannah Frost, in 1861 an eighteen-year-old single weaver, lived with her elderly parents in Old Tanyard, a yard off the High Street only two minutes' walk from the mill entrance. Her father was a former mill machinery attendant who had been moved to spindle cleaning and her mother was a former weaver.

Mary Merryweather frequently visited the homes of the silk workers, especially when one of them was ill. In her description of a visit to a man dying of consumption in one of the old handloom weavers' cottages, she provides a detailed view of the interior of one of the 'better class' homes:

I passed through a neatly furnished parlour downstairs, into which the street door opened, then mounted stairs which led to one large room, the windows of which extended the whole of the two sides of the house, back and front. At the top of the stairs was also a very small bedroom, without any fireplace, in which the poor man I came to nurse was lying.[12]

She continues by describing the inside of this bedroom

As I sat in this room by the light of a wood and coal fire, made brighter than usual for my reception, with the addition of one dim candle, the shadows of the looms flickered strangely over the whitewashed wall and ceiling, whilst the many reminders scattered about me of the daily toil and thrift of the inmates, made me feel for the costly fabrics they contained, contrasting with the old threadbare, but well-kept greatcoat which 'Father', as the good woman always called her husband, had extended on the back of the armchair to protect me from draught.[13]

As she sat there she looked around and noted the contents and furnishings of the room:

On the narrow mantle-shelf were a few well worn books of family devotion, besides some of the small tools used for their work. On one side was the ticking clock, with its swinging pendulum; on the other, the little safe, or cupboard, with all the etc. of their small house keepings; and around, were sundry articles of personal attire, such as you often see hung up in cottage homes. Stowed up in another part of the room were gathered seeds tied up in bundles, and other matters, telling that 'Father' had an allotment garden, and worked in it, too, for the benefit of the household. On the little table beside me, were all the restoratives provided for their poor, sick son, arranged with the thoughtful care of their kind hearts, before they retired for the rest they so much needed after many nights of anxious watching. Silent and alone, the thought of the hundreds of lives which are spent almost entirely in rooms like this, came vividly before me, waking intense sympathy with them in their many trials.[14]

'TWO WORLDS IN ONE'

The home life which Mary Merryweather observed was
inextricably intertwined with life in the mill. The 'myth of
separate worlds'[16] is no more evident than in this 'townlet'[17]
where the shared cultural identity cut right across the threshold
between cottage and workplace. What has frequently been
described for those living in such a 'townlet' (or 'village folded
within a town') as a 'mass experience',[18] was in reality a highly
gendered experience. Mary Merryweather herself noted some
aspects of life distinctive of women's experience. She was only
too aware that as well as six days toiling in the mill the
womenfolk faced a day of household chores every Sunday:

> Sunday morning is the time of general tidying up, and
> cooking a bit of meat dinner, which usually cost threepence
> or fourpence per pound, fried or stewed, and a few potatoes.
> The working clothes are mended, patched, or washed, ready
> for Monday morning.[19]

Meals had to be cooked and housework done every other day
of the week too and it was usually the women who did it.
This was not the only extra burden they faced either:

> Drunken and idle ways made wife-beating at that time a
> common thing. If we said to a poor woman who came for
> relief, 'I hope your husband is kind to you', the answer
> often was, 'well ma'am he don't pay me' (beat me) implying
> that she was grateful for that amount of goodness. If we
> said, 'I hope your husband is good and sober', the answer
> most often was 'oh, ma'am he can't get enough out of his
> wages to drink much'.[20]

It is true that Mary Merryweather's middle-class preoccupation with the moral virtue of temperance might have filtered
her view but newspaper reports in the local press[21] confirm
the widespread occurrence of violence, particularly by men
towards their wives. Also, Mary Merryweather cites one
particularly graphic case where drink was not involved:

One poor woman told me that her husband did not wait to be drunk to ill-treat her; that many a night he had come home and turned her and her five or six children out of the cottage, sometimes with a knife in his hand, declaring he would kill her; and she and the little ones had been obliged to crouch together in the garden, whilst this brutal man would sleep just inside the door to keep them out.[22]

These experiences indicate the patterns in which the domestic division of labour and authority relations were being carved out. So too does the location of women silk workers in the organization of resources and income in working-class households. Mill employment was clearly central to the organization of many Halstead households and represented a key thread in the binding together of home and workplace. There were very few households in Halstead which did not contain one or more silk workers at some point in their life cycle. The main exceptions were some of the shopkeeping, traders' and professional households. There was little 'family employment' in the sense often used,[23] because of the low proportion of men in the workforce.[24] Yet ideals of family life were being forged in the midst of household situations which were far more fluid than the prevailing stereotypes.[25]

Historically, labouring households have always been organized around a pooling of labour and resources.[26] Far from being a neutral or random process such distribution within households is structured according to age and gender. This continued to be as central a principle in nineteenth-century Halstead as it was in earlier centuries (see chapter 1) – only the circumstances had changed. 'Family employment' in this industrializing township within its rural hinterland meant survival strategies for working-class households organized around a balance between agricultural employment for men and boys and silk work for women and girls. Average household size in Halstead had increased between 1827 and 1861 from 3.26 to 4.39[27] and households containing silk workers tended to be slightly larger than the average in 1861.[28] In these households an average of nearly one-half of all members were engaged in silk work, either in the mill or at handlooms in the house, at some point in their lives.

The life cycle characteristics of those living in these households underline many of the divisions within the mill workforce described in chapter 2 above. The census figures serve as a reminder, for example, that in 1861 one-third of all female silk workers were married, while the proportion among male silk workers was two-thirds. Similarly, more than 40 per cent of the men were over forty-five years old compared to only 18 per cent of the women. In addition, there were far more women than men silk workers who were over twenty-five years old and still living with their parents. Many of these women contributed their labour to households where parents had a low earning capacity and younger non-earning dependent children were present. Take, for example, two sisters, both weavers in Courtauld's mill, Susannah and Emma Driver, who lived in Mount Hill. Susannah was twenty-nine years old and Emma twenty-six and both were still single and living in their parental home. Their father Thomas, was an agricultural labourer, aged fifty-one, and their mother, also aged fifty-one, had no recorded occupation.[29] There were two more wage-earning children, aged fifteen and twelve, both winders and therefore on low wages, and two non-wage earners aged eight and five.

The contribution of these two women was probably crucial to the household's survival. Any freedom or independence their employment gave them has to be set in the context of their household as well as their work situation. Their household circumstances at this stage in their life cycle provide just one instance of a system still containing much that resembles the kind of household organization in existence a hundred years previously. The location and content of productive activity had changed without considerably shifting the organization of labour and resources involved. Also unchanged was the authority structure underpinning these arrangements. Of all the households in Halstead in 1861, five out of six had male 'heads' while the remainder were 'headed' by females. The distinguishing features of these different types of household bring some aspects of this authority structure into relief.

HOUSEHOLDS 'HEADED' BY MEN

The households where men were classified as 'head' in 1861 fall into two major categories. First, there were those where the men had low paying declining occupations, predominantly in handloom weaving and agriculture. Second, there were those where the men belonged to the incipient 'labour aristocracy' and held relatively high status secure positions either in the mill or in a local urban trade like grocery or shoemaking. What is significant about the arrangements in these households is that the former could *only* survive through the extensive labour of women while in the latter the male head's status as a member of the local labouring elite was magnified by the contribution of women's labour to the household. In both categories, men's patriarchal status was cushioned by women's employment.

In the declining male occupations there was certainly an erosion of the traditional role of master but this was largely reshaped through a process which ensured the propping up of these flagging livelihoods during a period of vulnerability and insecurity. In the changed circumstances of an industrializing economy the labour of women and girls provided the props until such time as the local labour market was reconstructed in a way which was far more favourable again for men. In the case of the male handloom weavers, these men undoubtedly experienced a change in status from the days when their craft skills and earning power were highly protected and widely envied.[30] In a description reminiscent of contemporary characterizations of the declining traditional journeyman weaver,[31] Mary Merryweather adds to her earlier descriptions of a handloom weaver's cottage:

> A weaver's shop must usually be both his kitchen and his sitting room, because he cannot afford a fire elsewhere, as well as a sufficient one there, warmth being very necessary for his work; and neither frequent cleaning, nor thorough ventilation, are very possible when delicate and expensive work is in the loom. Thus neatness and health often suffer.[32]

Samuel Courtauld himself referred to the handloom weavers

as solely a kind of buffer labour force[33] kept on to back up the hard silk manufacturing in the mill until the 1880s.[34] They were an extremely vulnerable group of workers subjected to frequent underemployment and severe restrictions in their wages during slump periods (see plate 17). To balance the internal resources of such households it was common for any daughters living at home to work in the mill. A soft silk weaver called James Newton, living in Parsonage Street in 1861, shared a cottage with his wife, Sarah. They were both aged fifty and worked at home, James on the handloom and Sarah on the preparation of velvet for weaving. Their two daughters, Caroline and Emma, aged twenty and nineteen, both worked as power loom weavers in the mill. In the same household was a son of ten who assisted with the handloom weaving and another daughter aged six who was too young to have regular employment. Both Caroline and Emma had been engaged in soft silk production at home when they were younger but entered the mill at seventeen when they were old enough to acquire more regular and secure wages as power loom weavers.

In other handloom households, particularly where there were no daughters of a suitable age to take up power loom weaving, mothers entered the mill. In these situations, childcare was often left to the male handloom weaver during the daytime. As Mary Merryweather, again observing through her own filter, commented on such arrangements:

> In such [handloom weavers'] shops are often to be seen the men sitting in the click-clacking loom, with half a dozen children toddling or trotting in and out. Sometimes one of these would creep away, and slyly hide her face behind the large rough stones, tied to the end of the 'harness' to keep it steady; sometimes a baby face would peep out of the high wicker cradle. The infant almost lost in what looked like dirty rags, whilst sitting on a tiny stool, or kneeling at the side of the cradle, might be seen another little one, scarcely larger than the baby, but taught to rock it till mother came from the factory.[35]

Women and girls in these housholds had few resources at their disposal and their labour was primarily channelled into

NOTICE

TO OUR

Soft Silk

WEAVERS.

THE universal and extreme depression of the Trade, compels us at length to limit the make of all goods but Velvets to Four days' work out of Six.

But feeling much for the Hands whose earnings will be thus reduced by One-third in these dear times, and at the beginning of winter, we mean to make up to them One-third part of the reduction of their earnings.

Thus a weaver whose average earnings have been 15s. a week, will now be restricted to the earning of 10s. But of the 5s. thus reduced, one-third, say 4d. in in the 1s., or 1s. 8d. upon the 5s. will be given to him to help him to bear up under his difficulties.

SAMUEL COURTAULD & Co.

H. GILBERT. PRINTER. HALSTED.

PLATE 17 Notice to soft silk handloom weavers posted by Samuel Courtauld in 1854 during a depression in the silk trade, indicating the vulnerability of this section of the population who were kept on mostly as a buffer workforce until the 1880s when soft silks (velvets and other luxury products) were phased out completely.

the maintenance of the whole household in highly unstable and impoverished circumstances. Their access to mill jobs did not allow them to usurp the status of the male handloom weaver as was feared by commentators in other parts of the country.[36] On the contrary, male handloom weavers survived as long as they did because of the labour of their female kin. Similarly, it was the collective survival strategies based on widespread female mill employment which enabled agricultural labourers to sustain their household position without too much difficulty until male employment opportunities in the area improved.

The failure of women's employment to oust male authority in the home lay in the segregation and subordination of their position in the mill workforce, as outlined in chapter 2. This certainly did not mean that such authority went unchallenged. The cottages of the Courtauld workers represented an important arena of conflict and tension over decision-making and control. The interconnection between the workplace and home shaped the terms of the struggles in which women found themselves involved. If the pervasiveness of workplace relations extended into households where husbands and fathers did not work in the mill, this was a process which was even more marked where male 'heads' occupied the highest positions in the mill hierarchy. Recalling the life of Frederick Hawkes, whose career illustrated the rapid upward mobility of male millworkers in chapter 2 (see p. 57), 1861 finds him living in a household in Trinity Road with his wife, Mary Ann, their two children, Clara, aged eleven, and Frederick (Junior), aged nine, and Mary Ann's mother, Lydia Pretty. At this time, Frederick was thirty-three years old and earning 17 shillings per week as an overseer in the winding department. Lydia Pretty is recorded as a 'house manager' and, since Mary Ann had a job in the mill, probably looked after the house. Most men working in the mill had wives who also had mill jobs. The wives of overseers like Frederick Hawkes were also likely to be in the few higher paid female positions. Mary Ann, for example, had been a waster for some years, but after her marriage to Frederick 'had become an assistant overseer on the Winding Floor of the Old Mills, a job to which she was promoted, at a wage of 8/6d per week, in 1848'.[37]

Even at the height of her earning power, Mary Ann scarcely received half the amount of her husband's wages and her position in the authority structure of the mill was below that of her husband and other men in his position. Even though her spouse was among the highest paid and highest status men in the mill there was no question at this time that a married woman like Mary Hawkes should give up her job. Her employment record shows her continuing at work on the winding floor 'where the stock of silk etc. is kept and the duties are rather heavy' throughout the 1850s.

Although men like Frederick Hawkes were part of an emerging 'labour aristocracy', it is only much later in the century that such a status is accompanied, in Halstead, by the expectation that wives should stay at home after marriage. In this respect, it is probably appropriate to view the 'labour aristocracy' as a 'sub-category' of the combined employment of men and women in factories.[38] The crucial qualification is that it was precisely women's wage contributions which *enabled* these men to secure an even higher standard of living and whose labour became such a threat to the men's status by the 1890s. Women and girls in this kind of household made essential contributions not only to the household economy but also to the superior status of their husbands and fathers. Moreover, this was a process which continued across generations until women's employment was increasingly expected to be confined to the period between school and marriage. The Hawkes children, for example, entered the mill and experienced a very similar form of job segregation as their parents. Clara became a weaver by the late 1860s at wages around one-third of her father's. Frederick (Junior) started out as a ticket boy in the steaming room in December 1865 at a wage of 5 shillings per week. He followed a similar path of upward mobility as his father, being transferred to the drawing room in 1866 and trained as a ledger clerk in the store room in 1867 at wages increasing to 10 shillings per week by 1869, when he had to leave 'on account of his health'.

The Hawkes household comes closest to resembling the 'family employment' situation prevailing in northern textile towns.[39] While far fewer households fitted this description than among northern millworkers,[40] age and gender were shaping distinctive patterns of experience in the range of households 'headed' by men. Where male 'heads' were employed in the mill, the occupational and gender segregation practices assured them of a superior position in both the workplace and the home. This process was passed on across generations. Silk work in the mill had very different meanings for men and women with implications which straddled the 'two worlds'. For men, work in the mill enhanced their position in the household. Women, on the other hand, provided labour and resources that kept them in a subordinate position in the workplace and the household, by rendering them vulnerable to both increased dependency and the burden of the 'double shift'. This meant a double dependency for women – on the father/husband who was 'master' of his household and on the master/employer who was 'father' of his workforce. This pattern had further implications for households where there was no male 'head'.

HOUSEHOLDS 'HEADED' BY WOMEN

The incidence of female 'headed' households is frequently taken as an indicator of the extent of poverty in an area. The figure of one in six such households in Halstead in 1861[41] signals not only the hardship in the locality as a whole but also the severe conditions facing women in these households and the kinds of strategies for survival which they developed. Women 'heads' of household were divided roughly equally between those who had jobs in the mill and those engaged in a variety of casual activities such as charring, washing and strawplaiting. Most women in the low paying casual occupations were widows belonging to households that must have been among the poorest in the town. There was more variety in the marital status of the women 'heads' employed in the mill. This group was evenly split between widows, married women and single women, indicating that mill employment for women acted to a certain extent as a basis for different kinds of household structure.

In the case of the married 'heads', the form which their households took was also influenced by the lack of male employment in the area. Some of their husbands were away looking for work while some had deserted their homes and families.[42] The increased likelihood of outdoor relief for these women and the uncertainty of any income which they received from absent husbands was compounded by the burden of dependence of non-earning children. Particular strategies were required for coping with such circumstances. A weaver called Amelia Smith, for example, lived in Trinity Square in 1861 with four dependent children aged between ten years and a few months old. At this time she was thirty-four years old and had never been absent from the mill. There were no other adults in her household in 1851, 1861 or 1871. She started work in the mill in July 1851 and finally left in December 1868 'to keep at home'. She probably decided to stay at the mill until some of her children were old enough to bring wages into the household since by 1868 her oldest daughter was seventeen and engaged as a weaver in the mill.

Among the women 'heads' who were single some had children and some did not. Whether they were mothers or not a frequent strategy was to share the same house. One such household in 1861 had two single women, both weavers, sharing a small cottage in Old Tanyard. Martha Spurgeon was twenty-nine years old at this time and lived with Elizabeth Springett, aged thirty-two, who was recorded as a 'boarder'.[43] Martha was born in London and had worked in the mill since 1846. Her previous address was in Hedingham Lane where a Spurgeon household present in 1861 contained a husband and wife who were born in London. They were both wage earners and had three additional wage earning children living in the household. This was probably Martha's family of origin. Hers was probably a fairly uncommon situation where her income was no longer essential for the collective survival of her parents' household and she had left home to set up a household of her own. Elizabeth Springett, Martha's 'boarder', most likely came from a similar family of origin. There was a Springett household immediately adjacent to their cottage in Old Tanyard where there were several wage earners in residence. It is difficult to surmise the precise configuration of arrangements between these three households and the motivation behind the setting up of the household containing

the two single women. It is interesting to note, however, that
the latter arrangement was not necessarily a transient stage
on the way to marriage, for Martha and Elizabeth were still
living together in 1871.

Other ways of providing support and help probably developed
between households containing unmarried mothers where
mutual benefits included the care of children. For example,
two single weavers with children lived next door to each other
in Kings Inn Yard in 1861. Elizabeth Norman was twenty-
eight years old and lived with her son, William, aged five.
Her neighbour, Emily Beaumont, aged thirty-two, lived with
her daughter, Emily (Junior), aged ten. Again it is difficult to
deduce the exact nature of their relationship and the exchange
of resources which took place between them[44] but both women
worked in the mill, both had been winders and weavers for
several years and both had moved to these houses from
different addresses. Emily (Junior) would have been old
enough to undertake the common practice among girls aged
between seven and twelve of taking care of younger children.
Mary Merryweather noted this practice, mentioning that girls
of this age were too young to enter the mill but could bring
in extra money by being paid about 1/6d per week for their
services. She also reveals how another frequent form of
childcare support between women was that provided by elderly
women for younger, usually married, women working at the
mill:

> A poor woman, as soon as she could leave her house after
> the child was born, usually found some little girls to attend
> to the child, if her husband worked at home, and she had
> no elder children of her own. Sometimes, however, she
> took the poor baby, on the way to the factory at six o'clock
> in the morning, to a neighbour's house, probably an old
> woman who took charge of several others.[45]

The female networks developing between households of all
kinds were born largely out of conditions that were placing
increasing constraints on women's ability to combine wage
earning activity with childcare responsibilities. As women,
from necessity, took on more and more responsibility for
the 'double burden', the expectation of men's domestic

responsibilities correspondingly declined. The existence of households 'headed' by women, far from signalling a breakdown of male control, was actually a symptom of the reconsolidation of patriarchal organization. The principles that govern such organization attribute authority and status to the notional rather than the actual head of important social units. The attitude towards men's labour was based on the traditional notion that men were fathers/masters. The higher rewards that accrued to them both in terms of status and earnings carried through to the structuring of households. Households were assumed to be headed by a male with his higher status and earning power. In the conditions prevailing in nineteenth-century Halstead this was not always the case in actuality. Men left the area looking for work. Women were widowed and deserted. The female 'headed' households which resulted, from compulsion or choice, were far more vulnerable than those 'headed' by men. A further vulnerability in living arrangements among women in the town lies in the kind of lodging patterns in existence at this time.

LODGING ARRANGEMENTS

While there were a few young labouring men who lodged in Halstead, most people who adopted this kind of living arrangement were young single women who worked at the mill. In a small number of households elderly women took in either 'lodgers' or 'boarders' as a means of livelihood where there was little access to alternative sources of support.[46] The predominant pattern, however, was for households headed mostly by low paid male workers, in which there were few or no other wage earners present, to take in young women under twenty-five years of age, some of whom were unmarried mothers. The majority of the women were weavers who came from households in outlying rural villages like Gosfield, Great Maplestead, Greenstead Green and Colne Engaine where the occupational structure was dominated by agriculture and strawplaiting.

For the households in which these women lodged, the rent contributed towards survival where wages were particularly low. For the households from which the young women originated, decisions must have been based upon whether the daughter's presence in the house detracted or added to the collective resources. For many, the decision to send the daughter to the mill and to lodgings was probably shaped by the need for the higher income she could command even when rent for lodgings was deducted. The many statements by Mary Merryweather and the local Board of Health[47] suggest that incomes earned by youngsters in the mill, even when they did not reside at home, were still channelled back into the parental household. This is made even more likely by the fact that many of the lodgers went home every weekend.

Although these young women were living in different surroundings it is not likely that this gave them an 'indepedent' status. They were being transferred from one patriarchal household to another. Even though the 'heads' of the households in which they lodged were low paid they were male and earned more than the young women silk workers. Just as in previous centuries the 'master' was not necessarily related by kin to all those considered as part of his 'family' in the household, so the male 'head' in these households assumed a father role over young women lodgers, whether or not they were related by kin. Indeed, in some cases households were reconstituted along just such familial lines. A forty-one-year-old unmarried agricultural labourer, called Thomas Wilks, for example, had lodging with him in 1861 a twenty-four-year-old weaver called Elizabeth Bocking and her son, aged two, together with a forty-two-year-old strawplaiter called Sarah Bocking, who was possibly Elizabeth's mother.

It seems likely that male 'heads' and their households benefited not only economically from having young female lodgers but also via other services like childcare, support for elderly and sick household members, domestic activities like cooking and cleaning and in some cases perhaps even sexual services. Some of these benefits, and certainly the economic ones, were also present in situations where 'secondary kin'[48] were part of the 'one census family'.[49] In 1861, about three-quarters of the households in Halstead containing one or more silk workers were nuclear 'one census family' types. Of those that departed from the nuclear form, many contained extended kin. (By this time, the identification of 'the family' with a household consisting of husband, wife and children was well under way.)[50]

The most significant feature of these households was that the kin relationship was usually based on a female connection and that the ensuing organization of resources tended to benefit male more than female members of the household. Where there was just one other kin member present, apart from the nuclear kin, it was usually one of the parents of the woman in the 'primary' nuclear unit. It was more frequently the father than the mother of the woman. These men were recorded as elderly and as no longer employed. Whereas widows provided services to kin and non-kin, men who were widowers appear to have looked mostly to their female kin, especially daughters, for support. This process involved an abdication of patriarchal status in old age to men of the next generation, usually sons or sons-in-law. In a context where landless wage labourers have no property to pass on, increasing age and infirmity among men reduces male privileges just as youth denies but portends patriarchal authority.

In households where there was more than one 'secondary kin' member present the connection between 'primary' and 'secondary' kin was also usually provided by females. The most common situation was for a daughter of the 'head' of the household to be present together with her children, if she was single or widowed, or with both husband and children, if she was married. In circumstances like the latter, where a whole group of husband, wife and children were living in a relative's household, it was usually the wife's parents rather than the husband's parents who shared their household. Mutual exchanges of support and resources were probably made possible in these kinds of household. In one household where there were two 'secondary kin families', for example, two daughters had returned to live with their parents who were soft silk handloom weavers living in Parsonage Street. One of the daughters, a twenty-nine-year-old widowed weaver called Phoebe Wicker, had a ten-year-old son and the other was a twenty-two-year-old married weaver called Harriet Allison with no children and no husband present. Their parents, John and Mary Davey, had one more child in the house, a seventeen-

year-old son called John (Junior) who was a draper's assistant.
Phoebe and her sister, Harriet, by living in their parents'
house, did not have to rely totally on their own resources.
Phoebe also probably got help with childcare since both her
parents worked at home. Meanwhile, John and Mary Davey,
dependent on their own low wages from handloom weaving
and those of their son, gained from having two more adult
wage earners in the household.

The kinds of living arrangements experienced by Halstead
labourers cannot, however, be seen solely in terms of 'mutual
accommodation'[51] between the changing face of industry and
the rhythms of family and individual lives. Nor can they be
explained entirely in terms of 'rational calculation'.[52] Structural
inequalities of gender and age were central to experiences in
the house as much as in the workplace. This is because
patriarchal relationships were being refashioned across boundaries between household and workplace in such a way as to
shape the experience of women whose employment was based
outside the home as much as those whose paid activities
lay predominantly within the home. Patriarchal status still
combined the familial and the economic. At one time these
had been united in the one role as father and master in the
domestic system of production. In the new configuration of
economic activities accompanying industrialization there was
an apparent separation of 'family' and 'work' roles. In actuality,
however, women continued to provide essential economic
services via both paid and unpaid labour, both inside and
outside the home.

Survival in these circumstances was a different experience
– and held different meanings – for men and women. The
distinctions were perhaps most marked in households 'headed'
by women where there was a daily struggle to manage without
the presence of adult male wages. But there were differences,
too, for women and girls living in households where wages were
sometimes spent disproportionately for male consumption[53] and
where patterns of authority continued to be focused around
the male 'head'. Even if wages were paid directly into the
hands of women and girls the persistence of traditional notions
of patriarchal authority were buttressed both by the structural
relations of workplace and home and by legal controls such

as the denial of women's rights to their own earnings up until the 1870 Married Women's Property Act. These factors acted as a brake on any major changes in decision-making processes stirred by women's access to individual wages.[54] The general trend towards earlier independent status after the 1850s[55] took much longer to show an effect anyway in this part of Essex. The economic contribution of both girls and boys was an essential part of most households throughout the nineteenth century. For girls this contribution tended to last longer and additionally they provided domestic and childcare services. Access to control over their own lives for girls and women was seriously limited by the systematic channelling of resources into the household – first as daughters, then as wives.

Men, who were increasingly being defined as breadwinners with jobs outside the home, continued to benefit from a position of authority over women and children both outside and inside the home. The hierarchy which had formed the foundation stone of the silk industry in former centuries lived on in different circumstances. Samuel Courtauld's conception of himself as a benevolent father of his workpeople provided many of the conditions in which such a hierarchy could flourish.

NOTES

1 *Kelly's Directories of Essex*, 1855, 1862 and 1866. See also P. Bamberger, *A Pictorial History of Halstead and District*, Halstead and District Local History Society, 1979.
2 Courtauld paid £33,400 for Gosfield Manor and its 2,000 acres of land. He also paid £29,850 for 1,200 acres of adjoining land. See D. C. Coleman, *Courtaulds: An Economic and Social History*, vol. I, p. 127, Clarendon Press, 1969.
3 Mary Merryweather, *Experience of Factory Life: Being a record of 14 years' work at Mr. Courtauld's silk mill at Halstead in Essex*, 3rd edn, Emily Faithfull Publishing Co., 1862, pp. 6–7.
4 ERO D/F 3/3/39. Lodging is discussed further later in this chapter.
5 *General Memorandum Book*, 1879–1909, ERO D/F 3/2/39.
6 Letter from Reverend W. Billopp, Chairman of Halstead Sanitary Committee and vicar of St James' Church, Greenstead Green, 27 August 1849, to General Board of Health, PRO, MH 13/83.
7 Letter from Charles Burney, Vicar of St Andrew's, Halstead, 18 November 1852, to General Board of Health, PRO MH 13/83.

8 Letter from Harvey Bridges, of Blue Bridge House, Halstead, 13 January 1863, to General Board of Health, PRO MH 13/83.

9 The Courtaulds' objection to rates was confined primarily to a Nonconformist objection to levies supporting the Church of England. For a famous incident involving Samuel Courtauld in the 1830s see below, chapter 4, p. 98 and n. 8.

10 Report on Housing, 1867.

11 The report of a case in the Petty Sessions Court in March 1860, for instance, refers to a complaint by Frederick Norman, a mill machinery attendant at the silk mill living in Mount Pleasant, that his next-door neighbour's chickens had damaged his cabbages, *Halstead Gazette*, Thursday, 8 March, 1860.

12 Merryweather, *Factory Life*, p. 32.

13 Ibid. pp. 32–3.

14 Ibid., p. 33.

15 Elizabeth Pleck, 'Two worlds in one: work and family', *Journal of Social History*, 10(2), Winter 1976.

16 Ibid.

17 Patrick Joyce, 'The factory politics of Lancashire in the later nineteenth century', *The Historical Journal*, 18(3), 1975, p. 152.

18 Ibid.

19 Merryweather, *Factory Life*.

20 Ibid., pp. 19–20.

21 *Halstead Gazette* and *Halstead Times*. Violence towards women at this time was strongly attacked by Frances Power Cobbe in 'Wife Torture in England', 1878. It has also been documented by some recent researchers such as Nancy Tomes, '"A Torrent of Abuse": crimes of violence between working class men and women in London, 1849–1875', *Journal of Social History*, 11, 1978, pp. 323–45.

22 Merryweather, *Factory Life*, p. 20.

23 It is usually taken to mean husband, wife and children employed in the factory. See, for example, Patrick Joyce, *Work, Society and Politics: the Culture of the Factory in Late Victorian England*, Harvester Press, 1980; Neil J. Smelser, *Social Change in the Industrial Revolution*, University of Chicago Press, 1959.

24 A 17 per cent sample from the 1,015 employment records which were constructed for workers present in the mill in 1861 were followed through to the 1861 census enumerators' books to provide information about household circumstances. Only 7 per cent of individuals in this sample were male silk workers. In order to avoid producing only 'snapshots' of household situations some households were also followed through to the 1871 and 1851 census books. Most of the examples used in this chapter are taken from the record linkages between the employment registers and the census data. See T. Hareven (ed.), *Transitions: The Family and the Life Course in*

Historical Perspective, Academic Press, 1978; T. Hareven and R. Langenbach, *Amoskeog: Life and Work in an American Factory-city in New England*, Methuen, 1979.

25 This chapter explores actual household circumstances of Halstead workers while the next two (chapters 4 and 5) describe the kind of family ideology which was being promoted by the employers.

26 Alice Clarke, *Working Life of Women in the Seventeenth Century*, Routledge and Kegan Paul, 1982; see also C. Creighton, 'Family, property and relations of production in Western Europe', *Economy and Society*, vol. 9, May 1980; J. Goody, J. Thirsk and E. P. Thompson (eds), *Family and Inheritance: Rural Society in Western Europe, 1200–1800*, Past and Present publications, Cambridge, 1976.

27 1827 manuscript, Halstead Household Listing, ERO, and 1861 Halstead Census Enumerators Books, PRO.

28 The average household size among the 17 per cent sample was 5.31.

29 A major problem when using census data is that census enumerators used their own subjective and varying forms of classification. A common practice among nineteenth-century enumerators was the omission of any occupational designation to married women. They often either left the category empty or simply added the description 'wife' to the occupation of the woman's husband. Because of the widespread nature of women's employment in Halstead there are not a great many married women in the local census books who evade classification. Activities which were frequently under-estimated, however, were strawplaiting and other 'casual' work like taking in washing and cleaning. On the other hand, the extent of male occupations was sometimes over-emphasized since enumerators sometimes classified an elderly man by his former occupation without prefixing the entry with 'formerly'. This particular error was less likely to occur with elderly women. Some of the standard procedures for handling occupational categories in the census data are described in W. A. Armstrong, 'The use of information about occupation', in E. A. Wrigley, *Nineteenth Century Society*, Cambridge University Press, 1972.

30 See chapter 1, 'The thread of patriarchy', pp. 12–15. See also D. Bythell, *The Handloom Weavers*, Cambridge University Press, 1969; E. P. Thompson, *The Making of the English Working Class*, Pelican, 1968, ch. 9, pp. 297–346.

31 See, for example, W. Radcliffe, *Origin of the New System of Manufacture Commonly called Power Loom Weaving*, J. Lomax, 1828.

32 Merryweather, *Factory Life*, p. 34.

33 Coleman, *Courtaulds*, vol. I, p. 81.

34 An entry in one of the firm's General Memo Books (1879–1909), dated 17 October 1884, comments that, 'It is decided to take all the

handlooms down after the Canes that are being woven now are finished, those from the Lodges, the various Factories included. [The lodge keepers at each factory were put to work on handlooms and on organizing the putting out of work to handloom weavers in their homes.] As the firm can no longer employ the weavers engaged on this work out of the Factories. The Lodgemen will be found other employment and they will present each weaver with the sum of £5, which amounts can be either drawn at once, or left in the Firm's hands and drawn on as required', ERO D/F 3/2/39.

35 Merryweather, *Factory Life*, p. 34.

36 See, for example, F. Engels, *The Condition of the Working Class in England in 1844*, first published London, 1892, Panther edition, 1967.

37 Other men in the high status positions in the mill were also married to the few women who managed to ascend to the top of the female hierarchy. George Firmin, the principal clerk in the Store Room in the 1850s, was married to Jane Firmin, a gauze examiner. James Prentice, an assistant overseer in the Store Room, was also married to a gauze examiner, Anne Prentice. Furthermore, the timing of these marriages tends to coincide with the promotion of the women. The men were already overseers when they got married. Anne Prentice was promoted shortly after her marriage to James; Mary Ann Hawkes was promoted at about the same time as her marriage to Frederick.

38 P. Joyce, *Work, Society and Politics: The Culture of the Factory in Late Victorian England*, Harvester Press, 1980.

39 Smelser, *Social Change in the Industrial Revolution*.

40 Only 8.8 per cent of households in the sample followed through to the 1861 census books, for example, contained husband, wife and children all employed in the mill.

41 Halstead Census Enumerators' Books 1861.

42 A case appearing in the *Halstead Gazette*, 18 April 1861, for example, reports that a man called William Hunt had gone to Canterbury, Kent, to seek work in May 1859 and had stopped sending any money to his wife, Sarah, a weaver in the mill, after three months. Hunt claimed that he was ill but it was established that he was earning between 16 shillings and 26 shillings per week and had been living with a young woman whom he left pregnant in February 1861. Sarah had been granted outdoor relief since the beginning of 1860 and even had to enter the Union Workhouse for fourteen weeks as she had several children. Mr Manning, the assistant overseer of the workhouse at this time, reported that he knew of at least nine cases of unsolved desertion in the parish in April 1861.

43 The designation of 'boarder' in the census books signified an arrangement where the individual shared the same table as the

householder, indicating a closer sharing of resources than someone classified as a 'lodger', see Census 1863, vol. LII, p. 33.

44 Similar issues are explored in Diana Gittins, 'Inside and outside marriage', *Feminist Review* 14, Summer 1983.

45 Merryweather, *Factory Life*, pp. 50–1.

46 See L. Davidoff, 'The separation of home and work? Landladies and lodgers in nineteenth and twentieth century England', in S. Burman (ed.), *Fit Work for Women*, Croom Helm, 1979.

47 For example, Report of enquiry into petition for separation by Robert Rawlinson, Inspector, 1864, Halstead General Board of Health and Local Government Office correspondence 1849–1871: 'There are large silk factories in Halstead, paying some twenty to thirty thousand pounds per annum in wages. It was stated that most of the agricultural labourers of the Parish reside in Halstead to enable the children to work in the silk mills.'

48 Households with 'secondary kin' present, e.g. a father, mother, sister or brother of the husband or wife, together with households with lodgers or boarders present, constituted 8 per cent of all the 'one census families' in Halstead in 1861.

49 According to most tabulation procedures in the census enumerators' books a 'census family' is taken to be the co-residing group. See, for example, M. Anderson, 'Standard tabulation procedures for the census enumerators' books, 1851–1891' in Wrigley, *Nineteenth Century Society*. The co-residing group, as defined in the 1851 census, is the group who lives with an 'Occupier – understanding by "occupier" either a resident owner or any person who pays rent, whether (as a tenant) for the whole house or (as a lodger) for any distinct floor or apartment . . .', 1851 Census Report, part I, cxlii. This unit is most often taken to be 'the household'.

50 For example, *Encyclopedia Britannica* for 1860 defines 'the family' as husband, wife and their immediate offspring.

51 T. Hareven, *Family Time and Industrial Time*, Cambridge University Press, 1982.

52 M. Anderson, *Family Structure in Nineteenth Century Lancashire*, Cambridge University Press, 1971.

53 See Merryweather, *Factory Life*, and for other examples elsewhere in the country see Laura Oren, 'The welfare of women in labouring families: England 1860–1950', *Feminist Studies*, Winter 1973.

54 As Leonore Davidoff has remarked in relation to domestic service, 'The existence of cash payment *in itself* does not mean escape from paternalistic control; it only creates possibilities for an alternative way of life', see 'Mastered for life: servant and wife in Victorian and Edwardian England', in A. Sutcliffe and P. Thane (eds), *Essays in Social History*, Oxford University Press, 1986. The implications of paternalistic control in relation to silk workers and the possibilities

for alternative ways of life for women are explored in the following chapters of this present book.

55 Michael Anderson, 'Family work and household in Britain, 1851–1981', University of Essex Social History Seminar, November 1981.

4

FATHERING THE WORKPLACE

The notion of paternalism is most frequently associated with feudal relationships based on a fixed social hierarchy of positions each with its own clearly defined set of obligations, rights and duties. During the nineteenth century, a 'new paternalism' blossomed among many Victorian 'Captains of Industry', seeking legitimacy as a new social elite fashioned out of the rise of urban employment within a largely rural context.[1]

Employers were not united over attitudes and strategies concerning the management of industrial relations in larger, more collectivized workplaces. One main school of thought emphasized the rational and methodical control of workers whose welfare was not seen as the responsibility of the employer. The other took an approach of enlightened self-interest preferring moral persuasion to force. Human welfare was seen as both morally desirable and practically profitable. This stance was more common among the most powerful industrialists like Titus Salt, Henry Ashworth and Thomas Ashton. It also frequently accompanied Nonconformist allegiances. Samuel Courtauld, with his strong Unitarian background, identified himself from an early stage as a member of the latter camp.

COURTAULD'S 'NEW PATERNALISM'

Courtauld's style of paternalism combined a traditional adherence to the 'theory of dependence' with an espousal of individualistic principles of self help. The 'theory of dependence', modelled on aristocratic relations between rich and poor, was succinctly summarized by John Stuart Mill in 1848:

> the lot of the poor, in all things which affect them collectively, should be regulated for them, not by them. They should not be required or encouraged to think for themselves, or give to their own reflection or forecast an influential voice in their own destiny. It is the duty of the higher classes to think for them. . . The relation between rich and poor should be . . . affectionate tutelage on the one side, respectful and grateful deference on the other.[2]

Courtauld actively attempted to foster these kinds of relationships, previously associated with small industrial units, in his fast-expanding enterprise throughout the nineteenth century. This network of relationships was mainly advanced through the development of a host of institutions such as schools, libraries, working men's clubs, mechanics' institutes and sick clubs based on the principle of self-improvement. The Nonconformist belief in freedom from state interference and in a strict moral code of diligence, thrift and sobriety coincided with the widespread popularity of 'success literature', epitomized by the publications of Samuel Smiles.[3] This literature emphasized the virtues of hard work, thriftiness, education, punctuality, a prudent marriage, a good home and attention to small particulars.

This powerful combination of beliefs engendered a strongly individualistic creed which paradoxically nurtured a deep commitment to social improvement. Since every person is of equal and particular interest according to Nonconformist precepts, opportunities should be extended and restraints removed for all to develop their full potential. This was underpinned by the notion that it was the duty of the wealthy to assist the poor. In the context of the influence of the political economists' argument that relations between master and servant were governed by immutable laws, Courtauld's paternalist stance was aimed at promoting a harmony of interests between employers and employed. Courtauld shared the widespread belief among paternalistic industrialists that workers needed capitalists to provide jobs and capitalists needed workers to labour in their enterprises.

An emphasis on harmony was important in a society troubled by social and economic tensions. A strong motivation for enlightened employers was the reconciliation of the social classes. Divisions of economic security separating the middle and the working class were heightened by the movement of the middle classes to the suburbs and the deterioration of working-class housing. In this context, working-class poverty was chiefly characterized by middle-class observers as a consequence of moral failure. Echoing Smiles's notion that 'Misery is the result of moral causes',[4] Samuel Courtauld's brother, George, commented in 1846 that one of the 'grand miseries' of the millworkers was that the increased earnings of the men were spent 'too often in ministering to a selfish personal indulgence of a more or less pernicious character rather than to furnish the means of self-culture or to provide for this respectability and comfort of his own home'.[5] The other 'grand misery' was the neglect of home duties by the female silk workers.[6]

Employers like the Courtaulds felt that the solution to the problems of the working class lay in their adoption of middle-class values through self-help. The middle class employer's role, according to this viewpoint, was to assist in this process by establishing institutions for encouraging self-improvement through prudent habits of hard work, thrift and sobriety. This was manifest in the Halstead mill in the development of a range of paternalistic practices reflecting the same gender and age divisions characterizing the structure of the workforce. The 'new paternalism' was rooted in an age-old distinction between 'master' and 'man'. (Indeed the formal terminology of 'master' and 'servant' in places of employment was not dismantled until 1870 in England.) It was enmeshed within a network of rights and duties pertaining to the ownership of property. One factor distinguishing it from earlier definitions however, was its intrinsic association with domestic ideology and the sharpening definitions of masculinity and femininity accompanying the growth of urban industrialism. In conditions increasingly differentiating the home from the workplace, paternalism allowed the mapping out of 'separate spheres' for men and women. Obligations expected of the workers were gender-specific and fashioned from the norms and values close to the hearts of their middle-class employers.

At the centre of Courtauld's paternalism was 'the family'. If the highly segregated and vertically ranked labour force represented a recreation of the hierarchical ideal of family life so too every aspect of factory culture emulated a strict ordering of organic paternalist principles. According to these principles, the whole local population worked towards common ends, but all from their specified positions, demarcated not only by class but by gender and age. The factory was thus modelled on pre-existing familial inequalities of status and authority which were presented as 'natural' differences. Moreover, the appeal to workers' loyalty extended from the factory and its 'master' to the surrounding territory – to the homes, places of worship, schools, places of entertainment, right through to the habits of dress and moral behaviour of the local inhabitants. The influence of the employers permeated all aspects of everyday life. Being an employer involved Courtauld in a particular relationship with his workers in which their status as dependants was especially significant. He was motivated 'to act towards dependents as a father does to his wife, his children and his servants'.[7]

As an active Unitarian, closely linked with the radical minister W. J. Fox, Courtauld supported a quest for moral reform centering on a revitalized religious consciousness. This reforming zeal had a heavily rationalist foundation, predisposing its adherents to an affinity with radical political beliefs which tended to compound their conception of themselves as self-appointed moral entrepreneurs. Samuel Courtauld made a public stand on issues both religious and political in which he saw himself defending against the encroachment of the state.[8] The connection between Courtauld and Fox also put him in touch with a wider circle of radical views including those promoting women's rights to paid employment. Fox's journal, *The Monthly Repositary*, saw the first public airing of Harriet Martineau's writing.

Courtauld's self-appointed role as protector of his own 'family' of workpeople and his accompanying belief in the civilizing mission of industry helps to explain how paternalism rested so comfortably beside *laissez-faire* capitalism. The sense of moral and social superiority of employers like Courtauld facilitated their belief that it was the duty and responsibility of the industrial property owner, upon whom the livelihoods of his workforce depended, to create and maintain localized boundaries of interest in the face of interference from a remote national government. Employers were personal exemplars of authority to be set against the impersonal dictates of state legislation. In this role, it was impossible for Courtauld to countenance any form of government legislation restricting the employment of women and children. Arguing for the exclusion of the silk industry from the Factory Acts in the 1830s Courtauld stated that: 'Legislative interference in the arrangement and conduct of business is always injurious, tending to check improvement and to increase the cost of production.'[9]

This was a stand which Courtauld maintained for many years. In the custodial role which he assumed for himself he closely resembled a 'lord of the manor', a status which he undoubtedly cultivated in his search for a social position alongside the local landed aristocracy. In celebration of this role a huge festival took place in 1846, marking the beginning of a whole series of benevolent endeavours undertaken to strengthen the familial bonds between employer and employed.

'A FACTORY FESTIVAL' 1846

On 26 June 1846, the meadow in front of Folly House in High Garrett, the current residence of Samuel Courtauld, set the scene for

a spontaneous display of the goodwill and respect of the employed towards the employers, which speaks at once as much for the industry, and good habits, and right-minded gratitude of the one, as for the just, and liberal, and kind-hearted conduct of the other towards them. It is pleasant thus to see labour and capital sitting down together.[10]

Complete with banners, bands and processions this gathering epitomized the kind of public ritual that formed a central feature of factory paternalism signifying an important element in the encouragement of a 'company culture'.[11]

The whole spectacle was carefully stage-managed. Workers from all three of Courtauld's factories – about 700 in all from Bocking and Braintree and 800 from Halstead – were marshalled together in the morning for the march to High Garrett. The two great processions converged on their destination ordered in ranks displaying the status distinctions of home and workplace. The Bocking and Braintree contingent was led by male carpenters and blacksmiths followed by enginemen and mechanics. After them came various other male workers and finally in the tail of the great column came female dyers, dressers and packers. At the head of the Halstead procession were enginemen and mechanics and in the final ranks were vast numbers of female power loom weavers.

The banners and flags carried by the workers bore inscriptions reflecting the widespread paternalistic assumption that capital and labour were united in a common enterprise. The winders' banner proclaimed, 'By winders' aid Our wealth is made'. The mottos on the banners of the soft silk weavers and the packers declared, 'Weave trust with faith' and 'Honour to whom honour is due'. Other inscriptions heralded such ideals as 'Talent', 'Labour', 'Enterprise', 'Industry', 'It is good to see brethren dwell together in unity' and 'Blessed is he who considers the poor'. The whole display symbolized the notion that all those present were held together by a common familial bond in which the more vulnerable junior members were looked after and watched over by their elders and betters. How far the operatives shared this notion is difficult to establish. Evidence from other areas suggests that a degree of cynicism was apparent on many of these occasions, witnessed in comments that demonstrated a preference for higher wages rather than an occasional 'plate of beef and a glass of beer'.[12] Although the cost of this particular day's proceedings was borne by the operatives themselves there is no way of knowing who organized the collection of money and with how much duress.[13]

The event was certainly a large-scale affair involving thousands of local inhabitants and creating a public landmark of benevolence and goodwill in the area for miles around. A report appearing in the national press a few days later estimated that between 5,000 and 6,000 spectators waited at Folly House for the arrival of the processions at midday and that a further 3,000 or 4,000 visited the scene at some time during the course of the day.[14] The theme set by the banners was echoed throughout the day, particularly in the speeches after dinner. Lister Smith, the firm's secretary, set the stage with a robust tribute to the supposed mutuality of interests nurtured by the Courtaulds:

> We congratulate you on the era which has now dawned upon the sons of toil, when the buyers and the sellers of labour can regard each other as mutual friends, whose interests are the same, and who entertain towards each other no feelings opposed to their common welfare.[15]

Following this with a more personal reference to the paternalist qualities of Samuel Courtauld, Smith goes on to praise 'the patient and persevering manner in which you have attended to the complaints of the smallest child in your establishment [which] has inspired a confidence in your justice not often equalled, and exhibited you as *the father* rather than the master of those over whom you preside'.[16]

In his reply, Samuel's main concern seems to be to identify himself as a hard-working man whose motives are the benefit of all over and above personal gain. Amid the reported cheers of the workpeople, he announced that 'I too have known what it is to eat bread by the sweat of my brow' and thanked his employees for the great honour of referring to him as 'an ever-working man'. He proceeded to talk of his sympathies with the 'operative classes', adding that although 'I will not say that I did not calculate my profits', he had always been driven far more by the desire to provide employment since 'good masters make good servants and good servants make good masters'.

The paternalist emphasis on benevolent exchange between

employer and workers within a *laissez-faire* economy is
underscored by a celebration of the role of the employers'
wives in promoting harmony and well-being. Lister Smith led
the way in a tribute to the 'ladies of the firm', notably Samuel
Courtauld's wife, Ellen and Peter Taylor's wife, Catherine, by
waxing into a prolific eulogy of the selfless 'angel in the house',
complementing her husband's bustling role in the world of
business by her virtuous ministrations to all around her in her
'natural' sphere:

> Had *man* been destined to live alone
> His greatest blessing never had been known;
> This Adam proved when of the earth new made
> He stood the lord of all his eyes survey'd.
> Though rich in choicest gifts beyond compare,
> The child of happiness, creation's heir,
> Something was wanted still to crown his life
> And his creator blessed him with a wife;
> He found it better far to spare a bone
> Than do a world of business all alone;
> So gave a *spare rib* from his manly hip;
> And took his gentle Eve in partnership.
>
> But I am digressing from my purposed aim,
> Your warm reception of a worthy name.
> But why pronounce it? – will it not suffice
> To say the *Eve* of this fair paradise?
> Who e'er her sphere presides with angel sway,
> And all the virtues wait upon her way.
> Blest with an ample share of earthly wealth,
> Her time, her cares, her fortune and her health
> Are not expended on herself alone,
> But all around her generous bounty own.[17]

Smith's idealization of 'the perfect lady' shows how middle-
class men not only expected their wives to present the sanctified
face of their own wealthy and prestigious position but also
emphasized the 'natural' duties of their wives as mothers
bringing up the future owners of the business enterprise. He
went on, for example,

Tis Nature's law by Nature's God designed
That *mothers* should first form the infant mind . . .
Ladies! 'tis yours to act a noble part,
To store the mind and educate the heart,
With your own generous souls your sons inspire
And make your children worthy of their sire.[18]

Such sentiments represented the ideal irrespective of whether these 'ladies' actually bore children or not. In Ellen Courtauld's case there were no surviving children of her own. She had given birth some years earlier to a daughter, Nellie, who had died in 1841. Subsequent to this, in an act commensurate with the pervasive paternalism demonstrated in all their other activities, the Courtaulds adopted two girls Sarah Ann Causton and Ruth Harris, with whom they had been closely associated.[19]

Ellen Courtauld made extensive efforts to live up to the ideal of the ministering angel in her dealings both with her immediate and adoptive kin and with the wider 'family' of her husband's workforce and their kin. She was a constant helpmeet and confidante to her husband. He wrote to her in terms of endearment from wherever he travelled, sharing both his business anxieties and his emotional concerns. She was closely involved with the chapel that Samuel commissioned to be built in High Garrett for years after they moved from the village. As Mrs Sydney Courtauld recalled years later in 1895,

I have written of this chapel [High Garrett] as though it were mostly Mr. Courtauld's concern . . . but I fancy that she had as much to do with it as he; he always associated her name with it . . . It was Mrs. Courtauld who, with the help of Mr. Robertson, minister at Halstead at that time, selected and arranged the hymns we use; she also introduced various tunes we sing, and at one time she always led the singing . . .[20]

Her involvement with local activities continued long after her removal to Gosfield Hall in 1854. In his reply to Lister Smith's eloquent address her husband referred to her 'ceaseless ministrations to all around her', her 'instruction and moral guidance of the young', and her 'constant devotion to alleviation of suffering'.[21]

The speeches of those seated at the head table during the festivities reveal a web of intersecting political, religious and industrial bonds. The presence of at least two prominent Nonconformist ministers, W. J. Fox and the Reverend T. Craig, confirms the close interconnections between the Courtaulds' paternalist ideals and practices and their religious involvement. Indicating the advantages to be gained from educating the workforce, Craig proclaimed that, 'The head of the firm he had heard bear testimony that the more the mind was improved and expanded by education, the better was the artisan adapted to carry out all the work that might be required for him.' Other speeches, like that of an overseer called Mr Jones, echoed the organic ideals of the employers: 'In "giving honour where honour is due", we are happy that this day we sit down in company with our employers, with those above us in property and education, with one mind and with a common understanding of mutual interest.'

During the proceedings the die from which a number of medallions commemorating the occasion had been struck was presented to Samuel Courtauld. The medallions, of which some still exist, bore pictures of some of the banners and their mottos, together with an inscription on one side which read 'June 26th, 1846, Dinner given to Samuel Courtauld, Taylors and Courtauld by 1600 of their people', and on the other side, 'Wealth, Talent, Labour, each respecting all, united prosper but divided fall'.[22]

As a public display of harmony and goodwill between employers and employed, the 1846 festival stands out as a prime example of the many attempts among the Victorian middle class to recreate conditions favourable to a stable submission to traditional authority.[23] Central to this endeavour was the cultivation of deference among both male and female workers. As members of a rising industrial elite the Courtaulds had to seek ways of managing the potential tensions inherent in the polarized social and economic positions occupied by themselves and their workforce. The encouragement of a culture of unity and harmony provided the major means of pursuing this aim. Whether the workers shared their employers' commitment to unity is a different matter. Social relationships based on the fostering of deference contain possibilities of

PLATE 18   Commemmorative medallion produced on the occasion of a Public Dinner held in honour of the Courtauld and Taylor families on 26 June 1846. The mottoes on the medallion symbolize the paternalistic ethos of the occasion. Many of the medallions were distributed and the die from which they were cast was presented to Samuel Courtauld.

both subservience and rebellion since they emerge as the outcome, not the source, of an unequal social order.[24]

THE WAGE SYSTEM

In keeping with the practices of many other paternalist enterprises of the period, the management policies and principles in the Halstead mill were based on a finely organized system of differentiation and control. Although based in the place of work, these measures were not solely economic. Whether to do with wages or welfare they were also deeply imbued with cultural and moral significance. The wage system reflected both the pre-existing division of labour when the household had formed the central unit of production and the particular balance of sociopolitical power accompanying struggles around this division of labour in the years preceding large-scale mechanization.

Early labour requirements in the mill were amply met by the plentiful supply of young female hands in local workhouses. With the construction of a hierarchy of 'skilled' male workers at the top of a mass of low paid women workers Courtauld activated a customary calculation[25] which not only embodied but sharply rigidified gender and age distinctions in the labour process. In the years after the 1840s, often characterized as a period of increasing efficiency of labour utilization[26] and labour synchronization,[27] the paternalistic ethics of the Courtauld firm prolonged a wage system which added to the strong demarcations of gender and age already established in the workforce. The adult male employees of the firm were paid a weekly rate calculated, it would seem, according to the proximity of the tasks performed to the processes associated with craft status. Women and girls were paid on piece rates which were not only a fraction of the male wages but also far lower than wages in other industrial areas. Added to this, women and girls were far more vulnerable to fluctuations in production than men. Short-time working in the 1870s, for example, affected female workers engaged directly in the production of silk rather than men who were mostly in supervisory and machine-repairing positions.

Piece rates have been associated with the kind of motivational strategies increasingly adopted by employers in the second half of the nineteenth century. In the case of the Courtauld firm, where there were no trade unions until the 1890s and where Samuel considered himself as the 'father' and protector of his workforce, piece rates were used not only as a work incentive but as a status distinction between the male and female workers. The prime motivation proffered to the men was that of occupying a superior position, carrying both higher status and higher wages, over the mass of female hands who constituted the majority of the workforce.

Courtauld's style of paternalism kept the majority of his labour costs extremely low through persistent subordination of female labour. It also offset the need for methods pursued in search of greater labour efficiency in industries where the advance of the New Model unions and the growing knowledge of the 'rules of the game'[28] among the workforce were becoming significant factors in industrial relations. One of Courtauld's few concessions to the pre-'scientific management' strategies of nineteenth-century industrialists was the abolition of 'grace time' in 1873.[29]

These patterns illustrate how both 'custom' in wage practices and 'time-thrift' in industrial employment carried with them gender and age distinctions of the past and helped to sharpen these distinctions as industrial capitalism advanced.

FINES, FORFEITS AND REWARDS

In a statement to the Children's Employment Commissioners in 1833, Samuel Courtauld described methods of discipline among his young workers as 'a regular system of forfeits and rewards, the stimulus of piece-work, and dismissal in the last resort'.[30] He admitted that 'formerly something like a system of taskwork was adopted', but as the years went by he relied increasingly on forfeits and rewards. From the 1820s onwards beer allowances and other rewards were provided for both male and female workers. By the 1860s the firm's Rule Books enumerated the extent of beer allowances, overtime pay, coal allowances for enginemen and concessions for smoking in certain areas of the mills.[31]

Because of the division of labour in the mills, male workers tended to gain more benefits from the rewards offered than females. It was only men, for instance, who were eligible for the coal allowances and smoking was only allowed in the mechanics shops, dye houses and gas houses where only men worked. Smoking near the silk was strictly forbidden and, of course, it was mainly women and young people who were engaged on the processes dealing with the actual production of the silk. Male mechanics also received allowances for washing and clothing. Crimpers and carpenters received free newspapers and the mechnics were rewarded with an annual sum of £5 as 'feast money'.[32]

On the other side of the coin, women stood to fall foul of the fines system more than men since fines were imposed for bad work in producing the silk as well as for lateness. Since it was women and children whose work was directly connected to handling the silk it was they who were more likely to be admonished for bad work. Reasons given for imposing fines for bad work included 'dirty work', 'thick and thin places', 'refusing a cane' (refusing to work a particular beam of silk thread) and sometimes simply being a 'bad weaver'.[33] Added to these, female workers could be fined, and sometimes even dismissed, for 'misconduct', 'irregularity', and being 'abusive'.[34]

Men in the labour force came under scrutiny too but for different reasons. Lower status male workers, such as the loom attendants and mill machinery attendants were severely censured and cautioned if they arrived at work drunk. Overseers did not escape such criticism either. One overseer in the Old Mills at Halstead, Henry Garrod, was personally cautioned by George Courtauld. In a memorandum dated 9 July 1872, George Courtauld noted that,

> The Mill overseer, Henry Garrod, seems not at all competent to his place – Hands gossiping together or asleep – spindles empty for want of full balls (though the drawn stock at Halstead is now large to superfluity) – guiders badly adjusted – very large number of ends down [ends of silk thread not finished off properly]. – Altogether seems careless and without appreciation of his duties . . . Have cautioned him that we *must* dismiss him unless he does better.[35]

Two years later Garrod was finally demoted: 'After repeated cautions from Mr. George Courtauld who found him an inefficient overseer in allowing the Floor and Hands to be most disorderly he was put back to Spindle Cleaning,'[36] with a reduction of 4/6d weekly in his wages. It is clear that a chain of authority operated whereby the overseers kept order among the mass of workers while the Courtaulds themselves kept a careful eye on the performance of the overseers. Garrod was censured for failure to execute his proper authority.

Fines for being late were not abolished until 1889. Even then, late-comers were not allowed to commence work until after the next meal break or the next morning, so they missed earnings which probably amounted to more than the fines. Rewards were introduced at this time for punctual attendance.

Fines for bad work continued into the 1890s and even into the first decade of the twentieth century.

One further practice among this carefully balanced system of rewards and punishments was the payment of pensions to long-serving workers on their retirement from the mill. Policies regulating to whom these pensions were paid tended to vary over time and according to which Courtauld was in charge. Samuel tended to limit pensions mainly to 'skilled' men of long service. In September 1857, for example, Seth Scott, power loom overseer, retired after more than thirty years' service in Courtaulds' employment, with a pension of 10 shillings per week.[37] George Courtauld III, who was in charge in the 1890s, extended pensions to the wives of 'skilled' workers and to some ordinary hands as well as to skilled men. In the latter category, George Amey, an assistant overseer in the weaving sheds, was awarded 10 shillings weekly on his retirement in 1898. Among the lower status male workers, John Simmons, power loom attendant, received 6 shillings per week upon his retirement in 1895. Even the recalcitrant Henry Garrod was put on the allowance list at 3/6d weekly when he had to be dismissed because of the closure of the Old Mills in March 1896.

George Courtauld III gave bonuses to other workers, male and female, on their departure from the firm, but most of the 'perks' were reserved for men – and senior men at that. In the 1870s and 80s twenty-three of the highest status male employees were even sent on paid holidays to Paris.[38] Nowhere in the employment registers is there any mention of female workers being put on the allowance list.

HIRING AND FIRING

Paternalistic employers took a personal and moralistic interest in the behaviour and performance of their workers. Dismissal was a frequent reason for leaving employment in the mill.[39] Throughout the nineteenth century, even during times of more limited labour supply, the Courtaulds never hesitated to fire hands who met with their disapproval.

Some dismissals were occasioned by similar forms of

behaviour on the part of both men and women. Irregular attendance, 'idleness', abusive behaviour and bad language fall into this category. Another action equally likely to meet with dismissal by either male or female workers was leaving work without permission. References to workers staying away 'without leave' are reminders of familial notions of authority. This is extended in the case of some of the men who are sometimes referred to in more militaristic terminology as 'absent without leave' alongside fears about 'defecting' to another firm. Secrets such as those surrounding the mysteries of crimping were jealously guarded from other silk firms – the crimpers at Bocking, in fact, had to swear an oath of secrecy concerning their work in front of a Justice of the Peace. The military terminology is not altogether surprising if it is remembered that paternalism was a very important strategy among military as well as industrial elites in the nineteenth century.[40]

Other reasons for dismissal are closely allied to the gender of the worker. As testimony to the Victorian 'double standard',[41] women and girls were far more likely than men to be fired for 'immoral' behaviour. Eliza Adkins, a weaver of Chapel Street, was discharged in May 1884 for having an illegitimate child and Mary Ann Rayner, a drawer of Chapel Hill, had to leave in August 1873 'on account of third illegitimate child'. Another woman, a weaver named Elizabeth Gurney of High Street, is also reported as having to leave in July 1871 'with two illegitimate children'. It is not clear precisely what policy was followed in relation to illegitimacy. There are several instances of women being allowed back after a period of time. The criterion seems to have been the number of illegitimate children each woman had and her attitude on re-applying for her job. The manager noted under Mary Ann Rayner's name, for example, that she 'applied again January 3rd 1882. Refused. Left impertinent and laughing!!'[42] Perhaps if she had promised to mend her ways she might have been more lucky.

Women with illegitimate children were also at a disadvantage in getting lodgings in Courtauld's cottages. In a letter to Samuel Courtauld, dated 22 September 1873, mill manager Carey Clements mentions that four of the out-town hands lodging in the town 'have an illegitimate child each living with them who under such circumstances could not lodge in the cottages'.[43] Promises of reform, whatever the 'misdemeanour', usually in the face of increased economic vulnerability, secured a more favourable attitude from the management. A Mrs Chaplin received the following comments in the employment register for example: '[She] was a winder on and off for many years. Not being at one time well conducted she had much to suffer in consequence. Ultimately married, was deserted by her husband and was glad to get a place as a winder at which she remained steadily for above a year'.[44] Another woman, Margaret Atkins, who was dismissed for misconduct in 1882, tried to get her job back in July 1893 and elicited the comment from the manager that 'she promises to be better behaved – is urgently in need of employment as a means of living'.[45]

Even more frowned upon than illegitimacy were single women living with men. Perhaps this was because such a lifestyle openly flouted middle-class moral ideals whereas an illegitimate birth could be put down to innate and uncontrollable male desires. A weaver called Marianne Rayner of Parsons Lane was summarily dismissed in April 1871 when it was discovered that she was 'living with a man unmarried',[46] and she was not taken back. On another occasion Ann Slaughter, a drawer, was discharged never to return, because she 'left with a married man' in October 1865. Women with reputations as prostitutes were given very short shrift at the mill. Mary Merryweather observes, for example, that 'Many such women were at work in the factory, have been since expelled'.[47] In the 1880s the manager, Carey Clements, recounts how a weaver called Mrs Kibble received 'all sorts of men at her home, especially Robert Beadle from the mills'. He added that 'Mr. Courtauld told me we cannot employ such women so must dismiss them'.[48] A lengthier report by Clements gives a detailed account of the events leading to the dismissal of another weaver, called Mrs. Newcomb:

> Last Saturday night a married man named Drury who has a wife and six children living in Hedingham Lane, was with this woman and had been there frequently before as well as many other men single as well as married. The wife Mrs.

Drury went there to fetch her husband at 12 o'clock at night, Saturday. A man named Raynor whose wife works at the factory lives in the same yard, and he, for drink given him by Newcomb, keeps the yard clear of the wifes [sic] who come down to look after their husbands by swearing at them and abusing them.[49]

The rest of the report makes a clear distinction between the 'respectability' of the woman who complained about these events and the 'disgusting' character of Mrs Newcomb, reflecting a powerful strand of contemporary male thinking which categorized women into 'virgins' and 'whores'.

Women were also fired for other moral transgressions. A weaver called Maria Blackwell was 'dismissed for helping a girl procure an abortion' in 1850.[50] A number of women were cautioned and sometimes dismissed for wearing dresses considered unsuitable for the mill. One weaver by the name of Sarah Fitch was discharged in May 1863 for having 'too much dress' and Clements had added that she 'could lower Hoops!'[51] She was obviously disobeying a ruling introduced in October 1860 prohibiting the wearing of hoops or crinolines on the grounds not only that they were dangerous but, significantly, that they were sometimes 'shockingly indecent' when the work necessitated the wearers to stand above floor level. Such objections are reminiscent of the type of outrage expressed at conditions in the mines where the state of dress or undress of the women and girls appeared to attract more concern than the dangers and hazards of the working conditions.[52] A notice produced by Samuel Courtauld to draw the women's attention to this new rule urged them to dress 'with as much BECOMING NEATNESS as they can'.[53] Such rulings represented both an area of control and a set of attitudes which were not brought to bear on the male section of the workforce (see plate 19).

Female workers seemed to be more vulnerable to being caught and dismissed for stealing from the mill. They were more likely to be caught because they were searched regularly before leaving the premises whereas men were not. This may have been because of their much closer proximity to handling the silk. Harriet Dodd, a winder, was dismissed in December

DRESS.

OCTOBER 9th, 1860.

IT is always a pleasure to us to see our workpeople, and especially our comely young women, dressed NEAT and TIDY ; nor should we, as has been already declared in a notice that has been put up at Bocking Mills, wish to interfere with the fashion of their dress, whatever it may be, so long as their dress does not interfere with their work, or with the work of those near them in our employ.

The present ugly fashion of HOOPS, or CRINOLINE, as it is called, is, however, quite unfitted for the work of our Factories. Among the Power Looms it is almost impossible, and highly dangerous ; among the Winding and Drawing Engines it greatly impedes the free passage of Overseers, Wasters, &c., and is inconvenient to all. At the Mills it is equally inconvenient, and still more mischievous, by bringing the dress against the Spindles, while also it sometimes becomes shockingly indecent when the young people are standing upon the Sliders.

FOR ALL THESE REASONS

We now request all our Hands, at all our Factories, to leave HOOPS AND CRINOLINE at home when they come to the Factories to work ; and to come dressed in a manner suitable for their work, and with as much BECOMING NEATNESS as they can.

And OVERSEERS at all the Floors are hereby charged to see that all the Hands coming to work are thus properly dressed for factory work—without Hoops or Crinoline of any sort ; and Overseers will be held RESPONSIBLE to us for strict regard to this regulation.

Licking Bobbins.

WHEN a Bobbin is fastened off, it has been a common practice to touch the end with the tongue to smooth it down, and there is no harm in that.

But out of this practice has arisen another practice, both nasty and mischievous, of licking the Bobbins all over to make them weigh heavier.

And to put an end at once, and altogether, to this nasty and mischievous practice of Licking the Bobbins, we now make it

A RULE

Not to touch the Bobbins with the Tongue at all ; and Overseers are hereby authorised to enforce this rule by Forfeits.

SAMUEL COURTAULD & Co.

PLATE 19 Notice posted in the Halstead mill in 1860 concerning the dress to be worn by women workers. The reasons for the ruling include the danger and inconveniences of hooped dresses but also the 'indecency' when wearers are 'standing upon the Sliders', which were raised platforms above floor level. It is interesting to note the additional rule concerning the licking of bobbins and the sanction of forfeits attached to it.

1862 for refusing to be searched, and on a different occasion, another winder, Emma Gallifant, was 'discharged for hiding work in her stocking'.[54]

Such incidents brought wider public censure and severe prison sentences. Matilda Rutland was charged with stealing 7lb 6oz of silk valued at £8 from Courtaulds and concealing it in bottles on the train. She said in her defence that she was simply receiving the goods and that 'others are as bad as I am: there was another party went off with another bottle by the same train'. She added that 'the person who took it from the mill, that I had it of, took it on bobbins and it was wound off the bobbins on to these skeins'.[55] She was found guilty and sentenced to twelve months' hard labour. The newspapers frequently referred to the extensive and systematic disappearance of quantities of silk from the Courtauld mills. Pilfering silk may have been one way in which female workers sometimes attempted to compensate for their very low wages.

The reasons for men's dismissals from the firm diverged from the pattern common among women. Men were rarely fired on the grounds of suspected sexual 'misdemeanors'. The only instance of a man being fired in connection with such activities is that of Robert Beadle, the man mentioned in Carey Clements's account of Mrs Kibble's censured behaviour. There were, however, several other criteria for Beadle's dismissal. Clements mentions that Beadle, a mill cleaner, 'had not been seen since Saturday to work through being drunk and fighting . . . [He] was drunk Saturday and Sunday, been fighting, had his head knocked about so bandaged up. Mr. Courtauld said he must be dismissed. Mrs. Kibble says he has frequently been down to her house, and disgusting stories are told of his conduct there.'[56]

Disapproved vices for men were drunkenness and violence. In December 1852 a power loom attendant called William Miller was dismissed 'for insubordinate and disorderly conduct'. In keeping with the policy regarding the re-employment of women, in March 1855 he was 'received back on apology'. By the 1870s he had progressed to the position of engine driver but in the early 1880s he was in trouble again. In June 1881 he was suspended for five days for negligence at his job and on 1 March 1883 it is recorded that 'a bottle of beer was found in Miller's pocket by Mr. Carter [assistant manager of the Halstead Mill at this time] whom he abused in the strongest language, for this he was dismissed'. A few weeks later, 'he applied to be again taken on, expressing great regret for his conduct. Mr. Courtauld said he would give him a month's trial on condition he brought nothing of the kind into the Factory, apologised for his abusive language and returned at lower wages – 20/- instead of 22/6.'[57]

Another longstanding male employee, Joseph Scott, also had an employment record chequered with suspensions for misconduct and was finally dismissed on 6 June 1876, 'never to be employed again by Mr. George Courtauld's orders – was most abusive and violent in his conduct'. The same fate met a winding overseer called Alfred Beadle for 'repeated insobriety' during twenty years of service in the mill.[58]

Sobriety was a virtue much cherished and emphasized by all the Courtaulds by the 1860s. Samuel supported the setting up of Temperance Societies in Braintree, Bocking and Halstead and urged his male employees to attend. As part of the network of religious, moral and industrial interests of the town, the Reverend Clements, the local Baptist minister, with whom Samuel had a long and close association, sat on the committee of the Halstead Temperance Society. It held regular meetings where speakers on the platform, flanked by 'perfect ladies' (wives of the Courtaulds and local ministers), delivered oratories urging those present to pledge themselves to total abstinence. One newspaper reported that in January 1860 the Halstead Society had approximately 140 members.[59] Both the town's newspapers, the *Halstead Gazette* and the *Halstead Times*, were pro-temperance and carried regular advertisements for the Temperance Refreshment Rooms where non-alcoholic beverages could be consumed. In connection with the Temperance Society, a Halstead Band of Hope was set up that reputedly drew up to 500 and 600 children and young people along to the festivals and sermons that it organized.[60] A Young Men's Christian Association was also reported to be a thriving concern in the town by this time.[61]

To what extent the influence of these groups was exaggerated by partisan newspaper proprietors and just how far employees of Courtaulds were involved in their activities are largely matters of speculation. The evidence suggests, though, that the local culture, centred on the factory and woven together in a series of interlocking institutions integrally connected to the Courtauld firm, was shot through with the values and beliefs of the mill employers. In the accompanying structuring of institutions and experiences, the moulding of family and gender relations was central to the attempts to bridge the gulf between the middle class and the working class. The criteria which the Courtaulds adopted in their dismissal policies represent systematic, but not always conscious, attempts to shape masculinity and femininity in their own image. The ideals of the virtuous asexual respectable working-class woman were juxtaposed to those of the upright and sober working-class 'family man' and combined to represent a prototype of familial ideals and behaviour upon which the whole workforce was encouraged to model itself.[62] Working-class men and women and their offspring were regarded in terms which constructed them almost as a different species from their middle-class employers. As a result these ideals were expected to be incorporated into a way of life whose conditions of existence were vastly different from those of the industrial elite. Such expectations centred on a belief that it was the 'natural' lot of both males and females of the working classes to labour for their daily existence but that, under the paternalistic guidance of the employers, this was to be conducted in ways that were appropriate to the gender and age of the labourer.

This profound belief in the 'natural' order of authority relationships and moral duties surrounding class and gender also characterized the ways in which the Courtaulds dealt with disputes that occurred within the workplace.

THE HANDLING OF DISPUTES

The Courtaulds commended themselves on having no serious industrial disputes for at least the first forty years of their operation. When open conflict did surface, periodically from 1860 onwards, they reacted with characteristic paternalistic outrage, hurt pride and an intransigent reassertion of control and authority. Sometimes, however, the actions of the workers combined with changes in the local labour market to put constraints on the amount of power the employers were able to wield.

The first major dispute was a strike by the power loom weavers in May 1860. It was occasioned by a notice appearing in the mill announcing a reduction in the piece rates owing to a speed-up of the machinery. The employers argued that the speed-up would enable the weavers to produce more so a cut in the rates was justifiable. The weavers' reaction was that a speed-up would increase the likelihood of accidents which would add to the time it took to produce finished batches of woven silk and increase the likelihood of forfeits due to flaws in the work. They therefore wanted to maintain the existing piece rates. After hearing that the prices were definitely settled, the weavers struck on the following Monday afternoon. In the absence of a trade union the weavers' action was organized spontaneously by some of the women and supported by the vast majority of the weavers.

As a result the rest of the workforce had to stop work and the whole plant was brought to a halt. By the middle of the week, Samuel Courtauld, who was suffering from an illness in Bournemouth at the time, sent a telegram to the manager, William Davidson, which was duly read out to many of the hands. The weavers stayed out and about 600 of them held a meeting on Market Hill on the Friday. It was addressed, according to one of the local newspapers, by 'of course a *female* [who] delivered an *oration* as we gathered from the cheers of those immediately surrounding her, but not one word could we catch, nor was it easy to distinguish her from the crowd with whom she stood on a level'.[63]

The outcome was that the assembled hands 'agreed to "stick by the mess"'. It was by all accounts a very orderly gathering, the news report pointing out that 'we did not hear one insulting remark, or observe a single act calculated to disturb the public peace'.[64] By Monday a notice addressed 'To the Power Loom Weavers' was being circulated all over the town containing a message from Samuel Courtauld in which he roundly condemned the strike action of the weavers claiming that they

have by that *hostile and injurious*, but at the same time in
the present case *most wanton and unfitting*, and certainly as
they will find MOST VAIN ATTEMPT AT INTIMI-
DATION, made it impossible for us to confer with them in
the friendly spirit in which they must know in their hearts
we have always acted towards them.[65]

Like a deeply offended father, he went on to disown the
workers, saying, 'while they are out they are no work-people
of ours, and I will not meet them as though they were' (see
plate 20). He followed this with the threat of a lockout and
added a warning that if the weavers had not returned to work
by the end of the week, he would make plans to move his
mills permanently to other parts of England. The notice
concludes with a request to Davidson to 'report to me the
names of from 20 to 50 of those who have been foremost in
this shameful disorder, for immediate and absolute discharge'.[66]

Since the letter was not received till the Monday morning,
Davidson extended the deadline for a return to work until
Tuesday at 2 p.m. After reading the contents of the notice,
'the great bulk of the workpeople entered the factory at the
time specified', although some stayed out and taunted those
going in. True to his word, Courtauld did dismiss a number
of women who were considered to be ringleaders of the strike,
including a woman called Elizabeth Rayner, who was known
by the nickname of Betsy Piper and is described in the
employment records as 'conspicuous in the strike'. Betsy Piper
does not reappear in the employment records but some women
who are recorded as having left at the time of the strike do
show up again later in the records. It is not clear whether
Samuel Courtauld was simply relenting on his former threat
of absolute dismissal or whether the exigencies of the local
labour market persuaded him to be more lenient.

Courtauld's intervention in the strike was personal and
direct. His success in winning this particular dispute was largely
attributable to the scarcity of alternative employment in the
area at this time and his unhesitant use of threats inherent to
the dualistic notions of benevolence and obedience embodied
in paternalism. In later disputes, Courtauld had other circum-

TO THE POWER LOOM WEAVERS.

HALSTEAD, MONDAY, MAY 21st.

To the Power Loom Weavers,

Yesterday (Sunday Morning), I received a letter from Mr. Samuel Courtauld, which I at once print for your information, and at the same time I also place before you a telegraphic message sent by him, before he knew that you had left your work.

WILLIAM DAVIDSON.

Telegraphic message from Mr. Samuel Courtauld, received May 16th, at 12.30 p.m.

" BOURNEMOUTH.

" I am in bed with sore throat. If there is any dissatisfaction, I will meet the Hands as soon as I am well enough,—I hope in a few days; meanwhile they should continue quietly at their work, but need not take out particular canes they don't like. It will grieve me very much if they are so foolish and so wrong as to do otherwise, and will oblige us in the end to discharge those who now mislead the well-disposed."

Letter from Mr. Samuel Courtauld, received May 20th, at 7.30 a.m.

BOURNEMOUTH, MAY 17th.

To William Davidson, Esq.

MY DEAR SIR,

I am deeply grieved by the folly, and the bad spirit, shown on this occasion by the Halstead Power Loom Hands.

The regulation of prices for some particular works was shown to be most reasonable; at the same time we made the acceptance of those works perfectly voluntary; no one was obliged to take out those works who preferred other works, and in fact we should care but little whether many of those works were made, or not.

Nevertheless, we should have been, as we always have been, quite ready to listen to, and to fairly consider, whatever the Hands might have to represent to us in a proper spirit for our consideration, and we confidently believe we should have been able to satisfy them of the reasonableness and propriety of our regulations.

They have, however, chosen to at once *strike*, and have by *that hostile and injurious*, but at the same time in the present case *most wanton and unfitting*, and certainly, as they will find, MOST VAIN ATTEMPT AT INTIMIDATION, made it impossible for us to confer with them in the friendly spirit in which they must know in their hearts we have always acted towards them.

Under these circumstances we can have nothing whatever to say to them. While they are out they are no work-people of ours, and I will not meet them as though they were,—even when I may be well enough to leave this place, which at present I am not.

On Monday morning you may get the steam up, and the Hands may resume work if they please; if they come in, well and good, and let me have the names of the first 50 who do so come in. If by the breakfast hour they do not come in, close all the Factories for the whole week. And if by the end of that week they still chose to be idle, we shall then take instant and vigorous measures to get a large portion of our goods at all events, permanently made in other parts of England.

Of absolute necessity the Mills and Winding must stop, if the Looms stop, and however painful it is to us to stop the Mills and Winding for no fault of the Hands therein employed, we cannot in this case help it.

Meanwhile, report to me the names of from 20 to 50 of those who have been foremost in this shameful disorder, for immediate and absolute discharge.

Yours very truly,
SAMUEL COURTAULD.

N.B.—Not having received Mr. Courtauld's letter in time to make known that the Looms would resume work on this (Monday) morning, or else be closed for the week, I now name Tuesday, at Two p.m., as the time at which they will so resume or be closed.

WILLIAM DAVIDSON.

PLATE 20   Notice addressed to the power loom weavers of Halstead from Samuel Courtauld on the occasion of a strike in 1860. The tone underlines the double-edged character of paternalism in which the 'carrot' is readily accompanied by the 'stick', especially when the workers appear to be rebelling against their master/father.

stances with which to contend. On 7 April 1873, Davidson's successor, Carey Clements, reported that,

> a number of the Mill Hands waited upon me in the office this morning to ask for more wages, saying that the increased wages they got for the increased speed was not in proportion to the extra hard work and difficulty of keeping up the ends, etc., and that everything being so dear now, washing, coals and provisions, they find their 8/- is not sufficient to keep them respectable. Their hard work quite unfitted them to do anything at home.[67]

The women, to whom Clements refers as 'better class weavers', presented other grievances too. One was that 'the Lodgers were treated better than the generality of the weavers, by having an extra shilling paid them for their lodgings while so many of the young girls who live in the Town have to pay their own lodgings.'[68]

Another issue was that a large increase in the number of weavers in the previous twelve months meant that the newcomers got the easier work while the experienced weavers were left with the more difficult work which had the effect of reducing their earnings. Their final grievance was once more to do with the speed-up of the machinery lessening their chances for rewards and increasing the likelihood of forfeits for flaws caused by breakages. At the same time the weavers objected to the increased use of bright silks which were more susceptible to continual snapping and breaking.

Speed-up seems to have been a contentious issue during these years. While the weavers were concerned about the effects on their pay, the employers were anxious about the decline in the quality of the silk goods. George Courtauld, in a letter written to Carey Clements on 23 June 1873, expressed his anxiety about the increased shaking of the looms lowering the quality of the weaving.[69] Both employers and managers were preoccupied with cost-effectiveness. The correspondence is full of discussions concerning the relative advantages of changes in the labour process from a three looms per three weavers system to a three looms per two weavers system (which was cheaper in wage costs but less productive) and the provisions for lodgers (which made the lodgers more expensive to pay than the other hands since lodgings were subsidised). The reduction in hours introduced with the implementation of the 1874 Factory Act added to the issues that were constantly being weighed up in the shaping of management strategies during this period.

By 1875 another major consideration emerged to tip the scales more in favour of the employees in the recurrent altercations concerning pay and conditions of work in the mill. This was the increased opportunities for local female employment in domestic service. In a letter to Samuel and George Courtauld, written on 16 February 1875, Carey Clements draws their attention to the fact that 'a great many of our younger weavers leave after they have been here for about eight to twelve months and lately most of these have gone to service their being a large demand just now for domestic servants, tempting wages being offered to young girls with no experience of service'.[70] He further commented that domestic service was better paid than formerly, with some girls going to London where they received between £14 and £18 per year. This reflection led him to state 'that the balance between Factory work and domestic service is very nearly equal if not in favour of service'.

Clements subsequently suggested that the employers offer an inducement to young women both by paying higher wages while they were learners and by prolonging the increased payment after their training. He also proposed various increases on the piece rates of established hands which would bring average earnings up from around 8/- per week to an estimated 8/6d per week.[71] These suggestions were put into practice, but the differentials between male and female wages remained since increases were also introduced for male workers.[72] Moreover, the earnings of women and girls still lagged far behind the earnings of female textile operatives in northern England.

The restabilized relations between employers and workpeople remained from the 1870s until 1890. Apart from a period of short-time working between 1877 and 78, Courtaulds enjoyed a boom unknown to most other industrial enterprises at this time.[73] Depression hit the firm by 1886, however, and this continued into the 1890s. Wage rates did not fall but

employment declined and short-time was introduced again.
Growing competiton from producers of different fabrics and
changing fashions, particularly the decline of ritual mourning,
impressed a need for diversification and changed methods on
the owners of the firm.

A change to joint stock ownership was accompanied by
many other changes during this period. Among these was the
introduction of a new member of the management called
Tetley who was brought in to reorganize the manufacturing
processes and the importation of male textile workers from
Bradford to implement some of the new processes working on
finer silks. These men were paid more than their male
counterparts in Essex and this caused considerable resentment.
They also antagonized the women weavers leading to a
disturbance in 1894, a year when there were many dismissals.
This was followed by a strike in February 1897 over the
behaviour of some of the Bradford loom attendants.[74] The
cause of the weavers' complaints is not clear but it would
appear that the male attendants were abusing their authority
by harrassing the women in various ways, including sexually.
After leaving work from Friday till Monday, the issue was
resolved when one of the attendants was fired and two were
cautioned.

In June 1898 a week-long dispute was sparked off by an
order calling upon the weavers to clean their looms between
each new warp, a task for which they were to be paid 2d
each.[75] The women objected on several grounds. They claimed
that this was customarily the work of men and boys, 'that it
is not properly women's work', and that the pay promised
was insufficient. They further stated that they had cleaned the
looms but had not received any payment for it.

A series of meetings among the weavers followed, in which
they were addressed by Mrs A. Marland Brodie of the
Lancashire Weavers and Spinners Association and the Women's
Trade Union League. A resolution was dispatched to the
directors of the firm, stating their grievances and requesting
an interview. The directors acted with the same summary
power as Samuel Courtauld had used nearly forty years
previously. A lock-out was announced, which was to last until
such time as 'a sufficient number of weavers inform Mr. Carter

[the Halstead mill manager at this time] that they are desirous of resuming work according to our regulations'.[76]

Although they had the support of a trade union and an organizer the women met with no success on this occasion. One major drawback was that the male workers apparently did not support the women's action since during one of the open air meetings on Market Hill, Mrs Brodie upbraided 'the men of Halstead with having less pluck than the women'.[77] Many women pointed out the irony of this in that the men and boys were in danger of losing their jobs if the new order was implemented and that, indeed, some of them had already been told that their services would not be required after the coming week. The weavers in Braintree passed a resolution that they would not replace the Halstead weavers during the lock-out. Several meetings between the directors and a committee of weavers followed, but finally, at the end of the first week of the lock-out the weavers agreed to the management's proposals.

The disputes of 1897 and 1898 are significant for the way in which they revolved principally around relations and demarcations between men and women in the workplace. Having established a rigid sexual division of labour within the mill the firm now experienced some of the unintended consequences in terms of the kind of dissension to which such distinctions could give rise in different conditions. All the forms of unrest which took place from 1860 onwards demonstrate the ability of Courtauld's women workers to resist and challenge the paternalistic control which he wielded. They also underline the centrality of gender divisions to industrial relations during this period. The relative degree of success or failure of the contending parties depended greatly on a balance of forces shaped partly by the fluctuations of the local labour market (itself rooted in gender assumptions and distinctions guiding the recruitment of labour), partly by the resources upon which each party could draw, and partly upon the possibilities for strategic alliances which could strengthen their respective hands. Towards the end of the century the local labour market became relatively more favourable for women. The resources upon which they could draw, however, were always heavily outweighed by those of their employers and they were increasingly hampered by the tendency of the male workers to ally themselves not with the women but with the bosses.

ON-SITE WELFARE MEASURES

The other side of a paternalist coin that could deal out intransigent and authoritarian ultimatums to its workforce was the provision of a variety of welfare measures both inside and outside the workplace. One of the 'non-work' arrangements of mill life which Courtauld sought to regulate was the provision of facilities for meal times. Since there was always a substantial number of women employed at the mill who came from outlying villages and lodged in the town, it was considered necessary to make some provision within the factory for breakfast and dinner. A factory kitchen was therefore provided and furnished with a range, an oven, a boiler and a copper for making soup.[78] There was also a scullery and a pantry with a sliding shutter and a dresser which served as the hatch from which the provisions were dispensed. Mary Merryweather provides a description of the food available in the kitchen and the advantages which she considered it offered to the women.

> Soup was made from Soyer's recipe twice a week in winter, and sold at a penny a pint. Flour and suet dumplings were boiled in the soup, and sold for one halfpenny each; thus our factory women could, on those days at least, if they brought their bread with them, have a comfortable dinner for three halfpence. Mothers, who had no possibility of cooking at home, could when they left the factory, take home something for their own and their children's dinner. A good fire for the women at meal times, and tea made for them at cost price at breakfast, render the kitchen a most valuable establishment.[79]

This facility was widely used by the women workers: Mary Merryweather comments upon the fact that it was not large enough to accommodate all those who wished to utilize it. That it was a facility that could be withdrawn and was thus used within the chain of paternalistic threats and promises is also clear from Mary Merryweather's observation that:

The conduct of these people in the kitchen some time ago was such as made me doubt if we must not close the kitchen to them at mealtimes; but on certain measures of reform being taken, coupled with a threatening to report delinquents, it was found unnecessary.[80]

Mary Merryweather reports that gratitude for the kitchen accommodation was frequently expressed, but uncritical appreciation could not have been universal or unambiguous in the Courtauld plants since extensive inquiries were made at the Braintree mill as to the reasons why the operatives there did not like the firm's soup.[81] By the 1870s the rules governing meal-time facilities demonstrated another trajectory of work-discipline reflecting the gradual erosion of autonomy in the daily routine of the female workforce and the encroachment of employer control over all areas of the labourers' lives.[82] In a notice posted in the Bocking mill in March 1873[83] precise stipulations were laid down as to which women could use the kitchen facilities and what tasks could be carried out (see plate 21).

Only women living beyond a certain geographical boundary were permitted to remain in the mill at meal times and these women were restricted to eating their meals in the dining room provided. They were not permitted to eat their meals amongst the machinery. A woman was appointed to be in charge of the kitchen and her duties spelled out. She was to attend to the boiling of potatoes and to the warming of food in basins in the stove. She was also, for the meantime, to continue providing boiling water for those who wanted tea first thing in the morning. This was a practice which the employers considered to be 'inconvenient' and which would probably soon be discontinued. The kitchen and dining area were out of bounds to the operatives except at meal times and it was strictly forbidden to use the stove or furnaces for 'any but Business Purposes'. The peeling of potatoes 'or anything of that kind' was likewise prohibited by unauthorized people and in unauthorized areas. In addition, the women were no longer allowed to have food warmed or tea prepared to take away with them. Finally, the custom of taking tea and other refreshments at 11 a.m. and 4 p.m. was forbidden from thence

NOTICE

As a Rule only those women employed in the Finishing whose homes are beyond the Cemetery on the road to Braintree, or beyond the "Bricklayers' Arms" in Church Street, can remain on the premises at Meal Times.

All women who do remain, will take their Meals in the Room which has been fitted up for the purpose.

A woman will be appointed to attend to the arrangements of this Room.

She will attend to the boiling of Potatoes, and to the warming of Food in basins in the Stove upstairs (so long as it may not be found inconvenient or undesirable to make use of the Stove for that purpose), and will provide boiling water at meal times.

For the present she can also provide boiling water for those who want Tea the first thing in the morning, but this practice of Early tea drinking is found to be in many respects inconvenient and may, not improbably, have to be discontinued.

None of the other women must go upstairs except at meal times, and none of them can be allowed to make use of the Stoves or Furnaces downstairs for any but Business Purposes.

No Peeling of Potatoes, or anything of that kind, must be done downstairs.

No women who do not remain on the Premises for Meals can get food warmed or tea prepared in order to take away with them.

The practice of giving up work for a time, in order to have tea or other refreshments, at 11 a.m. and at 4 p.m., or at any other times but the regular Meal Times, must be entirely discontinued.

                                        SAML. COURTAULD & CO.
Mar. 4th, 1873.

Mem^m. June 1874.   It is to be clearly understood that no Beer drinking is allowed during the Hours of Work and the Overseers are enjoined to see that this Regulation is duly attended to.

                    SAML. COURTAULD & CO.

PLATE 21   Notice posted in the Bocking mill in 1873, with an additional memorandum dated June 1874, introducing regulations concerning the consumption of food and drink on the mill premises. Such rules signify the ever-extending encroachment of paternalistic control over the lives of Courtauld's workforce.

forward.   These directives clearly indicate that all these issues had been matters of contention between the employers and the operatives and that the women had been attempting for a long time to exercise autonomy in respect of the consumption of food and drink and the use of the kitchen facilities in the mill. Sections of the Bocking Rule Book[84] indicate that the management frequently admonished women for flouting the rules concerning these arrangements and that it took many years for the employers to get satisfaction on these issues. Even when the rules had become extremely narrow, there is every indication that instances continued of quiet subterfuge whereby food was eaten outside the dining room and illicit use was made of the kitchen facilities.[85]

Another attempt to regulate women's daily lives and practices appeared in the 1870s over the issue of nursing mothers. This was an issue over which the Courtaulds sought medical opinion, demonstrating the incorporation of medical definitions into the paternalistic framework of industrial and moral principles. Describing the routine practices of nursing mothers in the workforce, Carey Clements commented in 1875 that

> Mothers working at the Factory generally after confinements return to work some time within a month after the confinement, but the practice of bringing the infants down to the factory to be nursed by their mothers during working hours has for many years since ceased as 'bottle feeding' has come generally into use. The mothers nursing their infants only at their own meal hours and after they leave work at night, having them 'bottle fed', by the girl left in charge during the time the mother is at work, so that the child is fed at intervals of two hours about.[86]

Apart from providing insight into the childcare practices of the time, Clements' letter indicates the way in which factory employment had already substantially altered traditional child-rearing patterns, significantly by necessitating the use of the bottle.

His letter outlines the recommendations of the local doctor in the face of the existing conditions:

> Dr. Hinds says that it would be far better that the infant should have nothing but its *mother's milk* for two months after its birth and that the *mother alone* would be able to supply all the nourishment it needed but that it is too long to go from the mother's meal to meal, consequently if the child is not brought to its mother between each meal times it must be bottle fed . . . Mr. Hinds says the mother's supply of milk is not diminished by the long interval of four hours or more between the nursing. But he is strongly of opinion that it would be very much better both for the mother and her infant if she stayed at home for the first two months after confinement.[87]

The ensuing correspondence indicates that these recommen-

dations were met quite favourably by Samuel Courtauld. It is
not clear how far the women themselves followed the advice,
although the evidence suggests that there continued to be
many instances where mothers returned to work before two
months had elapsed after their confinement. It is difficult to
establish in such cases though, whether this was due more to
financial motives or to resistance to the values of the employers
and medical professionals.

One final instance of workplace welfare was the provision
of a sick club. It was Mary Merryweather's opinion that prior
to the establishment of the firm's sick club in Halstead in the
1840s the women workers suffered from illness more than the
men because they were less likely to subscribe to the existing
provident clubs.[88] This was most likely because the women's
earnings were a lot lower and therefore they were more loath
to part with them than the men. In addition, these early clubs
were mostly the domain of the higher ranking males whose
affiliation to craft status and all its associated perks represented
values and lifestyles far removed from those of most female
workers.

The illness most commonly referred to by Mary Merryweather and the managers of the firm was consumption. Mary
Merryweather, together with volunteers from among her school
charges, frequently visited girls and women absent from the
mill with what they commonly termed as 'decline'. The risks
of contracting consumption were increased among the female
workers in the Courtauld mills in their close daily handling of
the fine textile threads and the attendant hazards of lung
and respiratory problems.[89] The relatively damp and warm
atmosphere in which the silk thread had to be handled also
contributed to the health risks.[90] Another hazard frequently
mentioned among the weavers was bad eyesight produced by
prolonged concentration on the fine filaments of silk.

Men and boys were certainly susceptible to the same sort
of diseases as afflicted women and girls, particularly those that
were produced by hazardous health conditions in the home
and environment and which frequently reached epidemic
proportions. Women and girls were less cushioned against the
effects of ill health and disease, however, particularly in the
early years of the firm's existence because of their closer

proximity to the handling of the silk yarn and what Mary Merryweather refers to as their lack of 'any provision whatever for sickness when it came.'[91]

By the 1840s the manager of the Halstead mill helped to set up a firm's sick club especially catering for the women. In a twist of irony familiar among many paternalistic employers of the day, the Courtaulds contributed the money retrieved in fines from the workers to the sick club. Every member paid one penny a week into the fund. This was collected every Saturday afternoon after they had received their week's wages by club agents who were men employed at the mill.[92] The hierarchy of authority in the running of the sick club was such that men handled the money and women mostly implemented policy. William Davidson, the mill manager, was the treasurer of the club and a high-ranking male clerk was the secretary. The rest of the club committee was made up of six women who were elected by the members of the club from twenty-four who were nominated by William Davidson. The committee provided a sphere of influence for women workers but only in an area commonly considered to be within the woman's 'natural sphere'. The weekly subscription entitled members to 'a relief in sickness, adjusted according to the income of the Club, but amounting to about 3s.6d. or 4s. a week, for twelve weeks; and then half the amount for twelve weeks more, if still unable to return to their work; of course a medical certificate is required each week.'[93] While off sick, members received visits from two female members of the committee at monthly intervals so that the committee could hear regular reports of their state of heatlh.

In addition to these more formal procedures Mary Merryweather organized 'a little class' out of four of the women on the committee, who accompanied her every Monday evening 'for the purpose of reading, learning, and considering subjects relating to sickness and the means within the reach of most women for amelioration or prevention'.[94]

The evening school mistress considered such efforts to have only minimal effect so long as poor environmental conditions persisted. In the 1840s she was particularly concerned about the open ditches and drains extending in front of the 'tumble down cottages' and by the 1850s she thought that 'the town is still very imperfect in its sanitary arrangements'.[95]

These conditions, together with the lack of money among the female operatives, led Mary Merryweather to question how beneficial even the sick club was for the majority of female millworkers. In weighing up her judgements, she reflected that,

> I do not know with how much reason, but there was a prevalent feeling that many of the necessary medicines being too expensive were never given to the members of the club. The friends of the sufferer would often beg the doctor to let them pay extra for any medicine that would effect a cure; the answer to this appeal, as repeated to me, was invariably that, if they should pay pounds, there was nothing more could be done for the patient.[96]

In the light of such considerations she pressed for an officer of health in the town since most of the doctors' attention went to their better-off patients and the poor were left to rely mostly on the good will of 'some few ladies in the town'.

Her concern for health and hygiene also motivated Mary Merryweather's attempt to set up a factory wash-house in the 1840s. She proposed that the waste hot water from the steam engines could be used at a wash-house constructed close to the factory. For a small sum, she argued, factory women would be saved the inconvenience of trying to wash in the cramped conditions of their homes. In response, the women said they could not see 'how gentlefolks could possibly tell what they should want for *their washing*'.[97] It is unclear from Mary Merryweather's account whether the project got off the ground, but as there is no reference to the wash-house in any of the business records from the 1840s onwards it appears that this could have been another instance where the women's resistance to paternalistic pressures was successful.

The 'new paternalism' emerging in nineteenth-century Halstead was both complex and ambiguous. The employers demonstrated time and again their persistent belief in promoting a harmony of interests between capital and labour based fundamentally on familial ideals which incorporated strict imposition of authority as well as differential rewards and benefits. Since these benefits worked more to the advantage of male workers than female it was the women in the workforce who were more likely to resist the pressures of paternalism. Their resistance strongly affirmed a tradition of 'independency'[98], but one which came not from a heritage of male-defined Chartism and trade unionism. It came rather from a longstanding insistence on autonomy over eating, clothing and child-rearing arrangements bestowed by centuries of dominion over household duties. It came also from a determination to earn a livelihood which would enable women to continue to have as much control as possible over their standard of living.

In the other major textile producing areas of the country an 'accommodation' between a predominantly male-defined 'independency' and the industrialist employers had emerged by the 1860s and 70s.[99] In the small town of Halstead in Essex, where one silk mill provided the major source of survival for most working-class households depending heavily on female labour, 'accommodation' was delayed until the 1890s via the elaborate extension of the web of paternalism way beyond the factory gates.

NOTES

1 P. Joyce, *Work, Society and Politics*, Harvester Press, 1980.
2 John Stuart Mill, *Principles of Political Economy*, vol. II, Longmans, Green, Reader and Dyer, 1848, p. 314.
3 Samuel Smiles, *Self-Help*, John Murray, 1859, *Character*, John Murray, 1871, *Thrift*, John Murray, 1875, *Duty*, John Murray, 1880.
4 Samuel Smiles, *Workmen's Earnings*, John Murray, 1876, p. 14.
5 George Courtauld, in S. L. Courtauld (ed.) *The Courtauld Letters 1782–1900*, vol. vii, p. 3193.
6 Quoted on p. 8, chapter 1 above.
7 D. Roberts, *Paternalism in Early Victorian England*, Croom Helm, 1979.
8 A famous example of this is the Braintree Church Rate Case. Starting as a local issue in 1834 when Samuel Courtauld, supported by other Dissenters, opposed the levying of a rate for the repair of the Anglican Church in Bocking, matters escalated to national proportions, reaching a climax in a House of Lords' decision in 1853 which largely went in the Dissenters' favour. For a full discussion of this case, see D.

C. Coleman, *Courtaulds: An Economic and Social History*, vol. I, Clarendon Press, 1969, pp. 219–23.

9 Report on Handloom Weavers' Petition, 1834, vols. xix and xx.

10 *Essex Herald*, 30 June 1846.

11 R. Martin and R. H. Fryer, *Redundancy and Paternalist Capitalism*, George Allen and Unwin, 1973.

12 Joyce, *Work, Society and Politics*, p. 149.

13 D. C. Coleman surmises that this Public Dinner was almost certainly organized by a committee of senior workers and that the motivation of the lower status workers to participate must inevitably have been linked to their complete dependence on the Courtaulds for their livelihoods in an area so wracked with poverty and unemployment. See Coleman, *Courtaulds*, vol. I, pp. 254–5.

14 *Daily News*, 2 July 1846.

15 *A Factory Festival – Report of the Proceedings of a Public Dinner given to Messrs. S. Courtauld, Taylor and Courtauld by their workpeople*, commissioned by the firm and printed by Meggy and Chalk, Chelmsford, 1846, ERO.

16 *A Factory Festival*, 1846, my emphasis. All the following descriptions of the festival are taken from this account.

17 Emphasis in original.

18 Emphasis in original.

19 Letter from Ellen Courtauld to Sophia Courtauld, 13 January 1845, in S. L. Courtauld, *The Huguenot Family of Courtauld*, vol. 3, London, privately published, 1967, p. 92. These details of the personal lives of members of the Courtauld family themselves help to illustrate how domestic ideology was being enacted among their own ranks. Ellen's role as a substitute mother and organizer of a household of servants by this time was particularly significant. The boundaries of 'the family' in this context were markedly fluid. They expanded to incorporate adoptive children and a host of servants (who, while being waged, were still regarded at this time as under the paternal wing of the master and the maternal eye of the mistress and whose ranks increased to thirteen, according to the 1861 census for Gosfield Hall where the Courtaulds lived by then, and to twenty-one by 1871). The domestic ideal was also shaping the desirable role of unmarried middle-class women. Samuel's sister, Louisa, took up a position as a school teacher before she got married. The middle-class ideal of family life was taking a very specific form by this time and influencing the attitudes and principles by which factory life and the lives of workers were being governed.

20 Mrs Sydney Courtauld, 'Other days: a personal reminiscence', *The Accumulator*, 1895, cited in Courtauld, *The Huguenot Family of Courtauld*, p. 91.

21 In keeping with the expected modesty and virtue of her role, Mrs

Ellen Courtauld could not be persuaded to reply to Mr Smith's address, so Samuel did so on her behalf.

22 My thanks to Fred Brown, former overseer at Courtaulds' Halstead mill, for showing me these medallions.

23 See L. Davidoff et al., 'Landscape with figures: home and community in English society', in J. Mitchell and A. Oakley, *The Rights and Wrongs of Women*, Penguin, 1976.

24 H. Newby, 'The deferential dialectic', *Comparative Studies in Sociology and History*, 17(2), April 1975.

25 E. J. Hobsbawm, 'Custom, wages and workload in nineteenth century industry', in *Labouring Men*, Weidenfeld and Nicolson, 1964.

26 Hobsbawm, 'Custom, wages and workload'.

27 E. P. Thompson, 'Time, work-discipline and industrial capitalism', *Past and Present*, No. 38.

28 Hobsbawm, 'Custom, wages and workload'.

29 *Halstead and Earls Colne Wage Book 1852–76*, ERO D/F 3/3/27, p. 80.

30 Report from Commissioners on the State of the Handloom Weavers, 1840, vol. xx, p. 370. For accounts of similar systems in other contemporary factories see S. Pollard, 'Factory discipline in the industrial revolution', *Economic History Review*, 2nd series, vol. xvi, no. 2, December 1963, and R. S. Fitton and A. P. Wadsworth, *The Strutts and the Arkwrights 1758–1830*, University of Manchester, 1958.

31 For example, *Rules and Instructions – Bocking Mill, 1863–1894*, ERO D/F 3/2/25.

32 *Rules and Instructions – Bocking Mill.*

33 *Register of Employees*, ERO D/F 3/3/1–3/3/11.

34 Ibid.

35 *Wage Book*, Halstead and Earls Colne Factories, 1852–1876, ERO D/F 3/3/27, emphasis in original.

36 *Register of Employees*, 1873–1899, ERO D/F 3/3/10.

37 Ibid.

38 Business records of Bocking factory of Samuel Courtauld and Co., ERO D/F 3/2/72.

39 See chapter 2, 'Courtauld's: a "Family" Firm'.

40 See, for example, Cynthia Enloe, *Does Khaki Become You – the Militarisation of Women's Lives*, Pluto Press, 1983; Myna Trustram, *Marriage and the Victorian Army at Home: The Regulation of Soldiers' Wives*, Cambridge University Press, 1982.

41 Keith Thomas, 'The double standard', *Journal of the History of Ideas*, 20, 1959; E. Trudgill, *Madonnas and Magdalens: the origins and development of Victorian sexual attitudes*, Holmes and Meier, 1976.

42 *Register of Employees*, 1830–1918, D/F 3/3/5.

43 *Letters Book of Carey Clements 1873–1890*, ERO D/F 3/3/22.

44 *Register of Employees*, D/F 3/3/5.
45 Ibid.
46 Ibid.
47 Mary Merryweather, *Experience of Factory Life*, Emily Faithfull Publishing Co., 1862, p. 43. For a fuller discussion of prostitution in nineteenth-century England see J. Walkowitz, *Prostitution and Victorian Society*, Cambridge University Press, 1980.
48 *Rough Diary of Carey Clements*, Tuesday 17 July 1888, ERO D/F 3/3/26.
49 *Rough Diary*, Monday 16 July.
50 *Register of Employees*, D/F 3/3/3.
51 *Register of Employees*, D/F 3/3/2 and 3/3/3, emphasis in original.
52 See Angela John, *By the Sweat of their Brow: Women Workers at Victorian Coal Mines*, Routledge and Kegan Paul, 1980.
53 I am grateful to Fred Brown for providing me with a copy of this notice.
54 *Register of Employees*, D/F 3/3/5.
55 *Halstead Times*, Saturday 17 May 1861.
56 *Rough Diary*, Tuesday 17 July 1888.
57 Ibid.
58 Ibid.
59 *Halstead Gazette*, Thursday 5 January 1860.
60 Ibid.
61 *Halstead Times*, Saturday 27 April 1861.
62 In addition, by 1868 the further extension of the franchise to working-class men was serving to enhance ideals of respectability among the male working class.
63 *Halstead Gazette*, Thursday 24 May 1860, emphasis in original.
64 Ibid.
65 'To the Power Loom Weavers'; I am grateful to Fred Brown for providing me with a copy of this notice. The full text of the message was also reprinted in the *Halstead Gazette*, Thursday 24 May 1860, emphasis in original.
66 'To the Power Loom Weavers'.
67 *Letters Book of Carey Clements*.
68 Ibid.
69 Ibid.
70 Ibid.
71 Ibid.
72 Ibid.
73 See Coleman, *Courtaulds*, vol. I, ch. 7.
74 *Essex County Standard*, 27 October 1897.
75 Ibid., Saturday 18 June 1898.
76 Ibid.
77 Ibid.

78 Merryweather, *Factory Life*, p. 30.
79 Ibid.
80 Ibid.
81 Business records of Bocking factory, D/F 3/2/56, January 1872.
82 Thompson, 'Time, work-discipline and industrial capitalism'.
83 I am grateful to Fred Brown for providing me with a copy of this notice.
84 *Rules and Instructions – Bocking Mill*.
85 Ibid.
86 *Letters Book of Carey Clements*, letter to Samuel Courtauld, 9 June 1875.
87 Ibid., emphasis in original.
88 Merryweather, *Factory Life*, p. 71.
89 Modern research has drawn attention to the high incidence of byssinosis, or 'brown lung', among textile workers. See, for example, W. Chapkis and C. Enloe (eds), *Of Common Cloth: women in the Global Textile Industry*, Transnational Institute, 1983.
90 This was a feature of the working conditions in the mill that Mary Merryweather commented upon, *Factory Life*, p. 10.
91 Merryweather, *Factory Life*, p. 71.
92 *Letters Book of Carey Clements*, letter to George Courtauld, 22 October 1874.
93 Merryweather, *Factory Life*, p. 72.
94 Ibid.
95 Ibid., p. 11.
96 Ibid., p. 12.
97 Ibid., p. 57, emphasis in original.
98 See H. I. Dutton and J. E. King, 'The limits of paternalism: the cotton tyrants of North Lancashire, 1836–1854', *Social History*, 7(1), January 1982.
99 Dutton and King, 'Limits of paternalism'.

5
'IMPROVING' THE TOWN

Courtauld's intention to promote self-help and harmony reflected all aspects of local social life. The three towns of Halstead, Bocking and Braintree contained landmarks which testified to the paternalist philosophy of successive generations of Courtaulds. Samuel and his brother George regularly donated money to schools, hospitals, mechanics' institutes and various charities. In their wills[1] money was left to local schools and after Samuel's death in 1881 many municipal projects bore witness to the Courtauld presence. Water fountains[2] were erected in 1888 in Halstead and Braintree, and public parks received large endowments in the 1880s and 1890s. In the same period a cottage hospital was built from Courtauld funds in Halstead, to be followed in 1921 by another in Braintree.[3] After the First World War, twenty homes of rest for retired millworkers were built on the site of the old Union Workhouse in Hedingham Road in Halstead; nearly forty more houses appeared nearby. A 'civic centre' was presented to Braintree, at this time, and a village hall replaced in Bocking.[4]

In Halstead alone so pervasive was their influence that one lifelong resident and former weaver in the mill remarked that 'Courtauld's was the town'.[5] From public endowments through to philanthropic ventures in religion, recreation, childcare and mothering, Samuel Courtauld's activities embraced not only the values and culture but also the very bricks and mortar of the local community. His inspiration came partly from a visit

PRESENTATION

OF A DRINKING

FOUNTAIN

TO THE TOWN OF HALSTEAD

By

Geo. Courtauld, Esq.

IN COMMEMORATION OF HER MAJESTY'S JUBILEE,

On

TUESDAY, MAY 15, 1888.

The Fountain will be declared Open to the Public by MISS SPARROW, of Gosfield Place, at Ten Minutes past One o'clock, after which there will be a

PUBLIC LUNCHEON

In the TOWN HALL at 1.30 p.m.

J. R. VAIZEY, ESQ.,

Of Attwoods, will preside

In the Evening there will be a

PROMENADE ✠

✠ CONCERT

OF VOCAL & INSTRUMENTAL MUSIC

In the Town Hall, commencing at 7 o'clock. Admission, 4d. each.

The HALSTEAD STRING BAND have offered their services.

A BRASS BAND

Has been engaged to play during the Afternoon.

It is hoped that the Tradesmen of the town will close their establishments at noon, so as to enable all to take part in the proceedings.

Tickets for the Luncheon, 2s. 6d., may be obtained of Messrs. Carter and Son, R. L. Hughes, W. W. Turnell George Hotel, and of the Secretary, Edwin Bentall, Halstead.

25

R. L. HUGHES, PRINTER, HALSTEAD.

PLATE 22 Notice announcing the presentation of a drinking fountain to the town of Halstead by George Courtauld III in 1888. Such municipal gestures marked the significant social position secured by the Courtauld family in the locality by this time.

PLATE 23 The fountain presented to Halstead in 1888 as it stands today, situated at the junction of Hedingham Lane (now called Hedingham Road) and High Street.

in 1859 to Titus Salt's town of Saltaire near Bradford. The town, built around a vast alpaca works, symbolized the ideal of a harmonious community so cherished by Courtauld. In a letter to his wife, Ellen, he described the place as

> Truly wonderful, compared with which *our* factories are all nothingness . . . our walk through occupied an hour and a half – the buildings are all so large and handsome – the mountains of wool in the warehouses – the machinery so wonderful to my eye . . . a town of cottages and a most beautiful church (chapel by denomination) with a splendid organ – built at a cost of £11,000 – splendid school rooms, in which all the children are taught so many hours every day; it is said to be the largest factory in one building in the world – and all handsomely built of hewn stone. Titus

PLATE 24   The Cottage Hospital in Halstead as it is 100 years after it was originally built from Courtauld funds. It stands not far from the water fountain along Hedingham Lane (Hedingham Road).

Salt was left £1,000 by his father – made much money by mills in Bradford with alpacas, and four or five years since erected these buildings at a cost it was said in the railway carriages of £250,000 for the buildings *alone* – but that I think must be a great exaggeration (and now he is *only* 56).[6]

The visit served to strengthen the Nonconformist drive behind Courtauld's activities. The significance of religion for him lay more in its political and ethical principles than in the transmission of doctrinaire beliefs and rituals. His involvement with radical Nonconformist ministers and local chapel life contributed to shaping a social milieu uniting the different classes. His approach was non-sectarian and he chose non-sectarian ministers whom he believed embodied the religious, moral and political ideals to which he wanted his work people to aspire. A regular visitor to the local chapels established by Courtauld was William Fox, former editor of the radical

PLATE 25   Some of the Homes of Rest, built by the Courtauld firm after the First World War, as they stand today on the site of the old Union Workhouse near the Cottage Hospital.

Unitarian journal *The Monthly Repository*. In a letter to him Courtauld writes

> The more I re-cogitate your service of yesterday the more I admire it for its beauty, and the more exceedingly I am satisfied with it as fulfilling my ideal of what such a service should be for our village people; it turns their traditional reverence for the Bible to the best account – enriching their readings of it by associating so many true thoughts and moral lessons with its beautiful passages, while also those moral lessons, sympathies and sentiments, which otherwise might fade from their minds, will continually be revived.[7]

While a chief characteristic of many of Courtauld's ventures was their non-sectarianism they were constructed upon a familial model requiring marked distinctions between the responsibilities and activities of men and women. At the head of this 'family' was the dutiful Victorian father-figure of Samuel Courtauld, steering an equivocal passage through the straits of protection and control.

PATERNALISM TOWARDS WOMEN

The major arenas for paternalism towards the women and girls of the town were education, housing, childcare and recreation. These arenas were based on gender segregation – sometimes physically, sometimes ideologically, sometimes both. The maxim of 'separate spheres' was central to Courtauld's projects, shaping every activity accordingly.

For employers of a Unitarian persuasion education was a major platform for religious and moral revitalization. Education nurtured 'cultivation' and 'respectability' and could also, as Reverend Craig had astutely pointed out at the Public Dinner in 1846, (see p. 104 above), be used to adapt workers to their tasks. One of Courtauld's first ventures was the setting up of the Halstead Factory Evening School in the year after the famous Public Dinner. Since this school was aimed at the young female members of the workforce, women among the middle class were deemed appropriate to run it. This scheme brought Mary Merryweather to Halstead. A woman from a middle-class background originating from Devon, she was living in London when she first heard about the silk mill in Halstead. As a young woman drawn to philanthropic activities, she was attracted by the Courtaulds' wish for 'some lady who would undertake to read and lecture to the factory girls, who, now that the Ten Hours' Bill had come into operation, had much more time at their command, without much wisdom, as to how to employ it'.[8] She was impressed by 'these noble-hearted employers, and more particularly the wife of the senior partner [who] had been wishing to do more in the way of education and kindly oversight for the working people of their largest factory'.[9] She applied for the post, was accepted and spent six weeks at the Normal School in Borough Road in the East End of London preparing herself for her new life.

Mary Merryweather, arriving in Halstead in November 1847, vividly described the scene in the old Town Mill:

At one glance from the door of the basement-floor of a large brick building, I could see 500 looms at work by steam-power, with a woman tending each. It was a clean, airy and well-arranged factory, though to a newcomer it seemed very confusing, with its click-clacking of machinery and the great swift bands which kept all going; almost suspending thought by their manifestation of impelling power. Above this larger room were two floors partly devoted to the weaving of gauze for crape, and partly to the other processes of winding, etc. At that time there were 937 women and girls, and about 76 men, employed in the Halstead factory.[10]

Soon after her arrival, Mary Merryweather professes 'a longing sympathy with this large mass of women' who have been 'taken unnaturally from the school and the cottage – from tending the cradle, the children, the husband, the aged parent – in fact, from *all* the peculiar duties and loves of their womanly natures!'[11] There is an irony in this concern as she reflects upon 'the small daintily formed hands of the weavers' whose work required a feminine delicacy that would certainly be impaired by domestic tasks in their 'proper' domain. Mary Merryweather grapples to understand this contradiction, commenting that 'I have since seen this smallness to be, in a domestic point of view, a great disadvantage to women in that condition of life, at the same time that it is the result of their particular occupation; indeed should a weaver have to wash and scrub at home, she spoils her hands for touching the delicate filaments of the silk loom'.[12]

Domesticity as woman's natural domain was a central theme in the organization and activities of the Evening School. The first session took place in the Girls' British Schoolroom in premises adjacent to the mill buildings. One hundred and twenty girls and young women between the ages of thirteen and twenty-five entered the school in the first week. No charge was made. Fearing disruption and disorderliness from some of the girls who might be attracted by this novelty, the factory management offered to send one or two overseers to keep order. Mary Merryweather declined the offer but expressed some shock at the crowds who converged upon her for registration commenting that, 'some of those who came were coarse, noisy girls, with no womanly reserve or modesty; they pushed, jested and even swore at each other'.[13] Despite their

behaviour, the 'Firm's lady', as she was called, became attached
to the young women, admitting that she 'did already love
them in a certain sense'.

Three evenings passed before she organized any teaching.
She appointed eight monitors and set about delivering lectures.
Among the subjects included were 'moral questions', astron-
omy, geography, human physiology and health. She attempted
to introduce ideals of hygiene alien to her charges. Her
suggestion that they wash themselves all over every day, for
example, was considered 'a most absurd and impossible thing'.

Soon lessons in basic literacy began. Many young women
speedily developed the skills of letter writing. The curriculum
diversified with lectures on biology and botany interspersed
with poetry readings from popular Unitarian writers like Eliza
Cook and James Hogg and from journals like *Douglas Jerrold's
Magazine*. Some pupils left the mill to become teachers
themselves. To provide avenues of mobility for a few women
was probably not entirely counter to the employers' objectives.
A more significant aim, though, is summed up in a letter to
Mary Merryweather from Ellen Courtauld in 1849. Soon after
another of the factory festivals which became a regular feature
of local life, Ellen Courtauld wrote that, 'I could have counted
out your girls from Halstead by their quiet, enjoying,
respectable behaviour. This is very encouraging and delightful.
Labour is never thrown away, so we must "work away".'[14]
The young women living in lodgings tended not to attend
school as much as those whose homes were in Halstead.
Foreshadowing a phenomenon which was to become common
with the spread of state education later in the century,[15]
'domestic duties' kept many girls from attending regularly,
which the schoolmistress always excused since she 'encouraged
their serving the home affections first.'

Since many young women millworkers were dependent upon
lodging, providing such accommodation became an important
concern of Courtauld's. His intervention was as much to do
with moral control as with the physical well being of the
women. The stereotype of the 'fallen women' loomed large
in middle-class minds.[16] Young women from agricultural
households 'away from home and parents, without restraint
from within or without', were, in Mary Merryweather's view,

especially vulnerable to 'a class of women particularly adverse to morality'.[17] She feared 'many and sad immoralities, especially the very common habit of frequenting the public houses; not only did the men congregate there, but many women also, wasting their time and money, and enticing others comparatively innocent into their shameful ways.'[18]

To counteract these influences and the 'evils resulting from the bad accommodation in the ordinary over-crowded cottages and in the common lodging-houses',[19] Courtauld provided a house, called Factory Home, in November 1849, at the southern end of the town, five minutes' walk from the mill. Described as 'a large, pleasant, airy dwelling with spacious offices, flower and kitchen gardens, coach-house and stables',[20] it contained eight bedrooms, a dining room and a residents' sitting room. Each bedroom contained between two and five single beds. A housekeeper was installed in her own room near the entrance door and Mary Merryweather moved into rooms at the back of the house, separated from the rest by a green baize door. The rent of 1 shilling per week included washing. A charge of 2 pence per week was kept for the lodgers until the sum reached 5 shillings and was to be used for payment of rent in case of illness. This practice caused much dissension among the young women lodging at the Home as did the other ten rules posted up in every room. These mostly concerned the strict regulation of hours during which the lodgers should and should not be present and the kind of behaviour expected of them, such as: 'Modest and gentle manners, decent and becoming language and habits of cleanliness, are expected in all the lodgers; and no one guilty of misconducting herself in these respects will be permittd to remain in the Home.'[21]

The Factory Home and its rules met with much resistance. Young women were frequently excluded for not keeping the hours. 'Disorderly conduct' was common and even included 'the copies of the rules [being] taken from different rooms and *burnt* by the girls!'.[22] The lifestyle expected of the residents contradicted their 'intense love of some sort of independence'[23] and the house closed after seven years through lack of use. There were never more than nineteen young women lodging there at any time; during the entire seven years a total of sixty-seven lodgers passed through, many staying only for a short time.

Mary Merryweather regretted the failure of the Home to infuse 'the *true home spirit*'[24] amongst the young women, but drew comfort from the greater success of several social occasions held in the building. They usually consisted of evening parties intended to 'induce higher tastes among them, in their dancing, their singing, and their conversation'.[25] Whether or not 'higher tastes' were desired or achieved, these functions provided a welcome respite from the daily round of work in the mill.

Surveillance was also Courtauld's main preoccupation in establishing lodgings in Factory Terrace. The sixteen three-storey cottages in this row adjacent to the mill were built in 1872. Tenants were usually male employees at the mill while lodgers were usually young female weavers. Moral rectitude was always a primary criterion for admissions: 'If any girls are found to be unsatisfactory in conduct out of doors [we are] to strike off the lodging house from our books.'[26]

Similar moral concerns, combined with expedient consider-ations about labour needs in the mill, led the employers to try to influence working-class childrearing patterns. The mothers' interests were secondary to promoting ideals of motherhood symbolizing respectability in both the social and spiritual order. Attempting to attain such ideals would also furnish valuable evidence of children's health and well being in the current debates about the effects of mothers' industrial employment on their offspring.

Mary Merryweather expressed some anxiety about children's health when she first arrived in Halstead, remarking later that 'few results of Factory Life impressed me more painfully, when I first mingled with the inhabitants of Halstead, than the neglect of *infants* whose mothers worked at the factory.'[27] She lamented the use of sleeping draughts by the mothers and the frequency of 'decline' among babies who were often left in the care of seven- or eight-year-old children. She had observed these children laying their wards on cold stone steps or damp grass 'besides standing in draughts, and running into all sorts of dangers, which a mother's oversight would at least in some degree have lessened'.[28]

The work of monitoring and changing the childcare habits of the millworkers was entrusted to Mary Merryweather and Samuel's wife, Ellen Courtauld. Their first task was to set up a nursery for children of married women working in the Halstead mill. The nursery was to operate during mill hours. It was located on the ground floor of the factory lodging house in which Mary Merryweather lived. It opened in December 1850 with six cradles. A charge of 4 pence a day was made for the care and food of each child. Admission was refused if the money was not paid each morning. The nursery was equipped for children aged between one month and two years:

> Besides the cradles, which were made of iron and not to rock, we provided for the nursery a cushion three yards square, covered with soft washing calico, and filled with cocoa-nut fibre, on which the children who were old enough were placed to roll about and play. There was also a railed swing, soft ball and other little playthings; in summer they could toddle out on the grass-plot and pick daisies.[29]

The rules, printed on a leaflet and distributed among the women in the mill, specified that 'The child's clothing must be perfectly clean. All extra linen is provided by the Nursery', and included the provision that 'Unweaned children may be nursed at the Institution by their mothers during the day'.[30]

Many millworkers expressed surprise and suspicion as to why the Courtaulds should provide such a facility. With some caution, three mothers brought their babies to the nursery in the first week, leaving them there in their night clothes shortly before six o'clock in the morning and collecting them at the end of the day. On arrival babies were given a warm bath and dressed either in their own day clothes or in clothes kept at the nursery if the mother did not provide them. Use of the nursery never became extensive because of the mothers' suspicions. They strongly objected to their children being washed all over, a custom common among a middle class preoccupied with cleanliness and its association with godliness, but alien to the majority of the working class. They also regarded the nursery diet of milk, water, bread and arrowroot as inadequate.

A number of factors combined to make the nursery short-lived. Not least was the resistance of the majority of mothers to the imposition of middle-class methods of childrearing. Rather than having to find 2 shillings a week to pay for the firm's nursery most women preferrred, as we have seen (see chapter 3, pp. 84–5), to use an elderly neighbour or relative who charged far less (or exchanged childcare for other services) or to pay girls of seven or eight years 1/6d a week. Mothers generally found it much less trouble, too, to have their babies fetched or even looked after in their own homes by local girls and women than to take the babies back and forth to the nursery. Added to this was the advantage for many 'of having little maids at home to light their fire, boil the kettle, or look after other children'.[31]

Additionally, it proved difficult to find nurses willing to work in the nursery. The maximum number of children present at any one time only reached fifteen over the next two years and by the spring of 1853 the nursery closed its doors for the last time, hastened by an outbreak of bronchitis among babies born during the severe weather conditions in the early months of that year.

Middle-class ideals of maternity and child welfare were also promoted through monthly 'maternal meetings' established in the same year as the nursery. Mrs Clements, the wife of the Baptist Minister in Halstead, ran the meetings with the full endorsement of Samuel Courtauld. Aimed at the mothers in the mill workforce, they focused upon readings and discussion concerning aspects of domestic and childcare arrangements. Much of the written material was taken from two journals among the wide range of contemporary advice literature, *The Mothers Friend* and *Readings for Mothers' Meetings*. Written from a strongly moralistic and philanthropic standpoint, these journals contained stories and hints embodying middle-class domestic ideology.

One of the main preoccupations of the 'maternal meetings' was once again the pursuit of 'cleanliness and order',[32] issues which were persistently disputed by the women who worked in the mill. In particular, they drew attention to the vast difference in living conditions between the middle class and the working class, causing Mary Merryweather to comment that 'great difficulties are experienced in these matters, as the uniform reply of Factory mothers is that they have no time for these things'.[33] Another key question for debate was discipline. Mrs Clements frequently attempted to impress upon the mothers 'the law of kindness, commenting on the bad effects of the harsh treatment, scolding, and the violent language sometimes addressed to children among the poor'.[34] Such admonitions were also resisted by many of the women who pointed out the greater pressures under which they lived.

As well as rejecting much of what they were told to do, the women made their feelings about the 'maternal meetings' clear by their lack of enthusiasm in attending. Whereas after 1840 the numbers of mothers in the mill workforce in most years exceeded 250, attendance at the meetings rarely reached the maximum level of thirty. The Courtaulds remained committed to such projects despite this equivocal response. In the 1880s the firm paid a woman called Mrs Richardson 5 shillings a week, together with helpers who were paid 3d and 6d a night, to teach sewing to the women silk workers. The classes were held twice weekly, from 7.30 p.m. to 9. p.m., in the Workmen's Hall.

The main motivation for women to attend functions like the 'maternal meetings' seems to have been the opportunity for some relief from their labours both in the mill and at home. The meetings provided a rare chance for social and educational gatherings, including tea parties which were far more popular, sometimes bringing together as many as eighty women. Poetry readings of mainly Unitarian writers like Mary Howitt and Mrs Hemans were often held at tea parties. Such activities paralleled, but never reached the same scale as, the literary pursuits common among female millworkers on the other side of the Atlantic.[35] Their significance for the employers lay in their reforming and edifying role since recreation represented the third pillar in the Unitarian strategy of improvement. The other two pillars according to prominent Unitarians like Henry Solly, another of Courtauld's friends via the religious and political network of chapel life,[36] were temperance and education. According to Solly, 'Recreation, Temperance and Education' were like a 'three-legged stool'; if one was removed the whole project collapsed.[37]

Solly, and the 'rational recreation' movement commonly

associated with him,[38] contributed towards the reformulation of recreation into a separate, self-contained sector of social life, forging a wedge between 'labour and life'.[39] Courtauld adhered to the movement's aims by emphasizing the need for a 'play discipline' to accompany the 'work discipline' of an industrial milieu.[40] Ellen Courtauld voiced the ideal of an ordered life of work and play when she wrote to the inhabitants of Gosfield in 1871

> Let us help one another through our dark days, nor forget to help one another to have bright ones. The longer I live the stronger is my belief, that it is just as necessary for the well-being of the working man and woman to have change and amusements, as for other perhaps less useful classes among us. Some people seem to have an idea that working people only want to work – were made for work and nothing else. I hope the Gosfield workers will undeceive those people, and show that they need, and want, much more than that; that with their work they wish to enjoy their *lives* – partaking of all innocent amusement, and accepting any pleasant invitation to tea that they receive.[41]

When Ellen Courtauld wrote this letter, recreation had been more fully absorbed into the organized structures controlled by the firm. This was achieved by two main strategies. The first was the provision from early on of large-scale semi-feudal celebrations, distinguished from their medieval counterparts by the lack of licentiousness. They were highly ordered occasions marked by respectability and discipline. One prominent example was the 1846 Public Dinner which was followed by huge open-air parties held every summer in the grounds of the Courtauld residence. Mary Merryweather remarks upon the *'great and careful supervision'*[42] needed on such occasions and how,

> Giving out tickets on these occasions was always a trying thing, lest we should overlook the quietly deserving, or, from solicitation, admit the unworthy. We would not but see how much moral weight such things had in our little

community; the admission to these treats being held as a
mark of respect and approval, understood and responded
to by all alike.[43]

The employers directed their endeavours to the 'deserving'
and 'respectable' poor, through whom the 'problem' of leisure[44]
could be resolved in reform rather than repression of popular
recreations. The huge parties embodied the principles of unity
and locality which formed the backbone of such endeavours.
After 1854 the grounds of Gosfield Hall were increasingly
used for local functions beyond the immediate realms of mill
life. Events like the Halstead and North East Essex Floral
and Horticultural Society's annual Floral and Musical Fete
were held there. Significantly, on such occasions, the Courtaulds were listed in the local press as members of the
'gentry'.[45]

A second way in which leisure pursuits were brought further
under employer control was through the provision of gender-
specific pastimes and organizations. Mary Merryweather,
reflecting on the tea parties and dances emerging from the
'maternal meetings', said: 'Some of our workpeople remarked
to me that the parties at the Home never made them feel
unfit for their work the next day, as was too surely the case
when they had "a chance time" attended the dances at the
public house.'[46]

These concerns were underlined by an event in 1857 which
led directly to the setting up of a distinctive organization for
the recreation of women. The mill was required by law to close
down for two days for an annual clean-up and whitewashing.
Usually, up to fifty of the women workers undertook this work
while the rest of the female workforce used the time to clean
and tidy their own homes.[47] At the end of the 1857 clean-up,
the women who had been whitewashing the factory asked to
use the factory kitchen for a party 'instead (as they said) of
going to a public house, which they knew we disapproved'.[48]
Mary Merryweather describes the women as 'perhaps the
roughest and least refined that I had ever had to do with' and
remarks upon the fact that many of them were 'past middle
life'. She recalls telling the women that she had not ordered
any music since she thought they would be too tired to dance;

however, as they told her they would be most disappointed
not to dance, she sent for a fiddler. To her surprise, 'they
took each other out for a turn with mighty energy of movement,
and between times sang songs which I had never heard before,
peculiarly adapted to *their* particular view of life, but with
certain touches of affection and pathos not discreditable to
their hearts.'[49]

Shortly after this, opportunities for such spontaneous
recreation were curtailed because the employers interpreted
the event as underlining the need for a company entertainments
organization. An Amusement Society was established with its
own bureaucracy of a commmittee of seven people, a president
and a secretary. Monthly committee meetings were planned
to administer parties to be held on the first Wednesday of
every month. No one under fourteen years old was to be
permitted to attend the parties and tickets were priced at 2d
for those employed in the Courtaulds factory and 3d for others.
Parties were to last from 7.30 to 11.00 p.m. and no 'intoxicating
drink' or tobacco was allowed on the premises. Members
'misconducting themselves' could be expelled. Most of the
parties were held at the Town Hall and consisted of dancing
and drama, with an occasional piano performance by a visitor.
Mary Merryweather records average attendance at the parties
as around 150. The Society was set up particularly for the
women but by the end of 1857 it was reported as having 149
men as well as 245 women as members. Of the total 389
members, 225 were employed in Courtauld's mill. In Mary
Merryweather's opinion, 'To belong to the Amusement Society
implied a certain moral standing, and it was much sought by
the young men and maidens. We have in some characters seen
quite a reformation worked apparently by its agent.'[50] Despite
the numbers of men attending, the Amusement Society was
mainly perceived as a women's organization and concentrated
its activities on middle-class feminine accomplishments like
singing, drama and piano playing. Most importantly, it never
became a forum of political or social power.

PATERNALISM TOWARDS MEN

A number of parallel developments were directed toward the men of the town. Again, education, recreation and housing were three of the most significant areas of intervention. About the same time as the Evening School for young women began, an equivalent organization was initiated for the men and boys employed in the mill. This was the Literary and Mechanics' Institute which was first accommodated in a room over the factory kitchen. The main reason for this provision was to create a separate space for the working-class man away from the public house and from the home 'where probably his wife, just returned from her day at the factory, had to wash and scrub'.[51]

Just as the Evening School, run by women, was modelled on middle-class notions of femininity so the Institute, run by men, was fashioned on ideals of masculinity common among middle class men. Samuel Courtauld was central in initiating the project and forming a committee of male workers from the mill to control its affairs. For a charge of 6d per quarter, members could retreat to a male dominated atmosphere resembling on the one hand, the middle-class gentlemen's clubs of the day and, on the other hand, a less politicized version of the earlier working-class trade societies. The quarterly fee entitled members to attend lectures, readings or debates held at the Institute. It also allowed free access to a library of books, periodicals and newspapers mostly of a liberal and Nonconformist persuasion. Chief among these were the *Daily News*, the *Nonconformist*, the *Illustrated London News*, the *Mechanics Magazine*, the *People's and Howitt's Journal*, *Chambers Edinburgh Journal*, *Domestic Economy*, the *Cottage Gardener*, *Punch*, the *Freeholder*, the *Essex Herald*, *Eliza Cook's Journal* and the *Essex Standard*.[52]

The Institute rules contained a range of moral prescriptions governing members' behaviour. Two rules, for example, were directed at controlling language, gambling and drinking:

> Any person using profane or immoral language, tossing, gaming, or causing any disturbance in the room, shall be fined one penny each offence; and if he persists in repeating

such behaviour, he shall not be allowed to continue in the room that evening.

No smoking or intoxicating drinks shall be allowed.[53]

Such precepts were aimed at cultivating respectable upright working men, who were expected to have a knowledge of the world and of their place in it. The furnishings of the room which housed the Institute included maps, a globe and a small wax model of 'the kind founder', Samuel Courtauld.

Proportionately, attendance at the Institute was higher than that at the Evening School, although it fluctuated a lot particularly in the earlier years. In the first three months 101 members enrolled. Shortly afterwards, a misunderstanding about which books would be allowed to circulate led to bad feelings reducing the membership to fifty-three by the end of the year, but numbers picked up again significantly in the following years.

The general effects of both male- and female-oriented educational ventures were to raise literacy levels and at the same time to extend the scope of Courtauld's influence. In the year preceding the 1860 Annual General Meeting of the Literary and Mechanics' Institute, 2,250 books, 154 periodicals and 420 newspapers were exchanged.[54] Mary Merryweather praised the 'increase of cultivation' brought about by the Institute, remarking that 'of those first admitted, so many could scarcely, if at all, read and write'.[55] By 1860, Courtauld's schools contained 'considerably over a hundred boys and young men, and nearly as many girls and young women', a fact for which 'the town is much indebted to the generous conduct of the Courtauld Firm in wholly sustaining these schools, since they are not confined, by any means, to their own workpeople'.[56]

Schools were not only set up in Halstead but also in the villages of High Garrett and Gosfield. Educational aims and employment policies were not always in harmony. By the 1870s girls and boys needed a certificate of school proficiency before they could be employed. A reward of between 1 and 5 shillings annually for good attendance gave an incentive to attend, while poor attenders received bad reports.[57] By this time it was increasingly difficult for girls under fourteen years old, even with a certificate, to get a job. In March 1877, for example, Florence Prior, a thirteen-year-old was refused a job as a winder until she reached the age of fourteen.[58] This encouraged many girls to say they were older than they were.[59] The Courtaulds attempted to overcome some of the legal restrictions on the employment of children in the 1870s by employing 'half-timers'. Children between the ages of eleven and thirteen were employed for mornings or afternoons only. They were engaged on winding at 1/6 per week for the first eight weeks increasing by 3d per week plus their earnings at winding for the next sixteen weeks. This practice clearly offended some of the school teachers in the area for Carey Clements wrote to the Messrs. Courtauld in April 1879, informing them that the Gosfield school teacher was objecting and calling for an end to the system.[60] It appears to have continued, though, at least into the 1880s.

The effects of Courtauld's educational ventures in terms of gender were even more far-reaching. On the one hand, educational provision created a context in which issues concerning men and women's position could be debated. By the 1860s young women employed in the mill began to join the Mechanics' Institute but they were only granted associate status. This seemed to stem directly from women's attendance at the evening classes for men set up by Reverend Clements in 1850. So despite the overall segregation of male and female educational milieux there was a small area of overlap and it was predominantly in this arena that social issues such as 'Women in intellectual capacity equal to man' and 'Woman's influence on society' were debated. It is not unlikely that Courtauld himself favoured or even instigated such discussions. Through his membership of the National Associaton for the Promotion of Social Science he was familiar with and sympathetic towards views put forward by women involved in the *English Woman's Journal* who believed in women extending their range of activities and influence without upsetting the ideological boundaries of the 'separate spheres'. Courtauld was very disparaging at a National Association for the Promotion of Social Science Conference in 1859 about the contributions of Lord Shaftesbury and Secretary Hastings, both of whom wished to curtail the industrial employment of women. He spoke against protective legislation, considering all arguments in favour to be 'utter bosh'.[61] By contrast, he praised 'a beautifully written and most interestingly read' paper delivered by Bessie Rayner Parkes, a member of the Langham Place Circle who produced the *English Woman's Journal*, on 'The market for educated female labour', and another, written by Jessie Boucherett, also representing the Langham Place Circle, on 'The industrial employment of women'. Courtauld's beliefs in an educated industrial workforce of women under his tutelage co-existed readily with the views promoted by the network surrounding the Langham Place Circle. Indeed, he used their arguments to support his own position.

At the same time as he vigorously upheld women's rights to be employed by him in his mills, Courtauld's educational ventures for men served to shape and strengthen the local male labour elite, thus helping to ensure that 'separate spheres' meant unequal spheres. The Mechanics' Institute contained the same possibilities for subversion and self-interest as did the women's meetings. Catering as it did, however, for men with high status in the workforce, subversion was far rarer than among the women, self-interest taking the form of an even greater consolidation of a labour aristocracy founded on a powerful hierarchy of gender. Serving on the committee for the year 1860 to 1861, for example, were familiar figures from among the highest ranking clerks and overseers at the mill such as Frederick Hawkes, George Firmin, John Bentall, Alfred Perry, Henry Garrod and Frederick Boley.[62] The Institute meetings provided a further milieu for the development of social relationships between these men and the mill manager, William Davidson, who was the president of the Institute for many years. This kind of forum, which constructed bridges between men of the working class and men of the middle class, helped to shape political allegiances to the detriment of working-class women in the community. The numbers of women joining remained relatively small[63] and associate membership bestowed a secondary status akin to the relationship which women had to the guilds in earlier centuries. Although women were allowed to attend Reverend Clements' evening classes they formed a minority, particularly as other male workers not employed by Courtauld were admitted. The

majority attending were 'men from the shops' and men drawn
from 'the better class of mechanics'.[64] Hardly any soft silk
weavers attended. Men employed in supervisory capacities in
the mechanized mills and men working in urban retail had
now completely superseded handloom weavers as the craft
elite of the labouring classes.

The definition of this new elite was completed by the two
remaining legs of Solly's 'three-legged stool' – recreation and
temperance. Courtauld was centrally involved in fashioning
these two legs partly through his religious influence in the
local community. The driving force of the 'rational recreation'
movement was the desire to bring the working class and the
middle class together in the joint pursuit of mutual progress.[65]
Although it partially embraced women, the movement's
political strategy was directed explicitly at working class men.
Henry Solly founded the Clubs and Institutes Union and
supported the setting up of Working Men's Clubs which were
designed expressly 'to form a centre of communication between
men of all classes interested in the welfare of the people; to
bring about a better understanding between men of different
occupations and standings'.[66]

The Halstead Mechanics' Institute was based firmly on this
model and, in common with many other clubs of its kind,
there was a unity between its middle-class founders and its
working-class membership in the desire to retain male control
and to develop a self-consciously masculine culture.[67] The
Institute had a higher status and was generally regarded as
having a far more serious educational content than the
Amusement Society, which was primarily for women. More
significantly, it gave a predominant circle of men access to
political expression defined and contained by their middle-
class employers.

These men became a close-knit group with interests increasingly allied to those of the employers. They even organized
separate dinners away from the Mechanics' Institute, pooling
subscriptions to hire the malting on the factory premises.[68]
Nearly thirty men employed as clerks, engineers, mechanics
and higher paid attendants arranged such a dinner in May
1861. The mill manager, William Davidson, presided and
Messrs. Harcourt, Runnacles and Sudbury, owners of a local

building firm, attended by invitation. Wives and 'sweethearts' were also present and music and entertainment were provided. Such occasions helped to cultivate an exclusive stratum of 'respectables' among the working class whose bonds with the middle class extended beyond the workplace. Recreational relations were as significant as employment relations in ensuring a 'coincidence of interests'[69] between these 'respectable' labouring men and their capitalist employers.

Intermeshed with relations of recreation were various activities connected to temperance and religion. Samuel Courtauld helped to set up the Temperance Refreshment Rooms in the High Street in the 1850s[70] and continued to finance and attend meetings of both the Temperance Society and the Band of Hope for many years. One of the main organs of the Temperance Society was the Working Men's Temperance Institute among whose key members were men of the elite group, like Frederick Hawkes, George Firmin, John Bentall and Henry Garrod. From the 1860s many religious groupings emerged in the locality reflecting the same values of honour, sobriety and respectability as both the Mechanics' Institute and the Temperance Institute. These groups were male dominated and promoted a specifically masculine culture. The Halstead Free Christian Church's Mutual Improvement Class had a completely male membership.[71] The non-sectarian Monthly Prayer Meetings held at the Halstead Town Hall, attended by all evangelical denominations except the Episcopalians,[72] were dominated by men in both the organizational hierarchy and the rank and file. The commissioners of the United Charities of Halstead were all male and structured their activities in much the same form as the Courtaulds' relief work – with men occupying the decision-making positions and women doing the day-to-day nurturing and caring.

Men involved in these groups developed a network of organizations enshrining many of the principles fostered by religion. Thrift and self-help informed the Halstead Penny Bank, which witnessed the opening of between seventy and eighty new accounts in 1859,[73] and the Halstead Friendly Society and the New Benefit Society,[74] both promoting insurance schemes for sickness and death. An Industrial Society based on ownership of dividends and accumulation of interest was also set up at this time.[75] Dividends were formally taken up only by men but informally 'some of the good husbands had promised these dividends to "the missus" as her share of the concern to do as she liked with.'[76] This practice was reminiscent of women's relationship to the guilds in previous centuries (see chapter 1).

The primary status of men as controllers of household income was boosted by Courtauld's entry into the provision of housing for his workers. Although mainly motivated by the moral concern which accompanied the setting up of the Factory Home, (see p. 144), one of the major effects of his housing programme was to strengthen the position of men as householders. Once again, it was the small elite band of 'labour aristocrats' who mainly benefited. The Courtauld firm only built fifty-eight houses altogether in Bocking, Halstead and Gosfield by 1900. The majority of these houses were erected for male millworkers, who assumed the status of tenants while they invariably took in lodgers, alongside their own families, who were predominantly young women. As well as the sixteen three-storey cottages built in Factory Terrace next to the Halstead mill in 1872 (see p. 69), ten two-storey cottages appeared in Church Street, close to the Bocking Mill in 1873. The Bocking cottages were provided for male crimpers, who were considered to be the most highly skilled craftsmen in the mill, and other senior male workers.[77] By 1875 twelve more houses were built next to the Halstead mill, along the Causeway. Eleven of these houses were occupied by male mechanics and overseers and their families. The twelfth housed the dining hall keeper who lived there rent-free as part of his employment.[78] The dwellings were among the first in the area to have gas fittings and running water and were regarded as substantial and modern.[79] The rents of those on the Causeway, Halstead and in Bocking Church Street were approximately 3/9d per week while those of the houses in Factory Terrace, Halstead, were on a sliding scale according to how many lodgers were in residence (see pp. 69–70).

The limited provision of company housing further sharpened some of the internal class and gender divisions in both the Courtauld workforce and the wider local labouring population. The better quality of the houses marked a status distinction between their occupants and those of the much poorer cottages rented from other members of the local landowning and business elite. Men in the highest status jobs lived in the finest of the Courtauld houses. The securing of men as tenants of these houses reinforced the distinction between males as householders and females as lodgers. All of these factors contributed to the acquisition of a 'culture of respectability'[80] among the local labour aristocracy, while also helping systematically to strengthen the material position of this elite through the promotion of their financial and legal security. Working-class women had little direct access to such security since their relationship to housing was mediated by their dependent status as wives, daughters, relatives or lodgers of male workers.

OUTCOMES OF THE 'NEW PATERNALISM'

The 'new paternalism' adopted by Courtauld was aimed at fostering a fictional unity based on a stringent adherence to familial ideology involving the personal cultivation and supervision of the male household head. In this aim it accorded with strategies followed by other benevolent industrialists.[81] The significance of this style of paternalism is frequently seen to lie in its influence on working-class consciousness, which in the main is characterized as an essentially masculine phenomenon.[82] The outcome of relationships mediated by paternalism is seen principally as 'accommodation' between the working class and the middle class.[83] The major problem with this approach is that while acknowledging the role of familial ideology it fails to analyse the significance of gender differences. In the first place, there is little attempt to distinguish between the consciousness of men and the consciousness of women.[84] Secondly, there is a failure to recognize that the 'respectability' cultivated among sections of the male working class was achieved chiefly at the expense of the subordination of large numbers of working-class women.

Developments in Halstead during the nineteenth century show that there were marked differences in working-class men and women's responses to the overtures of paternalism. The foundations of late nineteenth-century aspirations to

'respectability' among working-class men can be traced back
to the earlier decades of the century. East Anglian Chartism
was not renowned for its strength or militancy.[85] A Working
Men's Association, closely modelled on the London WMA,
existed in Halstead from 1838 to 1849 and there were periods
of considerable activity, particularly during the years from
1841 to 1843 and 1847 to 1848. But the Chartists of Halstead,
as elsewhere in East Anglia, adopted a more cautious approach
than their counterparts in northern England.[86] Women were
very active at a grass roots level in Halstead Chartism but, as
in most parts of the country, were not represented in key
decision-making positions.[87]

One factor which helps to explain the lack of militancy in
this region was the way in which the strong Nonconformist
belief in the power of adult education pervaded the political
conduct of the Chartists. In this respect Halstead Chartists
adopted more of a Solly-type of approach to reform. Solly
had himself supported the Chartist cause in the West country
in the 1830s,[88] but by the 1840s he conceptualized his desire
for reform as harmonious and concerted action by both
working-class and middle-class men influenced by education,
temperance and recreation. Chartists in Halstead had potential
middle-class allies in the Courtaulds with their support for the
Anti-Corn Law League and their promotion of education.
Halstead and Braintree Chartists condemned the Physical
Force movement and urged unity with the Anti-Corn Law
League.[89] After the Newport Rising they dissolved their
Association.

The revival of Chartist activism in the 1840s included
demonstrations of opposition to Samuel Courtauld. In
Braintree in 1847 a huge assembly of 1,500 men and women
workers rejected Samuel's attempt to persuade them to
repudiate the Charter. There was considerable unrest too
among Courtauld's handloom weavers who, experiencing
shortage of work in the depression of the 1840s, objected to
increased mechanization in the mills.[90] By the late 1840s there
were signs of a closer alliance with middle-class reformers. By
mid-century, links were forged with the local Mechanics'
Institute and a key Chartist activist, Lister Smith, was a
secretary employed by Samuel Courtauld. Lister Smith was

one of the major speech-makers, supporting adult education and the unity of capital and labour, at the 1846 Public Dinner (see chapter 4, pp. 101–3).

Nationally, Chartism did not draw much of its support from industrial workers.[91] Locally, many of the membership were drawn from handloom weavers. Journeyman artisans found in Chartism a way of struggling to maintain their status in the face of the widening gap between masters and journeymen accompanying increasing mechanization and the growing size of production units. Like other political and industrial conflicts characterizing the advent of industrial capitalism[92] this process embodied a patriarchal struggle involving attempts by different groups of men to maintain an authority which was both economic and familial.

In Halstead, as in other areas, handloom weaving decreased in even greater proportions after the 1830s and 1840s. By the middle of the century, some former handloom weavers found themselves working alongside sons of handloom weavers who had entered the mill earlier on.[93] The mill environment provided these men with a protection to their standing, other than progressing to traditional journeyman and then master status. As well as occupying superior positions in the labour force they had access to the reforming activities of the Courtaulds such as liberalism, education, temperance, recreation and opposition to state intervention. Samuel's long-standing battle over the Braintree Church rates case (see p. 131, n. 8) identified him as an ally in the fight against state control. Anti-Church feeling was inextricably bound up with the political causes espoused by the Courtaulds and their allies. Religion and politics went hand in hand.

By 1860 this growing alliance formed the basis of other self-help ventures in Halstead. Chief among these was the Co-operative society, which was fully supported by the Courtauld family.[94] By 1889 it had 629 members and was accompanied by a number of other benefit societies all dominated by a male membership. Among these was the Working Men's Mutual Loan Society, the Loyal 'Courtauld' Lodge of Odd Fellows, with Henry Garrod, an overseer at the mill, as secretary, the Foresters and numerous Clothing Clubs and Benevolent Societies.

Thus for certain sections of the male working class, 'skilled' jobs in the mill contributed to 'respectability' outside the factory gates and helped to shape a particular notion of 'independency'. Whether this notion arose autonomously or came directly from the employers,[96] it was a conception that was nurtured through the coincidence of interests characterizing the bonds for reform which united men of both the labouring class and the employer class.

For the majority of women workers in Courtauld's mill, 'independency' had much more to do with attempting to maintain control over those aspects of life which had always been central to working women's experience. It meant struggling against the imposition of alien forms of childcare, personal hygiene and dress, and fighting the more flagrant attempts by employers to restrict wages and control the content and pattern of work. In all these actions, whether by quiet refusal to use the company's nursery, more noisy rejection of the firm's lodging house, or massive demonstration of disaffection over speed-up proposals, there is little evidence of support from the men in the mill. During the strike of 1860 the men were notable in their absence. Their interests were clearly felt to be at odds with those of the mass of women workers.

The women most likely to be touched by the web of 'respectability' were the wives and daughters of the male elite, but their 'independent' status was not that of their husbands and fathers. It was the labour of these women in the mill, frequently in the higher categories of women's work such as assistant overseer and gauze examiner, which helped their menfolk to achieve a different lifestyle from the rest of the working population during the development of the industry. However, theirs was a derived 'respectability' which by the end of the century was increasingly associated with dependence on a man as the sole breadwinner after marriage. A male elite consciousness which had accepted married women's employment in the earlier years was by the 1890s espousing the 'family wage' ideal, infuenced by the greater availability of men's jobs in the locality [97] and fuelled by the arrival of male trade unionists from the north of England arguing for a strengthening of economic barriers against women.

These processes affected all women, not just those related

to members of the male elite, and hastened a progressive marginalization of women's paid employment. For many women the results were doubled-edged. The possibility of relying on a man for the household income offered some release from the 'double burden' of waged work and domestic work. At the same time, the failure to implement fully an adequate 'family wage' meant that many women continued to work, either full-time or part-time, in a job market which clearly attached a lower status and lower income to the labour of women. For much of the nineteenth century, women silkworkers in Halstead resisted the advances of paternalism more energetically than men did since it was women who had most to lose.

The role of middle-class women in these processes was complex. Unmarried women like Mary Merryweather were influenced by the domestic ideal but sought to redefine it in their own terms by expanding the domain of their activities. Falling as she did into Greg's category of 'surplus women',[98] Mary Merryweather needed an income of her own and found it by reinterpreting the 'angel in the house' notion to include paid employment ministering to women of another class. This kind of work was not financially necessary for married women like Ellen Courtauld and Mrs Clements. By mid-century, middle-class economic fortunes enabled more and more households to emulate the domestic ideal. For these women, philanthropic activity provided a way of combining an enactment of this ideology with a means of reaching beyond the constraints of their own four walls. Ellen Courtauld found activity in the day-to-day duties attached to local chapel life and the temperance movement. With Mary Merryweather she also fulfilled an important function visiting the sick among the labouring households. In this respect, she came to represent a symbolic mother figure to complement Samuel's role of 'father' to the local working population.

The channelling of middle-class women's energies into areas of work like health and education contributed to the acceptability of certain professions for women. The women whom Courtauld met through the National Association for the Promotion of Social Science were part of a whole network linked not only with the National Association for the Promotion of Social Science and the *English Woman's Journal* but also with organizations like the Society for the Promotion of Employment for Women, the Emily Faithfull Publishing Company, the Married Women's Property Committees and the National Union of Women's Suffrage[99] Mary Merryweather was closely involved in this network for many years after her departure from Halstead in the early 1860s.[100] As well as opposing the curtailment of industrial employment for working-class women, women in the network advocated the entry of middle-class women into types of paid employment needing the capacity to nurture and care for others and so not offending notions of femininity. Just as Courtauld argued for the continuation of labouring women's work in factories and mills he unwittingly contributed to the growing institutionalization of nursing as a profession for women through his extensive financial endowments of health care organizations.[101] He also unintentionally facilitated the transition of working-class women into the nursing profession since female millworkers joined Mary Merryweather and Ellen Courtauld on their visits to the sick particularly on Sunday afternoons. Frequent outbreaks of typhoid, smallpox, consumption and other diseases ensured a constant number of sick people to visit. The young women who visited the sick met on Monday evenings to learn more about sickness and ill health[102] and many of them went on to train as nurses. Similarly, through attendance at the Factory Evening School, a new avenue was opened up for working-class women in the locality to enter the teaching profession.

These developments were part of a chain of events extending back to the ideals of harmony and unity extolled at the 1846 Public Dinner. An emphasis on hygiene, health, domestic welfare and personal conduct was integral to the project of bridging divisions between the classes. Working-class women were central to this project, as instruments of order and virtue, a taming influence over their husbands and sons. A 'good clean home and hearth' would keep working-class men away from trade unions and other possible disruptive influences as well as from the public house.[103] Physical cleanliness in the home and personal hygiene as promoted through the firm's nursery and the 'maternal meetings' symbolized a wider social and moral purity identified clearly with the middle-class world view. If even a minority of working-class households could be steered into 'respectability' this could be used as an exemplary model for others to follow. Middle-class women, deprived of their former economic role in the household economy, partly acted as mediators of this ideology to working-class women. They also extended the boundaries of their own restricted domain. The bridges constructed across the social divide of class were fundamentally gender-specific, providing a point of connection between the women of each class[104] similar to the alliance of interests across the male section of each class promoted by the employers.

The evocation of a well-tended home as a haven from the workplace had a far greater appeal for working-class men than for working-class women. It was not men who were held responsible for the duties which would keep the home clean and comfortable. On the contrary, they were provided with an array of all-male retreats for filling their leisure time.[105] Working-class women forged their own distinctive responses to the paternalistic interventions into their lives. They took issue with domestic ideology and with the form in which it was mediated by middle-class women. But the proximity of middle-class women in their daily lives and their shared gender provided a means of identification quite different from the interests they shared with the men of their own class. They did not benefit in the same way as their menfolk from the privileges of the factory culture. This cut across the ways in which working-class men and women had common goals and objectives.[106] The women who wove for Courtaulds negotiated their own ideals and definitions in the context of their own particular experience. This embraced their perspective on family life, employment, contacts between women and even notions of what constituted womanhood. The 'family wage' which consolidated men's position as primary breadwinners offered its own palliatives to women beleaguered by the 'double burden'. It also strengthened the boundaries confining middle-class women's employment opportunities to lower status, lower paid professions compatible with current ideals of femininity. Any 'accommodation' of class interests procured in Halstead by the end of the nineteenth century was achieved

by the progressive marginalization of women's employment
which packaged such a situation as 'natural'. It was an
accommodation not of two genderless classes but of the men
in each class secured at the expense of the women in each
class.

NOTES

1 George died in 1860 and Samuel in 1881. For details of their wills
see D. C. Coleman, *Courtaulds: An Economic and Social History*,
Clarendon Press, 1969, p. 255.

2 Water fountains were particularly significant symbols of the temperance movement at this time. See B. Harrison, *Drink and the
Victorians*, Faber and Faber, 1971.

3 *Bocking Factory General Memoranda Book, 1879–1909*, ERO, DRF
3/2/38.

4 See H. C. Wilson, 'The geography of an industrial enterprise: the
Essex mills of Samuel Courtauld and Co. Ltd', unpublished thesis,
Jesus College, Cambridge, October 1970, ERO T/Z 75/11, ch. 8.

5 Interview with Ivy Mead, 1978.

6 Letter from Samuel Courtauld to Ellen Courtauld, 12 October 1859
in S. L. Courtauld, *The Huguenot Family of Courtauld*, vol. 3,
privately published, 1967, p. 121, emphasis in original.

7 Ibid., p. 90.

8 Mary Merryweather, *Experience of Factory Life*, Emily Faithfull
Publishing Co., 1862, p. 7.

9 Ibid.

10 Ibid., p. 9.

11 Ibid., p. 10, emphasis in original.

12 Ibid. Hands, of course, represent a powerful metaphor in Victorian
society, see Leonore Davidoff, 'Class and gender in Victorian
England: the diaries of Arthur J. Munby and Hannah Cullwick', in
J. Newton, M. P. Ryan and J. Walkowitz, *The Double Vision : Sex
and Class in Women's History*, Routledge and Kegan Paul, 1983.
Manual workers were referred to as 'hands' by middle-class employers.
At the same time, people's hands were an important indicator of
both gender and class. The working-class women whom Mary
Merryweather observed had the small, smooth hands of the middle-
class feminine ideal but they were constantly in danger of being
roughened by their domestic toil at home. Ironically, it was the work
in the mill that required smooth feminine hands. The necessity to
maintain such smoothness might have contributed to the symbolic
superior status of factory work over domestic service in the eyes of
many working-class women. Dirty rough hands were a sign of servility
and degradation.

13 Merryweather, *Factory Life*, p. 16.

14 Letter from Ellen Courtauld to Mary Merryweather, quoted in Merryweather, *Factory Life*, p. 27, emphasis in original.

15 See, for example, Carol Dyhouse, *The Education of Girls and Young Women in Victorian and Edwardian England*, Routledge and Kegan Paul, 1981.

16 See E. Trudgill, *Madonnas and Magdalens: The Origins and Development of Victorian Sexual Attitudes*, Holmes and Meier, 1976; J. Walkowitz, *Prostitution and Victorian Society*, Cambridge University Press, 1980.

17 Merryweather, *Factory Life*, p. 43.

18 Ibid., p. 18.

19 Ibid., p. 43.

20 Ibid., p. 44.

21 Ibid., p. 46.

22 Ibid., emphasis in original.

23 Ibid.

24 Ibid., p. 48, emphasis in original.

25 Ibid., p. 50.

26 *Rough Diary of Carey Clements*, Friday, 4 May 1888, ERO, D/F 3/ 3/26.

27 Merryweather, *Factory Life*, p. 50, emphasis in original.

28 Ibid., p. 51.

29 Ibid., pp. 52–3.

30 Ibid., p. 52.

31 Ibid., p. 55.

32 Ibid., p. 58.

33 Ibid.

34 Ibid., p. 57.

35 See, for example, B. Eisler (ed.), *The Lowell Offering : Writings by New England Mill Women, 1840–1845*, Harper, 1980; Lucy Larcom, *An Idyl of Work*, J. R. Osgood and Co., 1875, and *A New England Girlhood*, Houghton, Mifflin and Co., 1890; C. Knight, *Mind Among the Spindles: A Selection from the Lowell Offering*, Jordan, Swift and Wiley, 1845; Harriet H. Robinson, *Loom and Spindle: Or Life Among the Early Mill Girls*, T. Y. Crowell and Co., 1898.

36 The particular connection between Solly and the Courtauld family was established through Solly's ministry at Carter Lane Chapel in London in the 1850s where his congregation included the Martineaus, and many other radical Unitarian families, as well as the Courtaulds. See Coleman, *Courtaulds*, vol. I, p. 207.

37 H. Solly, *These Eighty Years, or the Story of an Unfinished Life*, 2 vols, Simpkin, Marshall and Co. 1893, vol. II, p. 160. See also, P. Bailey, *Leisure and Class in Victorian England: Rational Recreation*

and the Contest for Control, 1830–1885, Routledge and Kegan Paul, 1978.

38 Bailey, Leisure and Class.

39 E. P. Thompson, 'Time, work-discipline and industrial capitalism', Past and Present, no. 38, 1967.

40 Thompson, 'Time, work-discipline and industrial capitalism'.

41 Letter from Mrs Samuel Courtauld III to 'the Gosfield Tenants', Christmas 1871, in Courtauld, The Huguenot Family, p. 135, emphasis in original.

42 Merryweather, Factory Life, p. 64, emphasis in original.

43 Ibid.

44 Thompson, 'Time, work-discipline and industrial capitalism'.

45 Halstead Times, Saturday, 13 July 1861.

46 Merryweather, Factory Life, p. 63.

47 Letters Book of Carey Clements, 1873–1890, p. 95. ERO D/F 3/3/22.

48 Merryweather, Factory Life, p. 65.

49 Ibid., p. 66, emphasis in original.

50 Ibid., p. 68.

51 Ibid., p. 34.

52 Correspondence concerning the Factory Reading Room, 13 February 1857, from George Courtauld, ERO D/F 3/2/100.

53 Merryweather, Factory Life, pp. 36–7.

54 Halstead Gazette, Thursday, 4 April 1861.

55 Merryweather, Factory Life, p. 38.

56 Halstead Gazette, Thursday, 15 March 1860.

57 Letters Book of Carey Clements, pp. 123–4.

58 Ibid., p. 124.

59 A detailed family history study of a Halstead family with several generations of workers in the mill shows, for example, that Emma Goodey appears in the Courtauld employment registers as fourteen years old when she commenced work as a winder in February 1890. Her birth certificate states that she was born in April 1877. I am grateful to Carole Bagshaw of the Halstead and District Local History Society for this information

60 Letters Book of Carey Clements, p. 161.

61 Letter from Samuel Courtauld to Ellen Cortauld, 11 October 1859, in Courtauld, The Huguenot Family of Courtauld, vol.3, p. 120.

62 Halstead Gazette, Thursday 4 April 1861. These men represented what Dodd referred to as 'the higher order of Mechanics', W. Dodd, The Labouring Classes of England, J. Putnam, 1848, pp. 9–10; see chapter 1, p. 23–4.

63 In 1861, for example, there were 24 women and 102 men, Halstead Gazette, Thursday 4 April 1861.

64 Merryweather, Factory Life, p. 39.

65 See H. Solly's novel, James Woodford, Carpenter and Chartist, 2

vols, S. Low, Marston, Searle and Rivington, 1881, in which the hero chooses to work with, rather than against, middle-class reformism. See also, R. V. Holt, *The Unitarian Contribution to Social Progress in England*, G. Allen and Unwin, 1938.

66 Bailey, *Leisure and Class*, p. 111.

67 Ibid., pp. 119–20.

68 *Halstead Gazette*, 31 May 1860.

69 M. Barrett and M. McIntosh, 'The family "wage": some problems for socialists and feminists', *Capital and Class*, no. 11, 1980, pp. 51–72.

70 *Halstead Times*, Saturday, 27 April 1861.

71 *Halstead Gazette*, Thursday, 15 March 1860.

72 *Halstead Times*, Saturday 11 May 1861.

73 *Halstead Gazette*, Thursday, 19 January 1860.

74 *Halstead Times*, Saturday, 1 June 1861.

75 Ibid., Saturday, 8 June 1861.

76 Ibid.

77 *Bocking Factory Book*, p. 2.

78 *Bocking Factory Book*, p. 8.

79 Personal communication with Albert Cross, Halstead and Distict Local History Society.

80 See J. Lewis, 'Women lost and found: the impact of feminism on history', in Dale Spender (ed.), *Men's Studies Modified*, Pergamon Press, 1981.

81 See P. Joyce, *Work, Society and Politics*, Harvester Press, 1980.

82 E. Hobsbawm, *Labouring Men*, Weidenfeld and Nicolson, 1964; J. Foster, *Class Struggle and the Industrial Revolution*, Weidenfeld and Nicolson, 1974; E. P. Thompson, *The Making of the English Working Class*, Pelican, 1968; Joyce, *Work, Society and Politics*; D. Roberts, *Paternalism in Early Victorian England*, Croom Helm, 1979; H. I. Dutton and J. E. King, 'The limits of paternalism', *Social History*, 7(1), 1982.

83 Dutton and King, 'Limits of paternalism'.

84 Some important theoretical and empirical issues concerning the analysis of working women's consciousness are discussed in Sarah Eisenstein, *Give Us Bread But Give Us Roses*, Routledge and Kegan Paul, 1983, a study based on the United States experience between 1890 and 1914.

85 *Chartism in East Anglia*, WEA Eastern District publication, 1951; A. F. J. Brown, *The Chartist Movement in Essex and Suffolk*, Local History Centre Publication, University of Essex, 1979.

86 Brown, ibid.

87 D. Thompson, 'Women and nineteenth century radical politics: a lost dimension', in J. Mitchell and A. Oakley (eds), *The Rights and Wrongs of Women*, Penguin, 1976.

88 Bailey, *Leisure and Class*.
89 Brown, *The Chartist Movement in Essex and Suffolk*.
90 Brown, ibid.; *Chartism in East Anglia*, WEA.
91 R. G. Gammage, *History of the Chartist Movement*, Merlin, 1969.
92 See M. A. Clawson, 'Early modern fraternalism and the patriarchal family', *Feminist Studies*, 6(2), Summer 1980.
93 Of the core of senior male workers who appear on so many local committees, George Firmin 'was originally a Ribbon Weaver' (i.e. a handloom weaver) before he joined the mill labour force in 1834, Frederick Hawkes, John Bentall and Henry Garrod were sons of handloom weavers and Alfred Perry was the grandson of a handloom weaver. *Courtauld Registers of Employees, 1830–1919*, ERO D/F 3/3/1 to 3/3/10.
94 See A. E. Hodgkinson, *The Great Adventure*, Halstead Co-operative Society Ltd, 1960.
95 *The Essex Almanac*, 1889, p. 176.
96 Bailey, *Leisure and Class*. See also, G. Crossick, 'The labour aristocracy and its values: a study of Mid-Victorian Kentish London', *Victorian Studies*, March 1976; R. Gray, 'Styles of life, the "labour aristocracy" and class relations in later nineteenth centry Edinburgh', *International Review of Social History*, vol 18, 1973.
97 In particular, jobs for working-class men increased with the development of the brewery and maltings in Halstead, Portways' Ironworks next to Halstead Railway Station (producing 'Tortoise' Stoves, ranges, drilling machines, carriage jacks and fire globes), Rippers woodworks in Sible Hedingham, Hunt's iron foundry in Earls Colne and Rayners brickworks in Gestingthorpe and Sible Hedingham. See *Kelly's Directories of Essex* for 1870, 1874, 1878 and 1882; *Industries of the Eastern Counties*, British Industrial Publishing Company, 1890. See also, P. Bamberger, *A Pictorial History of Halstead and District*, Halstead and District Local History Society, 1979; J. Booker, *Essex and the Industrial Revolution*, ERO Publications, no. 66, 1974.
98 W. R. Greg, 'Why are women redundant?', *National Review*, 14, 1862, pp. 434–60.
99 See L. Holcombe, *Wives and Property: Reform of the Married Women's Property Law in Nineteenth Century England*, Univeristy of Toronoto Press 1983, ch. 4; Liz Stanley, 'Feminism and friendship in England form 1825 to 1938: the case of Olive Schreiner'. *Studies in Sexual Politics*, no. 8, University of Manchester.
100 Mary Merryweather's obituary refers to her involvement in a number of feminist and philanthropic concerns after her departure from Halstead. She died in 1880 at her nursing post in Westminster Hospital (*Work and Leisure*, June 1880, vol. v, p. 181). Through this network, Mary Merryweather was connected to key feminist figures like Bessie Rayner Parkes, Barbara Bodichon and Harriet

Martineau – see G. Weiner, 'Harriet Martineau – a reassessment', in D. Spender (ed.), *Feminist Theorists*, The Women's Press, 1983. A common link between many of these women was their Unitarian faith.

101 As well as setting up cottage hospitals in Halstead and Bocking and subscribing to local lying-in charities, the Courtauld firm made regular financial contributions to the London Hospital in Whitechapel Road, the City Road Hospital for Chest Diseases, the City of London Hospital for Chest Diseases, the London Fever Hospital in Liverpool Road and the Colchester Hospital, see *Bocking Factory Book*.

102 Merryweather, *Factory Life*, pp. 71–2.

103 See L. Davidoff et al., 'Landscape with figures'. Mitchell and Oakley, *The Rights and Wrongs of Women*.

104 The kinds of bonds to which such philanthropic connections could ' give rise have been explored by J. L'Esperance, 'Woman's mission to woman: explorations in the operation of the double standard and female solidarity in nineteenth century England', *Social History – Histoire Sociale*, 1979.

105 It is important to note how lines between 'work' and 'leisure' were never so clearly drawn for women as they were for men, mainly because of the greater demands of domesticity on women. For a discussion of this in a later period see M. Abendstern, 'Expression and Control, A Study of Working Class Leisure and Gender 1918–1939: A case study of Rochdale using oral history methods', unpublished PhD thesis, University of Essex, 1986.

106 This is the kind of tension which is ignored in accounts of class consciousness emphasizing unity within working-class households, see J. Humphries, 'Class struggle and the resistance of the working class family'. *Cambridge Journal of Economics*, 1(3), 1977. It seems more accurate to assume elements of both unity *and* tension in households.

6

DEBATING 'WOMEN'S WORK'

The Courtauld story represents one facet of a pattern of change and continuity characterizing life in the nineteenth century. Developments associated with industrialization were uneven over different geographical regions and the various sectors of the economy.[1] Many elements of domestic and workshop production persisted alongside the factory system well into the nineteenth century. At the same time, a shifting occupational structure signalled the expansion of jobs in the clerical sector[2] and the rise of professions such as teaching[3] and nursing.[4] There are common implications, however, for women's relationship to paid employment across different regional locations and economic sectors.

The simultaneous construction and continuing renegotiation of categories of gender and class during this time profoundly influenced the lived relationships of women and men in different economic positions. The issue of patriarchal authority was central. Notions of masculinity and femininity were directly connected to ideals of the patriarchal family which in turn were intrinsically harnessed to a hierarchical ordering of economic positions.

Many of the changes commonly taken to typify processes of industrialization embodied powerful messages of gender ideology. Technological developments became metaphors for masculine and feminine values. An increasing split between 'culture' and 'nature'[5] symbolized a division not only between

PLATE 26 Eighteenth-century painting entitled 'An Iron Forge' by Joseph Wright of Derby.

science and intuition, town and country, the intellect and the spirit, but also between work and home, the public and the private, man and woman. Paradoxically, these changes relied on a form of continuity with the past.

An eighteenth-century painting, 'An Iron Forge' by Joseph Wright of Derby (see plate 26) depicts a family gathered around a forge.[6] The husband stands taller and larger than the rest of the group, his muscular arms folded, one foot raised against the forge and his eye directed in a protective and paternal gaze downward upon his wife and children. He stands apart from his wife and two children who are physically entwined together, the mother cradling a baby, and a girl of about nine or ten encircling an arm around her mother's waist.

A workman, the son perhaps, crouches over an ingot of burning iron. As an idealization of an industrial workshop the picture reveals a view of gender ideals continuous with and yet long predating the adulation by Victorian writers of the 'angel in the house'. In choosing to represent the Industrial Revolution in this form rather than through a portrayal of, for instance, women nailmakers, Wright expresses a sensibility influenced by the pervasiveness of the patriarchal household. In symbolizing a desire to perpetuate the existing authority relations of production, the picture identifies masculinity with the power to dominate both nature and women through the control of technology. Correspondingly, feminine values are connected to nurturing and caring.

THE CHANGING FACE OF 'WOMEN'S WORK'

This ideology contributed to moulding a distinctive category of 'women's work' in several of the major industries and trades in which women had long played an important part. In those sectors of the economy undergoing mechanization women's labour was transferred from an unequal status within the household economy into categories defined as lower in skill and less well paid than those occupied by men. Developments along these lines in the silk industry, for example, were paralleled in other branches of the textile trades. In cotton producing areas the introduction of spinning jennies into factories was accompanied by an increase of status and earnings for the men who took over spinning while weaving passed mostly to female hands who suffered a lowering of status and earnings.[7] In the Leicestershire hosiery trade, the transition to factory production brought about a labour hierarchy similar to that in the Courtauld mills whereby women were at the bottom, employed in tending the automatic knitting machines, while men were mechanics and overseers.[8] In other trades similar patterns of marginalization took place. In printing women's work was limited to bookbinding, predefined as an activity requiring the 'domestic' ability of sewing and therefore lacking in both status and skill.[9]

Processes of deskilling, dilution and exclusion cut across the town and country divide. In London, women's activities mainly fell into categories coinciding with domestic labour and were 'unskilled', overcrowded and low paid.[10] In the countryside women were increasingly being displaced in farmwork by men and became restricted to seasonal casual activities.[11] In mining areas, women gradually became confined to the most 'unskilled' tasks at the pithead.[12] Many of these women had been characterized by the strength required of their work and a reputation of 'independence' which the work cultivated. Both attributes were increasingly outlawed in women in late Victorian society. Not only were women losing what little pay and status they had in some areas of work, they were also having to relinquish some of the sources of pride afforded to them by their work. Their lives did not accord with the image of 'respectability' being fostered in many working-class communities, closely linked to the efforts of men as 'skilled' workers to reshape a superior status for themselves.[13]

Domestic ideology, rooted in anxieties about a perceived threat to family life and to the whole social order, influenced the definition of 'women's work' so that it became associated with low paid, low status activities in certain restricted categories of labour acceptable only as long as it was secondary to domestic duties. The desire to perpetuate the gender divisions and authority structure of the patriarchal household coincided with working-class men's struggle to maintain their economic and familial standing in changing circumstances of production. Because economic and familial relations were still inextricably linked, radical activity in relation to employment reflected growing conflicts between male and female workers in a destabilizing market. The debates taking place through the publications of workers' organizations in the 1830s and 40s, for example, highlight how the 'wage earning wife, once seen as the norm in every working-class household, had become a symptom and symbol of masculine degradation'.[14] In a statement revealing the implicit connections made between gender and industrial employment, Engels wrote in 1844 that a married woman working 'unsexes the man and takes from the woman all womanliness' and 'degrades in the most shameful way, both sexes'.[15]

This viewpoint was fuelled by the fact that men's status,

and thereby their masculinity as represented through their patriarchal position, was under attack at the same time as it became increasingly difficult for women to combine household tasks with paid employment. Just as masculinity was being equated with economic primacy and familial authority so femininity was defined in terms of domesticity and subservience to husbands and fathers. It was these qualities, confined within the walls of the home, that marked out a 'lady' in the wealthier strata; they could be achieved for the working-class 'woman' only if she never let paid employment outweigh her other duties, especially when she was married. A clear distinction was frequently drawn between 'ladies' and 'women'. The most a working-class woman could hope for was to become a 'respectable woman' by following the middle-class ideal of allowing her husband to be the sole breadwiner while she fulfilled his physical, emotional and spiritual needs.

By the end of the nineteenth century most 'respectable' trades had contracted in terms of women's work and notions of respectability were moving towards the prescription that women either withdraw from paid employment altogether or engage only in occupations representing an extension of the nurturing capacities assumed to be their natural endowment. Supposedly appropriate activities were closely related to distinctions in social class and frequently accompanied by the expectation that marriage would mean forfeiting employment so that the woman could pursue her primary duty of ministering to the needs of the rest of the family. The prevailing attitude that employment was mainly a temporary stepping stone towards marriage for young women was one of the reasons for employers' strategies to downgrade women's work. Accompanying this notion was the idea that women were simply required to translate some of their innate abilities into the market but, since the market was not the ideal place for women, none of their jobs could be seen as careers. All these developments were a major source of the unevenness characterizing the economic structure throughout the nineteenth century. This much vaunted unevenness was produced by far more than the vagaries of an industrializing economy: it was the result of the particular and complex ways in which patriarchal interests vied with capitalist concerns.

Jobs no longer considered suitable for women were fast disappearing from their reach. Occupations that did not accord with current conceptions of femininity – and threatened both the control which men had over them and the sense of masculinity which this bestowed – were becoming more and more consolidated into men's hands. Only work which was considered feminine was offered to women and there was no shortage of public voices defining what constituted fit work for women. Women's potential freedom in the labour market was a threat to marriage itself. The reinstatement of the patriarchal household model within the labour market and institutions of a developing industrial economy prevented a large-scale loss of services provided by women within the marriage relationship. Instead, women were encouraged to extend those services into the public realm through work which was both subsidiary and cheap.

The possession of structural control in the public realm does not, however, preclude self-defined bases of power and autonomy within the larger culture.[16] Analyses characterizing developments like the growth of the clerical sector in terms of 'proletarianization'[17] depend upon a male-defined theory of stratification. The use of masculine experience as a yardstick by which to measure social mobility distracts attention from how women might have experienced employment. Proletarianization suggests downward movement from the ranks of the middle class to those of the working class but, as Meta Zimmeck points out, 'for middle class women there was nowhere to go but up'.[18] Many of the new job opportunities opening up to women in the second half of the nineteenth century established arenas which were paradoxically both peripheral and powerful. Those women whose work involved them in separate women-centred institutions like schools, colleges and religious houses, were finding alternatives to marriage and the nuclear family. These provided them with bases of power through which to actively transform and redefine the external constraints surrounding them.[19] Central to this experience was an identification with the common concerns of women and a valuing of relationships among their own sex.[20] Such recognition and consciousness could arise out of a variety of different circumstances in which women were situated. Apart from the women-controlled institutions occupied principally by single middle-class women, the confines of domesticity among those for whom the ideal was also a reality formed a basis for female friendships for married middle-class women.[21] Factories, workshops and mills employing predominantly women also provided settings for the formation of working-class female solidarity,[22] as did many of the homes and communities of the labouring poor.[23]

These networks added another dimension to the complex relationships of gender and class. Alongside developments simultaneously demarcating yet providing channels of allegiance across the boundaries between men of different classes, points of connection were emerging across similarly sharpening class divisions between women. All these dimensions played a part in the kinds of responses among women and men to changes in employment and familial patterns throughout the nineteenth century. Such responses were influenced by the fact that both class and gender are relationships:[24] they rely on the claiming of an identity with one group in relation to another. Because these identities are mutually constructed, an individual's loyalties depend upon identification with two groups some of whose interests coincide and some of which conflict. Race is also commonly built into this mutual constellation of identity and was no less present in the nineteenth century than it is today. The prevailing model of social difference in the Victorian period was one predicated on a naturally ordained hierarchy which placed white on a higher scale than black, 'ladies' higher than 'women', the familiar higher than the 'empire'.[25] Stratification was determined not simply by male occupational status but by a complex prism of dichotomies which placed white adult male aristocrats at the top of the social and biological pyramid dependent upon the subservience of women, children, servants, working-class people and black residents (and former residents) of the colonies.

This model owed much to former conceptions of a feudally organized system of rank and order but was being recast under the growing ascendancy of the industrial middle class who posed a challenge to the rule of the landed gentry. Religion continued to serve as a means of rationalizing the social order and was buttressed by scientific theories of evolution.[26] In the hands of members of the middle class, femininity became a new class ideal which had implications not just for the lives of women related by kin to middle-class men but also for women of labouring households.

In the case of the Courtauld enterprise, we have seen how as the business prospered the female members of the family became more isolated from the day-to-day activities of the firm[27] and were increasingly cast into a philanthropic 'angel of the house' mould. Meanwhile, women from local labouring families dependent upon the mill for employment were systematically encouraged to imitate middle-class ideals of domesticity alongside their labours in the mill (see chapter 5). The circumstances surrounding women across the social spectrum in the vicinity of the Courtauld mills in Essex are in many ways emblematic of the shifting meanings of class and gender in the nineteenth century and the wider responses which such shifts evoked.

'WOMAN'S MISSION AND WOMAN'S POSITION' IN THE 1830S AND 1840S

The rapid expansion of the Halstead mill in the 1830s depended upon an influx of women and children. At this early stage Courtauld defended the use of such labour, a stance to which he adhered for the rest of his life. The statement of an opinion was necessitated by the widespread visibility of working-class women entering employment in mills, factories and workshops at the same time as many middle-class households were attempting to institute the 'domestic ideal' in their own homes. Courtauld's was one voice among many during this period debating the extent to which the 'domestic ideal' should be applied to working-class lives. The key questions in this debate focused upon the nature of 'women's mission' in society and the issue of control over women's lives.

The framing of the early debates depicts a process of struggle between various groups of men in differing relationships to the state which parallel earlier antagonisms between journeymen and masters concerning the maintenance of legitimate patriarchal authority. The central bone of contention was whether or not legal reforms to control women's employment were necessary and desirable. The initial impetus to use legislative measures came from government representatives shocked by evidence not only of poor conditions of health and physical safety but of rising illegitimacy rates and other codes of conduct which affronted mdidle-class standards of decency and respectability.[28] Attention was selectively focused, however, upon factory labour and minework with little concern expressed about occupations like domestic service where women were located 'appropriately' in the home providing for the comforts of middle-class life.

By the early 1840s domestic ideology was more explicitly mobilized by parliamentary commissioners investigating women and children's employment. Under the terms of the Children's Employment Commission of 1841 female workers were asked 'how far their employment during childhood has prevented them from forming the domestic habits usually acquired by women in their station, and how it has rendered them less fit than those whose early years have not been spent in labour for performing the duties of wives and mothers'.[29]

Increasingly, women and children were presented as a special category beyond the tenets of political economy with its emphasis on a *laissez-faire* relationship between capital and labour. State intervention came to be seen from this perspective to be the only way to control the effects of industrial employment not only on women but on society as a whole. The Chief Factory Inspector, Leonard Horner, proclaimed in 1843 that:

> Twelve hours' daily work is more than enough for anyone; but however desirable it might be that excessive working should be prevented, there are great difficulties in the way of legislative interference with the labour of adult men. The case, however, is very different as respects women; for not only are they much less free agents, but they are physically incapable of bearing a continuance of work for the same length of time as men, and a deterioration of their health is attended with far more injurious consequences to Society.[30]

Lord Ashley, the most publicized proponent of restricted

hours for working women and children, gave this theme the greatest prominence in his campaigns for a Ten Hours Bill. Lamenting the harsh conditions under which factory women laboured he continually emphasized that the result of such a state of affairs would be the destruction of homes and families. In the parliamentary debates leading up to the final enactment of the Ten Hours Bill in 1847 his words encapsulated the whole range of anxieties that had been aired over the previous decade or more. In the course of one speech he asked, 'Where, Sir, under this condition, are the possibilities of domestic life? how can its obligations be fulfilled? Regard the woman as wife or mother, how can she accomplish any portion of her calling? And if she cannot do that which Providence has assigned her, what must be the effect on the whole surface of society?' He added, that, 'the females not only perform the labour but occupy the places of men; they are forming various clubs and associations, and gradually acquiring all those privileges which are held to be the proper portion of the male sex'. All of this, he maintained was 'a perversion as it were of nature, which [had] the inevitable effect of introducing into families disorder, insubordination and conflict'. Not far from his mind, as with other Tories and Evangelicals, was the threat of incipient unrest contained in recent Chartist protests. The family, as 'the mainstay of social peace and virtue, and therein of national security'[31] must be protected and woman's place in it secured if social turmoil was to be kept at bay.

Women's own interests were of no greater significance to the men who opposed legislation. Dr Andrew Ure had similar intentions of a primarily domestic definition of women's place but considered that wage differentials between male and female workers obviated the necessity for legislation:

> Factory females have in general much lower wages than males, and they have been pitied on this account with perhaps an injudicious sympathy, since the low price of their labour here tends to make household duties their most profitable as well as agreeable occupation, and prevents them from being tempted by the mill to abandon the care of their offspring at home.[32]

Meanwhile, employers like Courtauld and other liberal

manufacturers like John Bright of Lancashire, opposed any form of state interference on the grounds that they as enlightened employers should be entrusted to look after their workers and that government intervention ran counter to the laws of political economy which should be left unfettered at all times. Many middle-class men, both supporters and opponents of legislation, were united in their adherence to the ideal of 'True Womanhood'. Their disagreements concerned the extent to which it was the responsibility of the state or of individual employers to uphold the ideal and the exact form it would take in working-class households.

A similar concern with the role of the state characterized some of the more vocal responses of middle-class women to the issue of legislative regulation of women's employment. The emphasis in these responses, however, was not freedom for industry from interference but freedom for women to control their own destinies. A prominent female opponent of legislation was Harriet Martineau. As a well-known popularizer of the principles of political economy[33], Martineau firmly opposed any legal retrictions on women's access and rights to employment. She insisted that the rules of political economy should be applied equally to men and women. Treating women as a separate category had only detrimental effects: 'It is pleaded that half the human race does acquiesce in the decision of the other half, as to their rights and duties . . . Such acquiescence proves nothing but degradation to the injured party.'[34] Like Samuel Courtauld, Martineau was brought up in the Unitarian faith, but, unlike him, she experienced first hand some of the contradictions of a world view emphasizing personal freedom yet continuing to harness women to the strictures of the 'domestic ideal'.[35]

Other women writers entered the fray. In 1843, Anna Jameson published an article criticising both male proponents and opponents of legal reform. She identifies the main problem for all employed women as the double standard by which they are simultaneously adulated as the keepers of domestic and moral virtue and compelled through financial necessity to work. She forcefully draws attention to this anomalous condition which 'inculcates one thing as the rule of right, and decrees another as the rule of necessity' and declares that "woman's mission", of which people can talk so well and write 'so prettily is irreconcilable with woman's position, of which no one dares to think much less to speak'.[36]

Articles like this drew connections between issues of women's employment and other circumstances of women's lives such as the lack of the vote and legal rights.[37] The circles aligning themselves to such arguments reveal the kinds of interconnections forming foundations for varying types of alliance. The politics of some radicals crossed class boundaries to embrace the causes of women's rights, Chartism and anti-slavery. Unitarian and Quaker affiliations were often prominent among such activists. Chartists and abolitionists were involved, for example, in Joseph Sturge's Complete Suffrage Union. This was a milieu which also included women's rights supporters like William and Mary Howitt, editors of the *People's and Howitt's Journal*, W. J. Fox, editor of the *Monthly Repository*,[38] and Elizabeth Pease, the daughter of a Quaker family of industrialsts in Darlington who became a Chartist. Mary Howitt and Elizabeth Pease attended the 1840 World Anti-Slavery Convention in London when the position of women in the movement was raised.[39] Many of those involved in these circles strongly criticized attempts by government to control women's employment.

While some middle-class women entered such circles, others were equally vehement in backing restrictive legislation. In 1844, Charlotte Tonna, a well-known novelist, wrote a series of fictional accounts of working women published as *The Wrongs of Women*.[40] Even these accounts were written in the language of women's rights, however, invoking the home as the 'proper sphere' of women in order to attack the injustices of industrial labour. Writers like Tonna and Mrs Sarah Ellis, who assiduously catalogued women's obligations in the home,[41] feared not for the well being of society so much as the loss of a woman's right to remain in her 'natural' domain. They represented the other side of the coin concerning the kinds of rights attached to women defined by the 'domestic ideal'. The women aligned to Harriet Martineau and Anna Jameson accepted that women had 'natural' abilities but argued for the extension of individual rights to women by allowing them to take their 'natural' skills into employment thus rendering the public sphere a better place. Women like Charlotte Tonna and Sarah Ellis used their belief in women's innate caring and nurturing qualities to insist on women's rights to stay at home and avoid the evils of the market place.

Similarly, not all those involved in working-class reform held the same interpretations of women's rights. As in the debates triggered by parliamentary commissions into working conditions, the voice of women was the least heard. Chartist associations provided a focus of activity for many working women, even raising issues of enfranchisement for women and women's rights,[42] but it was franchise for their fathers, husbands and brothers that dominated women's energies. Despite the familiarity and even direct involvement of some Chartists with causes connected to women's rights, the insinuation of the 'domestic ideal' increasingly shaped the direction of Chartist struggles. Some male Chartists made explicit appeals to women for their support on the basis of their domestic burden:

> Women of Britain, you have ever been foremost in every good, in every noble cause . . . you have to bear the thousand varieties of domestic vexations, which to the impatient spirit of man would be worse than the actual distress; you are then even more interested than ourselves in procuring a fair day's wages for a fair day's work.[43]

The objectives of male trade unionists were also influenced by domestic ideology. Representations from working-class men on the short-time committees called for a division of labour which emulated that preferred by their employers. A deputation from the West Riding informed Gladstone and Peel in 1841 that they favoured the 'gradual withdrawal of all females from the factories' and that they believed that 'the home, its cares and its employments, is true woman's sphere'. They referred to the divine status of man's and woman's place and expressed fears for their masculinity, insisting that women's industrial work was 'an inversion of the order of nature and of Providence – a return to a state of barbarism in which woman does the work while man looks idly on'.[44] Such views had been encouraged by the notion expressed by the earlier Factory Commissions and opponents of the factory system that single working women were gaining a new form of independence through their access to an individual wage. Gaskell looked upon this as 'another evil of the factory system' and bemoaned how 'each child ceases to view itself as a subordinate agent in the household'.[45]

Despite such views, many women persisted in the setting up of female lodges, particularly after the establishment of the short-lived grand National Consolidated Trades Union in 1833.[46] Some lodges, like the Ancient Virgins in Oldham, worked with men in fighting for the ten hour day. In other instances, there were protracted battles between male and female workers over the division of tasks and pay within trades such as that witnessed in the tailoring business.[47] Voicing concerns close to those of Ashley, a tailor called George Edmonds argued against the setting up of a Grand Lodge of Women for those without paid employment on the grounds that 'The only way to make [home] attractive is to have the wife's company in the evening, when man has done his day's labour; for if she goes out to sport, he will go to the public house'.[48]

Many unions, like those in the printing industry, were busy fighting to keep women either out of their trades or in separate lower status categories of work. The idea of the 'family wage' was pursued among sections of the male tailoring trade as it was among many male workers in the mines and other industries by the 1840s. There were other instances where women and men fought together for equal rates of pay as in the Glasgow Spinners Association, but the motives of the men were coloured by a desire not to have their wages undercut.[49] On other occasions women strikers found it difficult to get the support of male workers.[50]

Many of the women active in trade unions and many of those questioned by government officials were ambivalent about their relationship to paid employment. For some, waged work, no matter what the conditions, was essential for survival of the household and this took overriding precedence. For others the conditions in which they were compelled to work were an understandable cause for grievance and lent weight to a wish for shortened hours. Few at this stage argued for their own complete removal from waged work.[51] Domestic ideology made far fewer inroads into working-class women's consciousness at this time than into that of working-class men. In terms of the distinctive conditions of working-class women's lives the 'domestic ideal' was neither realistic nor desirable.

The only alternative strategy to the 'domestic ideal' framed by women and men of both classes emerged in the Owenite socialist movement. Started by a small group of radical intellectuals in the early 1820s, the Owenite movement expanded and moved almost entirely into the hands of working people by the 1830s until its demise in 1845.[52] Part of its programme was a radical critique of power relationships between men and women based on a wider vision of a 'New Science of Society'[53] organized around communalized property and collectivized family life. It was among followers of Owen and other 'utopian' socialists like Saint-Simon that the word 'feminist' was first coined. The writings of feminist socialists like Anna Wheeler and Eliza Macauley contain far-reaching indictments of marriage and call for the emancipation of women from a form of sexual slavery.[54] Their words had much in common with those of Harriet Martineau, Harriet Taylor and John Stuart Mill. A strong interconnection existed at this time between the prominent Unitarian circle and the Owenties. W. J. Fox, the editor of the *Monthly Repository*, was eventually expelled from the Unitarian hierarchy for his Owenite views on marriage. Such groupings were very fluid and there was a great deal of interchange and overlap between their ideas, activities and friendships.

FEMINIST STRATEGIES FOR WOMEN'S EMPLOYMENT: THE 1850S AND 1860S

By the middle of the nineteenth century, Courtauld had consolidated a workforce made up predominantly of female workers and had increasingly made use of paternalism to reconcile his patriarchal and capitalist interests. Having been progressively marginalized from central economic functions in household and business, the women of Courtauld's class had a different relationship to paternalism. For them it offered a way of enlarging the female sphere. Mary Merryweather, who spent fourteen years as a 'moral missionary'[55] in Courtauld's employment, was a single woman from a middle-class home. As such, she would probably have been regarded by writers like William Greg as a 'redundant woman'.[56] When she entered teaching she was joining the ranks of many other women in her position. Her first job in the Courtauld factory evening school brought her into close daily contact with working-class women and girls. Through her work in the school she became involved in a whole range of related philanthropic activities. These were by no means straightforward in their execution or results. First, she provided a resource which could be used by the town's female inhabitants to their own ends. Secondly, there are signs that she learned a lot from the women with whom she worked and that her own values and beliefs changed as a result of this experience so that certain of her goals moved closer to those of the millworkers.

A key indicator of this shift lies in the way in which she wrote about her experiences, both in the autobiographical record published through the new feminist press established by Emily Faithfull[57] and in articles appearing in the *English Woman's Journal*. Both these organs were linked to the activities of the Society for the Promotion of Employment for Women with whom Mary Merryweather became closely associated. In an article called 'Cottage Habitations', she described the living conditions of Halstead millworkers. The article contains both an adherence to a middle-class notion of domesticity and a self-conscious recognition of the fact that this notion is an *ideal*. This realization stems from her first-hand experience of the workers' lives:

> Our young girls are sent, unformed in mind and body, to spend ten hours a day in the debilitating air of the factory; they come back in the evening just in that state which craves more excitement than is to be found in scrubbing a room, washing their clothes, or sitting down to make and mend them; shut up all day, they most naturally long for open air, and so used to company are they that it becomes an absolute necessity, and to stay at home is invariably thought by them *very dull*.[58]

A sentiment underlying the article is that an ultimate aim is to create conditions in which the domestic ideal was more likely to be achieved. Middle-class men were removed from direct contact with the inhabitants of such homes and blamed the existence of poor dwellings upon the labourers' own moral shortcomings. For Mary Merryweather it was 'an evil for which the class which inhabits them is not responsible'.[59]

The dullness of staying at home motivated many working-class women to seek outside recreation. Mary Merryweather was instrumental in providing sources of entertainment which were no less double edged than her pursuits in the school and lodging house (see chapter 5, pp. 142–51). She nevertheless acted as a resource for the female mill hands, a resource which helped them to distance themselves from, and in some cases, rebel against, the more directly censorious paternalism of the employers and the pressures exerted on them by their husbands and fathers. The female networks (see chapter 3, pp. 84–5) existing among them were in many ways facilitated by the separate realms of paternalistic activity set up by the firm. These networks, and the nucleus of women within the mill to which they were connected, formed a ready base for militant action, like the 1860 power loom weavers' strike, and for later involvement in the Women's Trade Union League.

The concerns expressed by Mary Merryweather reflect the wider character of feminist activity in this middle period of the century. There was a restlessness among middle-class women, particularly those who were single. There was an impatience with the lack of opportunities for middle-class women and the living conditions of labouring women. There was a philanthropic drive to use time fruitfully and to improve the lives of those to whom such services were directed. There was the influence of a Unitarianism which was variously experienced and implemented by men and women. There was the potential for both continuity *and* conflict across class and gender lines.

The first organized expression of this restlessness came through the activities of the women who in 1859 set up the Society for the Promotion of Employment for Women and the *English Woman's Journal*. They were known as the Langham Place Circle,[60] a network of single-sex friendships and alliances uniting an older with a younger generation of women. The older women, like Harriet Martineau and Anna Jameson, had wider connections stretching back to Harriet Taylor and Elizabeth Sharples. The younger women were in their twenties and thirties at mid-century. Foremost among them were Bessie Rayner Parkes, Barbara Leigh Smith, Eliza Fox and Anna Mary Howitt,[61] whom Anna Jameson, in her fifties, referred to as her 'adopted nieces'. The Unitarian and Quaker influence was strong among these young women[62] and their personal contact with Harriet Martineau introduced them to the tenets of political economy. A particular form of Unitarianism, known as Necessarianism,[63] combined with their knowledge of political economy to produce an outlook which emphasized every individual's right to follow the natural laws of motion governing the universe. These women, and others like them, produced a radical reinterpretation of religion and politics from their particular experience as women.

Meetings in Anna Jameson's house led to the emergence of two pamphlets in 1854. *Remarks on the Education of Girls*, written by Bessie Rayner Parkes, argued publicly for wider employment opportunities for women. *A Brief Summary, in Plain Language, of the Most Important Laws Concerning Women*, by Barbara Leigh Smith, showed how married women had no legal rights over their own earnings, personal property or children. These arguments came to the public eye with the presentation of a petition in 1856, signed by many well-known names like Harriet Martineau, Anna Jameson, Mary Howitt, Elizabeth Barrett Browning, George Eliot and Elizabeth Gaskell,[64] calling for a change in the property laws relating to women. Prior to this, little notice had been taken of the writings of the Langham Place Circle. Anxieties were stirred and public debate increased when the issues were openly linked to the status of marriage and the family.

Fears were directed at the foundation of marital life. When the Married Women's Property Report was presented to the House of Commons in 1856, one MP reacted by saying:

No doubt the evils which now existed required remedy and ought to be attended to, but to introduce into every house in England the principle of separate rights, separate interests and a separate legal existence between man and wife, was to nullify and destroy the law of marriage altogether as far as regarded its sacredness and sanctity.[65]

Proposals for reforming the divorce laws were before the House of Commons at the same time and prompted another MP to declare that 'Nothing could be more frightful than to teach wives that their interests were on one side and those of their husbands on the other'.[66]

The formation of networks among women of both the middle class and the working class provided a meeting point over the issue of property legislation. The petition referred to the legal situation of middle-class married women and to the worse plight of 'women of the lower classes', who had their own reasons for supporting a change in the property laws. Working-class women organized their own meetings on the issue. One meeting, held in Leicester Town Hall on 14 April 1856, was attended by between 150 and 200 middle-aged female factory operatives. It had been initiated by a group of women workers especially concerned about a recent parliamentary proposal for the flogging of wife-beaters. Physical violence towards women, or 'wife torture' as one contemporary feminist writer later called it,[67] was an important issue in working-class communities.[68] The feeling of the meeting was that control over their own property and wages would do far more than harsh penalties to reduce wife-beating. A resolution was passed to that effect.[69]

The strategy being developed by middle-class and working-class women involved in this struggle led them into direct confrontation with men because they threatened those central institutions which men were anxious to uphold – marriage and the family. This influenced the tactics adopted in the pursuit of legal reform. The Langham Place Circle became less critical of marriage, concentrating more specifically on the language of individual rights and pointing out that men would benefit from changes in the law whereby they were held responsible for their wives' debts. Many working-class women were critical of this conciliatory tone but nevertheless supported the campaign, highlighting the distinctive class responses to this gender-specific issue.

In May 1857 the Married Women's Property Bill was

defeated under the impact of the Divorce Act and did not resurface for more than a decade. It served, however, to highlight a realm of subordination which, though differently experienced, was common to women of divergent social and economic positions. It encouraged a political alliance which altered the traditional demeanour of philanthropic activity. There were continuing tensions in these cross-class contacts since middle-class feminists were affected by a world view bestowing on them a sense of superior social status in the Victorian hierarchy. The publicity surrounding the petition called forth wrath from within parliament and the traditional press. One MP accused feminists of attacking 'the distinguishing characteristics of English men – the love of home, the purity of husband and wife, and the union of one family.'[70] The *Saturday Review* railed against these 'strong-minded women' who were 'a little corps of orators' and 'unladylike' in their behaviour.[71]

This kind of invective probably had a bearing on the tactics of the Langham Place Circle. A group with no parliamentary franchise was sensitive to the reactions of those with political representation and power. They increasingly built on the earlier objective of extending the bounds of the 'domestic ideal' by arguing for the spread of opportunities for women in work that did not encroach on 'men's work'. Although addressing a wide range of issues such as education, politics, prisons, housing, sanitary reform, divorce, the franchise and various aspects of employment for women of all classes, the pages of the *English Woman's Journal* became dominated by a concern to direct women into the emerging service sector – shopwork, clerical work, telegraphy, book-keeping, art and design, watchmaking and piano-tuning. Alongside these activities, nursing and teaching were also encouraged. All of these occupations were consistent with an interpretation of 'feminine qualities' accepted by the early feminists as much as their contemporaries. In the hands of women like Anna Jameson, this interpretation was recast to claim a complementary sphere for women in which their qualities could be used for the larger social good. The key question for her was 'whether a more enlarged sphere of social work may not be allowed to woman in perfect accordance with the truest feminine instincts'.[72] Her answer was 'the communion of love and the communion of labour',[73] a means of turning the 'domestic ideal' on its head by accepting a distinctively womanly nature but using that as a basis for women's rights to particular types of work, particularly in teaching, nursing and social work. This work would help to regenerate society since women were needed 'on a larger scale [as] mother, sister, nurse and help'.[74]

Such a theme was echoed in the novels of prominent women writers connected to the Langham Place Circle. Characters in the books of Charlotte Brontë and Elizabeth Gaskell express struggles to use their special qualities as the basis for a fuller existence. George Eliot's *Romola* was closely modelled on the life of Eliot's friend Barbara Leigh Smith. Elizabeth Barrett Browning's *Aurora Leigh* echoes the notion of 'a communion of love and labour' with Aurora establishing herself as a poet before agreeing to marry her cousin and form a partnership of mutual commitment to the social good. Both fictional and polemical writings reflected this theme. Barbara Leigh Smith's article on 'Women and Work', written in 1857, extols the work of women inside and outside the home. She feels, with Elizabeth Barrett Browning, that,

> The honest man must stand and work;
> The woman also; otherwise she drops
> At once below the dignity of man
> Accepting serfdom[75]

Bessie Rayner Parkes's tone became even more conciliatory by the early 1860s with her proposal that women's employment should only be a temporary solution during 'a time of difficulty', a particular 'stage of civilisation'. She claimed that she did not wish to see 'the mass of women becoming breadwinners' since most women 'ought to be employed in the noble duties which go to make up the Christian household'.[79] More radical critiques of marriage were confined to the letters pages of the *English Woman's Journal*, one woman responding strongly to Bessie Rayner Parkes that 'every woman should be free to support herself by the use of whatever faculties God has given her', and concluding that 'this question of marriage and its motives has lain at the core of the whole matter'.[77]

The reshaping of domestic ideology was double-edged. It

could, on the one hand, open up new possibilities to women and, on the other, uphold a traditional form of gender segregation. Even the establishment of a feminist printshop by Emily Faithfull in 1859 bore these hallmarks for women were engaged on composing while men read proofs and worked the presses.[78] In nursing, too, the approach taken by Florence Nightingale, whilst contributing to the employment opportunities of women, helped to construct hierarchical divisions not just between doctors and nurses but among the ranks of nurses themselves.[79] One consequence, therefore, of feminist strategies in relation to employment was to reinforce the extension of a patriarchal sexual division of labour into the capitalist economy – a process already set in motion in the textile industry and other sectors of the economy. In simultaneously contributing towards the growth of women-centred bases of power, however, conditions were provided for a continuing process of redefinition and reinterpretation, including possibilities of translating philanthropy into solidarity.

UNITY AND DIFFERENCE IN THE 1870S and 1880S

Two main strands of development served to reshape the culture of paternalism in the Courtauld mills in the last quarter of the century. One was the increasing encroachment of state controls through the spread of restrictive legislation on women's employment and the regulation of education. The other was changing local employment conditions reflecting the expansion of 'women's work' in shops, offices and domestic service. The twin effect of these developments was to strengthen female millworkers' position at work. Their resistance to paternalism was aided and their bargaining power over wages and conditions increased. This enabled them to win wage increases in the 1870s and to acquire trade union representation in the 1880s. This happened at the same time, however, as the maturing of a male labour elite, weaned through paternalism into a patriarchal stance at home and work.

This complex web of gender and class relations binding household and workplace was reflected in the wider activities of men and women still struggling to resolve the 'Woman

Question'. Two prominent issues from the late 1860s to 1880s serve to illustrate this complexity. They both concerned seemingly unconnected questions of legislation: the continuing controversy over restrictive controls on women's employment and the fierce struggle over the regulation of venereal diseases.

By the 1870s the proponents of 'protective' legislation had made a series of inroads into women's employment. Successive acts in 1833, 1842, 1844 and 1847 had spread regulation of children, young persons and women from cotton mills to other textile factories and to mines. Further controls came with the extension of regulation in the 1860s.[80] The main result of the acts in coal mining was to push more women into competition with men for work at the pit brow.[81] The proportion of women working at the pit brow never exceeded 7 per cent of surface workers yet as the century progressed there were increasing attacks on their employment. The consolidation of a male labour elite and its espousal of the notion of a 'family wage' occurred earlier in the mines than in the silk mills of Essex. Male workers were far more numerous and had always maintained positions at the top of the labour hierarchy as hewers of coal and hirers of family members to carry out other tasks such as drawing the tubs of coal from the coal face to the pit shaft. The exclusion of women from minework was aided by the Miners Association who wanted to 'keep the women at home to look after their families' in order to decrease the pressure on the labour market and increase the 'chance of a higher rate of wages being enforced'.[82] This attitude became consolidated in a prevailing official union view culminating in a wholesale condemnation of female pitbrow work at the 1866 Select Committee on Mines.

The 1872 Mines Act failed to remove women from the pitbrows. The women themselves were opposed to legislation designed to exclude them completley from mine work. As in earlier instances, they stood against the interests of a powerful lobby of male MPs combined with those of the male mining community. Coal owners were divided: those who relied on women at their pits opposed legislation while those only employing men supported it. Just as Courtauld had a stake in female employment in textiles, it was in the interests of many coalminers, particularly those in Wigan where women were employed, to fight restrictive legislation. Further allies to the women's cause came from a number of disparate quarters, adding to the complexity and divergence of interests and motives involved.

One source of support was the increasingly vocal network of middle-class feminists active in the fight for women's rights, their voice mostly finding expression now in the successor to the *English Woman's Journal*, the *English Women's Review*, and publications like the *Women's Suffrage Journal*. Another was a growing group of advocates of individual liberty for both male and female adults.[83] In the campaign to protect pitbrow women's work in the 1880s, men and women with overlapping allegiances to groupings concerned about state interference and committed to women's rights were joined by an upper-middle-class lawyer called Arthur Munby who spent about thirty years visiting the Wigan coalfields to talk to pitbrow women. Munby had a lifelong obsession with working-class women and his motives for supporting the pitbrow women's right to work represented the reverse side of a male middle-class ideology which depended upon ever-sharpening definitions of masculinity and femininity.

In the hands of proponents of restrictive legislation this ideology reflected a deeply rooted anxiety about the gender identification and sexuality of the Wigan pitbrow women. Their 'masculine' attire and physical strength were repeatedly rebuked. This period saw the emergence of legal definitions of male homosexuality[84] and pseudo-scientific taxonomies of 'sexual inversion' creating the category of lesbians as women with masculine traits.[85] Upholders of these tightening definitions of gender and sexuality felt threatened by women whom they deemed to combine masculine characteristics with female immorality and sexual licentiousness. As neither 'virgins' nor 'whores' these women stood for a new category of female identity and behaviour undermining an intricate but fragile web of boundaries constructed to stave off disorder and chaos. Their visibility affronted a maturing domestic ideology which not only underlined women's commitment to home and husband but increasingly emphasized their duties as mothers and 'guardians of the race'.[86]

The flouting of gender boundaries, which disturbed the

collective sensibilities of those opposing the pit women, constituted a source of perverse individual gratification for Arthur Munby whose psyche represents another facet of the distortions produced by the extremities of Victorian ideologies relating to class, gender and race. His diaries and photographs[87] reveal an intense preoccupation with physical strength, blackness and manual labour reflecting an 'industrial Amazon' imagery current throughout the nineteenth century among white male middle-class commentators. Comparisons were frequently drawn between pit women and 'Negresses' and many of Munby's sketches of pit women appear to be caricatures of black slave women. In his idealization of working-class female strength and his rejection of middle-class female fragility Munby was, on the one hand, playing games with the rigid boundaries betwen masculinity and femininity. On the other hand, his world view accorded with the prevailing hierarchical conception of a scale between 'civilization' and 'savagery' in which the closer people were to blackness the lower down they were in Nature's order.[88] Working-class people were, in his view, a 'race apart' and akin to 'savages'. He upheld the 'right' of 'savages' to work but never questioned the social and economic hierarchy which determined what kind of work they did or what rewards they received. He never questioned the expectations surrounding women as wives and mothers and he consistently opposed women's suffrage. He also used his privileges as a white professional man both to assume the right to inquire into working women's lives and to extend his dubious obsession with slavery and servitude into a longstanding personal relationship with a female domestic servant.[89]

The agitation against the pitbrow women in the 1880s failed once again to deprive them of their jobs. This was left to increasing technological change and a gender-based restructuring in mining in the early twentieth century. The controversy highlighted, however, the way in which 'respectability' came to be associated not just with domesticity and the 'family wage' but also with clear boundaries of sexual and gender identity. This represents another strand of control over women. On the one hand, there were increasing legislative attacks on a diminishing group of strong, independent and physically distinguishable female manual workers. On the other, an expanding group of single professional women with their own incomes were increasingly cast under the shadow of the sexual deviant label.

The growing influence of sexual and gender stereotypes, together with male trade union support of the 'family wage', brought about a change in policy towards 'protective' legislation in the women's trade union movement too. Under the leadership of Emma Paterson, women trade unionists in the 1870s opposed such legislation because it reduced women's employment opportunities. [90] With the change of leadership to Lady Dilke in the late 1880s, official endorsement of 'protective' legislation grew, although some rank and file members continued to fight legal controls and, in some instances, even proposed communal childcare facilities as an alternative.[91] The official women's leadership called for equal pay in 1888 but this was principally a pragmatic move to prevent men's wages being undercut by women.[92]

The fluidity of alliances across lines of gender and class was also evident in another area of legislation directed at working-class women. This was the Contagious Diseases Acts of 1864, 1866 and 1869 aimed at preventing the proliferation of venereal disease among enlisted soldiers and sailors through the special policing of women identified as 'common prostitutes'.[93] The common ground between this legislation, together with the campaign to repeal it, and legislation designed to control women's employment was that both reveal a connection between perceptions of sexuality and women's economic position and both were opposed by groups with varying motives for upholding the rights of working-class women. In the case of middle-class women, the path from philanthropy to solidarity was taken further than in the fight against 'protective' legislation by the particular stance taken by the Ladies National Association for the repeal of the Acts under the leadership of Josephine Butler.

Butler was one of the many women connected to the wide network around the Langham Place Circle. She had a similar background in radical causes and, like other women of that circle, she extended religious beliefs in equality to the realm of gender relations.[94] For her, Christ's teachings asserted 'the equality of all men and women'.[95] Unlike male interpreters of religion who frequently used the scriptures to justify unequal treatment of women, Josephine Butler held that women's subordination was the 'act of men, not of God'.[96] This belief in the man-made, rather than God-given, laws of society combined with a rejection of current philanthropic practice. Her work with destitute women in Liverpool in the 1860s was inspired not by detached charitable concern but by identification with human pain and suffering arising out of her own experience of misery and loss after the death of her five-year-old daughter. Rejecting both the 'old fashioned Lady Bountiful' approach of private philanthropy and the large institutions of 'the masculine form of philanthropy,[97] she developed an active philosophy and practice aimed at publicly and privately transforming male behaviour and the laws which supported and perpetuated it.

For the leaders of the LNA, prostitution served as a paradigm for the female condition[98] and the Contagious Diseases Acts as a symbol of the interdependency of economic and sexual power relations in their attempts to institutionalize the double standard. In their acceptance of the dichotomy between 'whores' and 'virgins' the laws flagrantly victimized working-class women who were the most susceptible to the new police powers. Furthermore, Butler saw the legislation as a deliberate attempt to reinforce male-defined barriers between working-class and middle-class women in an effort to preserve male control of both. She identified the many layers of male domination in a recollection of the complaint of a woman detained under the acts:

> It is *men, men, only men*, from the first to the last, that we have to do with! To please a man I did wrong at first, then I was flung about from man to man. Men police lay hands on us. By men we are examined, handled, doctored . . . In the hospital it is a man who makes prayers and reads the Bible for us. We are had up before magistrates who are men, and we never get out of the hands of men till we die![99]

To this, Josephine Butler adds, 'And it was a Parliament of men only who made this law which treats you as an outlaw.

Men alone met in committee over it. Men alone are the executives.'[100]

Transcending existing philanthropic beliefs, Butler saw divisions between women as artificial barriers constructed by men which could be dismantled by political solidarity designed to overcome the way

> one group of women is set aside, so to speak, to minister to the irregularities of the excusable man. That section is doomed to death, hurled to despair, while another section of womanhood is kept strictly and almost forcibly guarded in domestic purity.[101]

The LNA contained tensions between equalitarian and custodial ideals[102] but its strategy was based on the necessity for change in male moral standards and behaviour. The rejection of the 'double standard' led members into closer contact with the conditions of working-class women's lives. The risks they took in campaigning publicly against the acts exposed them to physical violence on the streets which also bridged the gulf of experience between their lives and those of 'their sisters' for whom they were demanding 'their most sacred rights'[103]

The campaign for repeal also gained widespread support among working-class men. These were mostly 'respectable' skilled workers, usually trade union members, whose motivation was partly mobilized by the class basis of the legislation and partly by the ideals which 'respectability' entailed. Imbued with the values of the 'family wage' and the 'domestic ideal', processed through the filter of their own economic position, these men fought against legislation sanctioning 'immoral' behaviour and threatening the sanctity of women's place in the home. At varying conscious and unconscious levels, the campaigns also allowed expression of working-class men's hostility towards the sexual appropriation of 'their women' by middle-class men. Many of these working-class men went on to become a strong presence in the social purity movement, from whom Josephine Butler split, after the repeal of the acts in 1888.[104] Meanwhile, middle-class men had conspicuously low representation in the campaigns.

Laws designed to police working-class women's sexual behaviour were fashioned by the same men in parliament who were passing legislation in the 1860s to extend the regulation of women's employment. Resistance to repeal of the Contagious Diseases Acts came from those groups of MPs who were also debating the pros and cons of pitbrow work for women. Fears and disputes concerning women's employment were never far removed from fears and disputes concerning control over women's sexuality. Both were about maintaining double standards for men and women in public and private spheres. An array of motives and objectives characterized those who opposed both sets of legislation. Some women, like Josephine Butler, were active on many fronts – for education, the vote, wider employment opportunities, sexual autonomy – and made explicit links between dominant perceptions of sexuality and the economic status of women. Such was the extensiveness and diversity of response to the laws that there were many overlapping and sometimes contradictory connections across both political causes within the same social class[105] and social class differences within the same cause.[106]

Alliances were neither straightforward nor static. Female leaders in the trade union movement increasingly diverged after the 1880s from feminists outside the movement who continued to oppose 'protective' legislation. This was not a disagreement based on class since many of the women across the divide originated from similar class origins. There were further shifts when the women's trade union movement, and later the infant Labour Party, formed an organizational basis for new political allegiances between sections of middle-class women and skilled working-class men. Alongside these developments a strand of feminist activity continued to emphasize the role of male sexuality in perpetuating the subordination of women and to focus the need for change on increased responsibility among men rather than mounting legislative control of women.[107]

Between 1825, when Samuel Courtauld first filled his mills with women and children, and the 1890s, after his death, the 'family wage' model and the 'domestic ideal' had ensured that women's employment was confined mostly to the period between school and marriage. Paternalism had played a central role in keeping women in a subservient position at work and home and fostering the growth of a male labour elite whose patriarchal interests increasingly coincided with those of their employers. Working-class women had restricted resources with which to resist the combined power of their employers and menfolk but, through the contradictory effects of segregation and philanthropy, developed a power base of their own from which to distance themselves from middle-class ideals and initiate action for improvements in their conditions. They were also aided in this by another outcome of the complex forces contributing to the availability of other types of women's employment which loosened the monolithic hold on local labour wielded by Courtauld.

These developments were shaped and reshaped by a variety of different protagonists occupying disparate relationships to both patriarchy and capitalism. These were reflected in the wider debates about women's position taking place throughout the century. There was no single clear process. An ever-shifting constellation of middle-class men, middle-class women, working-class men and working-class women adopted different positions and different alliances both within their own ranks and across ranks. Sometimes class and gender coincided as uniting factors and sometimes they pulled in opposite directions. According to many conceptualizations of class and gender which see them as exclusive categories, common interests are more likely to occur where class cuts across gender. The debates and issues explored in this chapter highlight how at times common interests arise where gender cuts across class and that the diverse and complex possibilities require far more fluid conceptualizations of both categories.

NOTES

1 R. Samuel, 'The workshop of the world: steam power and hand-technology in mid-Victorian Britain', *History Workshop Journal*, no. 3, Spring 1977; M. Berg. *The Age of Manufactures 1700–1820*, Fontana, 1985.

2 See A. Davin, 'Telegraphists and clerks', *Bulletin of the Journal of the Society for the Study of Labour History*, no. 26, Spring 1973, pp. 7–9; L. Holcombe, *Victorian Ladies at Work*, Archon Books, 1973; Meta Zimmeck, 'Jobs for the Girls: the expansion of clerical work for women, 1850–1914', in A. V. John, *Unequal Opportunities*, Basil Blackwell, 1986, pp. 153–7.

3 See F. Widdowson, *Going Up Into the Next Class: Women and Elementary Teacher Training, 1840–1914*, Explorations in Feminism, no. 7, WRRC, 1980; Holcombe, *Victorian Ladies at Work*, ch. III; J. Burstyn, *Victorian Education and the Ideal of Womanhood*, Croom Helm, 1980; M. Vicinus, *Independent Women: Work and Community for Single Women, 1850–1920*, Virago, 1985, chs 4 and 5.

4 See E. Gamarikow, 'Women's re-entry into health care: medical reactions to the Nightingale Reforms,' BSA conference paper, *Gender and Society*, University of Manchester, April 1982; E. Gamarnikow, 'Sexual division of labour: the case of nursing', in A. Kuhn and A. M. Wolpe (eds), *Feminism and Materialism: Women and Modes of Production*, Routledge and Kegan Paul, 1978; Vicinus, *Independent Women*, ch. 3; Holcombe, *Victorian Ladies at Work*, ch. IV.

5 C. MacCormack and M. Strathern (eds), *Nature, Culture and Gender*, Cambridge University Press, 1980. See also S. Griffin, *Woman and Nature*, The Women's Press, 1985.

6 This picture is also reproduced on the front cover of Berg, *The Age of Manufactures* and discussed on pp. 11–12.

7 M. Berg, 'Responses to machinery in eighteenth century England', *Bulletin of the Society for the Study of Labour History*, no. 49, Autumn 1984. See also, J. Liddington and J. Norris, *One Hand Tied Behind Us*, Virago, 1978, ch. V.

8 N. G. Osterud, 'Gender divisions and the organisation of work in the Leicester hosiery industry', in John (ed.) *Unequal Opportunities*.

9 F. Hunt, 'Opportunities lost and gained: mechanisation and women's work in the London bookbinding and printing trades', in John (ed.), *Unequal Opportunities*, ch. 2; Cynthia Cockburn, *Brothers: Male Dominance and Technological Change*, Pluto Press, 1983, ch. 2.

10 S. Alexander, *Women's Work in Nineteenth Century London, A Study of the Years 1820–50*, Journeyman Press, 1983, p. 13.

11 E. Hostettler, 'Gourlay steel and the sexual division of labour', *History Workshop Journal*, no. 4, Autumn 1977; M. Roberts, 'Sickles and scythes: women's work and men's work at harvest time', *History Workshop Journal*, no. 7, Spring 1979.

12 A. John, *By the Sweat of their Brow: Women Workers at Victorian Coal Mines*, Routledge and Kegan Paul, 1984. See also G. Burke, 'The decline of the independent bal maiden: the impact of change in the Cornish mining industry', in John (ed.), *Unequal Opportunities*, p. 179.

13 For a discussion of the social construction of categories of 'skill' see A. Phillips and B. Taylor, 'Sex and skill: notes towards a feminist economics', *Feminist Review*, 6, 1980, pp. 79–88.

14 B. Taylor, *Eve and the New Jerusalem*, Virago, 1983, p. 111.

15 F. Engels, *The Condition of the Working Class in England in 1844*, first published London 1892, Panther edition, 1967, p. 174.

16 See, for example, Gerder Lerner's contribution to 'Politics and culture in women's history: a symposium', *Feminist Studies*, 6, 1980, pp. 52–3.

17 See, for example, F. D. Klingender, *The Condition of Clerical Labour in Britain*, Martin Lawrence, 1935; D. Lockwood, *The Black Coated Worker*, Allen and Unwin, 1958; and H. Braverman, *Labor and Monopoly Capital*, Monthly Review Press, 1974.

18 Zimmeck, 'Jobs for the girls', p. 170. This was true even for women in the upper echelons of the middle class owing to the greater separation between wives and the business enterprise, see L. Davidoff and C. Hall, *Family Fortunes: Men and Women of the English Middle Class, 1780–1850*, Hutchinson, 1987.

19 Vicinus, *Independent Women*, p. 7.

20 J. Rendall, *The Origins of Modern Feminism: Women in Britain, France and the United States, 1780–1860*, Macmillan, 1985, p. 214.

21 In relation to these sorts of friendships in the United States, see, for example, Carroll Smith-Rosenberg, 'The female world of love and ritual: relations between women in nineteenth century America', *Signs*, 1, 1975, pp. 1–29, and N. Cott, *Bonds of Womanhood: 'Woman's Sphere' in New England, 1780–1835*, Yale University Press, 1978.

22 See, for example, Liddington and Norris, *One Hand Tied Behind Us*.

23 See, for example, M. Pember Reeves *Round About a Pound a Week*, Bell, 1913 and M. Llewellyn Davies, *Maternity Letters from Working Women*, Bell, 1915.

24 E. P. Thompson discusses class as a relationship in *The Making of the English Working Class*, Pelican. 1968, p. 9.

25 L.. Davidoff, 'Class and gender in Victorian England: the diaries of Arthur J. Munby and Hannah Cullwick', in J. Newton, M. P. Ryan and J. Walkowitz, *The Double Vision: Sex and Class in Women's History*, Routledge and Kegan Paul, 1983.

26 Darwinian theories of evolution had implications for notions of both gender and race as well as class. For a useful discussion of their influence on perceptions of gender see J. Lewis, *Women in England 1870–1950*, Wheatsheaf, 1984, pp. 83–5.

27 See chapter 4, pp. 141–4. For a much wider discussion of this process amongst middle-class families see L. Davidoff and C. Hall, *Family Fortunes: Men and Women of the English Middle Class, 1780–1850*, Hutchinson, 1987.

28 Such evidence appeared in parliamentary reports arising from the Sadler Commission of 1833 and in books like Peter Gaskell's *The Manufacturing Population of England*, Baldwin and Cradock 1833,

and James Key-Shuttleworth's *The Moral and Physical Conditions of the Working Classes employed in the cotton manufacture in Manchester*, J. Ridgway, 1832.

29 *Children's Employment Commission*: Appendix A. Instructions from the Central Board of the Children's Employment Commission to the Sub-Commissioners, House of Commons, 1842, CXIV, 1, p. 226.

30 Quoted in B. L. Hutchins and A. Harrison, *A History of Factory Legislation*, P. S. King and Son, 1903, p. 84.

31 *Hansard*, 15 March 1844, pp. 1088–100.

32 A. Ure, *The Philosophy of Manufactures*, C. Knight, 1835, p. 475.

33 H. Martineau, *Illustrations of Political Economy*, 9 vols, Routledge, Warnes and Routledge, 1859. See also, V. Pichanick, *Harriet Martineau: the Woman and her Work*, University of Michigan Press, 1980.

34 H. Martineau, *Society in America*, 3 vols, Sanders and Ottley, 1837, p. 203, quoted in G. Weiner, 'Harriet Martineau – a reassessment', in D. Spender (ed.), *Feminist Theorists*, The Women's Press, 1983, p. 69.

35 See H. Martineau, *Autobiography, with memorials by Maria Weston Chapman*, 3 vols, Smith, Elder and Co., 1877, reprinted by Virago, 1982.

36 A. Jameson, 'Condition of the women and the female children', *Athenaeum*, 18 March 1843, reprinted as 'Woman's mission and woman's position', in *Memoirs and Essays Illustrative of Art, Literature and Social Morals*, Wiley and Putnam, 1846.

37 See, for example, M. Reid (Mrs Hugo Reid), *A Plea for Woman: being a vindication of the importance and extent of her natural sphere of action; with remarks on recent works on the subject*, W. Tait, 1843.

38 Both these Unitarian journals were among the publications provided by Samuel Courtauld in the Halstead Mechanics Institute, see chapter 5, p. 152 above.

39 See J. Rendall, *The Origins of Modern Feminism: Women in Britain, France and the United States 1780–1860*, Macmillan, 1985, p. 247.

40 Charlotte Tonna, *The Wrongs of Women*, 4 vols, M. W. Dodd, 1843–4.

41 Sarah Stickney Ellis, *The Wives of England: Their Relative Duties, Domestic Influence, and Social Obligations*, Fisher, Son & Co., 1843; *The Daughters of England: Their Position in Society, Character and Responsibilities*, Fisher, Son and Co. 1842; *The Women of England: Their Social Duties and Domestic Habits*, Fisher, Son and Co., 1838.

42 See D. Thompson, 'Women and nineteenth century radical politics: a lost dimension', in J. Mitchell and A. Oakley (eds), *The Rights*

and Wrongs of Women, Penguin, 1976, p. 125; D. Jones, 'Women and Chartism', *History*, 68, February 1983, pp. 1–21.

43 Thomas Wheeler, 'Address from the London Delegate Council to the male and female chartists of Great Britain and Ireland', quoted in Rendall, *Origins of Modern Feminism*, pp. 238–9.

44 Quoted in M. Hewitt, *Wives and Mothers in Victorian Industry*, Rockcliff, 1958, pp. 23–4.

45 Gaskell, *The Manufacturing Population*, p. 93.

46 See B. Drake, *Women in Trade Unions*, London, 1920, reprinted by Virago, 1984, ch. 1; S Lewenhak, *Women and Trade Unions*, Ernest Benn, 1980.

47 B. Taylor, *Eve and the New Jerusalem*, ch. IV.

48 Quoted in Lewenhak, *Women and Trade Unions*, p. 40.

49 See Drake, *Women in Trade Unions*, pp. 4–5; and Lewenhak, *Women and Trade Unions*, p. 39.

50 Lewenhak, *Women and Trade Unions*. On the contrary, male workers sometimes took strike action *against* women's employment. See N. J. Smelser, *Social Change in the Industrial Revolution*, University of Chicago Press, 1959, pp. 232–5; and Liddington and Norris, *One Hand Tied Behind Us*, p. 90.

51 Evidence of working women's resentment of the factory reform movement can be found in *The Examiner*, 26 February 1832 and *The Pioneer*, 12 February 1834. See Taylor, *Eve and the New Jerusalem*, n. 125, p. 317. The degree of such resentment depended greatly on the age and gender constitution of the household and the pattern of available employment in the locality. In north-east Essex during this period, for example, the lack of male employment in the area made female work in the mill desirable as far as both women and men were concerned, see chapters 2 and 3 above. A similar situation prevailed for power loom weavers in Lancashire – see I. Pinchbeck, *Women Workers and the Industrial Revolution*, Virago, 1981, pp. 199–200. Also, after the enactment of the legislation government surveys revealed that it was more popular with male workers than female, see W. Neff, *Victorian Working Women*, Cass, 1966, p. 76.

52 See Taylor, *Eve and the New Jerusalem*.

53 Ibid., p. 19.

54 Ibid., ch. III.

55 This is how Mary Merryweather is described in the 1861 Halstead census enumerators' books.

56 William Greg, 'Why are women redundant?', *National Review*, 14, 1862, pp. 434–60.

57 Mary Merryweather, *Experiences of Factory Life*, Emily Faithfull Publishing Co., 1862.

58 M. Merryweather, 'Cottage habitations', *English Woman's Journal*, vol. IV, 1 October 1859, p. 74, emphasis in original.

59 Ibid.

60 For a full account, see M. C. Worzala, 'The Langham Place Circle: the beginnings of the organised women's movement in England, 1854–1870', PhD thesis, University of Wisconsin–Madison, 1982. The following discussion owes much to this research and to that of Sheila R. Herstein in 'Barbara Leigh Smith Bodichon (1827–1891): A Mid-Victorian Feminist', PhD thesis, City University of New York, 1980.

61 These women were just a few belonging to a rich and extensive feminist culture which cannot be understood solely in terms of its organisational expressions. See L. Stanley, *Feminism and Friendship: two essays on Olive Schreiner*, Studies in Sexual Politics, no. 8, University of Manchester, December 1985.

62 Bessie Rayner Parkes, Barbara Leigh Smith and Eliza Fox all came from Unitarian families and Anna Mary Howitt was the daughter of the Quaker couple, Mary and William Howitt, who edited the radical *People's and Howitt's Journal*.

63 This was a movement associated with Joseph Priestley, great-grandfather of Bessie Rayner Parkes and a friend of Barbara Leigh Smith's grandfather, William Smith, who believed that the moral and natural universe moved according to laws set in motion by God. It was the duty of every individual to understand these laws and act accordingly. All people were thus capable of contributing both to their own destiny and to the advancement of the divine plan. See F. E. Mineka, *The Dissidence of Dissent, The Monthly Repository, 1806–1838*, University of North Carolina Press, 1944, and Herstein, 'Barbara L. S. Bodichon'.

64 See Holcombe, *Wives and Property*.

65 T. Chambers in *Hansard*, 3rd series, 142, 1856, p. 1283, quoted in Herstein, 'Barbara L. S. Bodichon', p. 139.

66 G. Phillmore in *Hansard*, 3rd series, 142, 1856, p. 1281, quoted in Herstein, p. 140.

67 Frances Power Cobbe, *Wife Torture in England*, London 1878 (reprinted in S. Jeffreys, ed., *The Sexuality Debates*, Routledge and Kegan Paul, 1987, p. 219).

68 See Nancy Tomes, 'A torrent of abuse: Crimes of violence between working class men and women in London, 1840–58', *Journal of Social History*, 11, 1978 pp. 323–45; Frances Power Cobbe also drew attention to the prevalence of wife-beating across all social classes, see *Wife torture in England*.

69 See Worzala, 'The Langham Place Circle', p. 95.

70 *Hansard*, 3rd series, 1857, p. 280.

71 *Saturday Review*, 19 July 1857.

72 Anna Jameson, 'The communion of labour', 1859, p. 17.

73 Ibid.

74 Anna Jameson, 'Sisters of Charity', 1859; see Vicinus *Independent Women*, p. 46.

75 Elizabeth Barrett Browning, *Aurora Leigh*, quoted in B. L. Smith Bodichon, 'Women and work', 1857 (Barbara Leigh Smith entered an unconventional marriage in 1857, to a French doctor living in Algeria and added his surname to her name; she spent much of her married life dividing her time between England and Algeria, see Herstein, 'Barbara L. S. Bodichon').

76 B. R Parkes, 'The balance of public opinion in regard to woman's work', *English Womans Journal*, IX, July 1862, pp. 341–4. This article in many ways represents a significant shift away from the views expressed in *Remarks* eight years earlier. Again, it is not possible to detect how far such a shift was attributable to tactical motives, although Parkes's subsequent conversion to Catholicism suggests that this was not entirely so.

77 E. W. F., letter to Open Council, *English Womans Journal*, X, September 1862, p. 70.

78 John (ed.), Introduction to *Unequal Opportunities*, p. 9.

79 See Gamarnikow, 'Women's re-entry into health-care' and A. Summers, 'Ladies and nurses in the Crimean War', *History Workshop Journal*, 16, 1983, pp. 33–56.

80 See Hutchins and Harrison, *A History of Factory Legislation*.

81 See John, *By the Sweat of their Brow*.

82 *The Northern Star*, 7 October 1843, quoted in John (ed.), *Unequal Opportunities*, pp. 24–5.

83 See John, *By the Sweat of their Brow*, ch. 5.

84 Criminal Law Amendment Act 1885. See J. Weeks, *Sex, Politics and Society*, Longman, 1981.

85 The most prominent producer of such taxonomies was Havelock Ellis. See S. Jeffreys, *The Spinster and Her Enemies*, Pandora, 1985, ch. 6, 'Women's friendships and lesbianism'.

86 John, *By the Sweat of Their Brow*, p. 194. See also, L. Bland, '"Guardians of the race" or "Vampires upon the nation's health"? Female sexuality and its regulation in early twentieth century Britain', in E. Whitelegg et al. (eds), *The Changing Experience of Women*, Martin Robertson, 1982.

87 See D. Hudson, *Munby: Man of Two Worlds – The Life and Diaries of Arthur J. Munby 1828–1910*, John Murray, 1972.

88 John, *By the Sweat of Their Brow*, p. 219.

89 This was Hannah Cullwick. The relationship and secret marriage, depicting the sado-masochistic character of their interaction, has been explored by Leonore Davidoff, 'Class and gender in Victorian England: the diaries of Arthur J. Munby and Hannah Cullwick' in

J. Newton, M. P. Ryan and J. Walkowitz (eds), *The Double Vision: Sex and Class in Women's History*, Routledge and Kegan Paul, 1983. Extracts from eight of Cullwick's diaries appear in L. Stanley (ed.), *The Diaries of Hannah Cullwick, Victorian Maidservant*, Virago, 1984.

90 See Lewenhak, *Women and Trade Unions*, p. 106.

91 Eva Gore Booth, for example, was associated with such efforts in the North of England. See Liddington and Norris, *One Hand Tied Behind Us*, pp. 238–40.

92 Lewenhak, *Women and Trade Unions*, pp. 89–91.

93 See J. Walkowitz, *Prostitution and Victorian Society*, Cambridge University Press, 1980

94 See J. Uglow, 'Josephine Butler: from sympathy to theory', in D. Spender (ed.), *Feminist Theorists*, The Women's Press, 1983, pp. 146–62; N. Boyd, *Josephine Butler, Octavia Hill, Florence Nightingale: Three Victorian Women who Changed Their World*, Macmillan, 1982, pp. 23–92.

95 Josephine Butler, *Woman's Work and Woman's Culture*, Macmillan and Co., 1869, p. liv.

96 Josephine Butler, Letter to Frederic Harrison, 9 May 1868, quoted in Uglow, 'Josephine Butler', p. 150.

97 Butler, *Woman's Work*, pp. xxxvi–vii.

98 Walkowitz, *Prostitution*, p. 125.

99 J. Butler, *The Shield*, 9 May 1970.

100 Ibid.

101 J. Butler, 'A woman's appeal to the electors', 1885, quoted in Uglow, 'Josephine Butler', p. 154.

102 Uglow, 'Josephine Butler', p. 158.

103 J. Butler, *The Shield*, 9 May 1870. Josephine Butler came under physical attack many times at public meetings and it was not uncommon for working-class women to defend her and offer her refuge in their own homes, see J. M. Murray, *Strong-Minded Women and Other Lost Voices from Nineteenth Century England*, Penguin, 1984, p. 296.

104 The split came over whether to tighten state control over both men's and women's behaviour or to aim for more freedom for women. While one strand within the social purity movement increasingly stuck out for the former there were groupings who continued the strategy adopted by Butler of increasing women's freedoms. See S. Jeffrey, 'Free from all uninvited touch of man: women's campaigns around sexuality, 1880–1914', in L. Coveney et al., *The Sexuality Papers*, Hutchinson, 1984; S. Jeffreys, *The Spinster and Her Enemies*, Pandora 1985; S. Jeffreys (ed.), *The Sexuality Debates*, Routledge and Kegan Paul, 1987.

105 In terms of those involved in a variety of feminist pressure groups,

Liz Stanley points out the futility of distinguishing different 'types' of feminists in the nineteenth century. She demonstrates the existence of elaborate and complex webs of friendship spanning ideological, age, class and religious differences. See L. Stanley, 'Feminism and friendship: two essays on Olive Schreiner'.

106 Norris and Liddington, for example, show some of the links between middle-class and working-class women in the suffrage campaign in *One Hand Tied Behind Us*.

107 Christabel Pankhurst's famous call for 'Votes for women, chastity for men' exemplifies this strand. See C. Pankhurst, *The Great Scourge and How to End It*, E. Pankhurst, 1913; also S. Jeffreys, 'Free from all uninvited touch'.

CONCLUSION

This book set out to explore the reasons why women's employment was such a contested issue in nineteenth-century England. It also aimed to examine some of the forms these contests took and what the consequences were for women. Such an inquiry produces no simple answers, but the way forward suggested here takes as its starting-point the need to approach the historical record with concepts capable of mapping the interconnections between 'family' and 'work' processes.

These interconnections were frequently obscured by the way in which differences between groups became emphasized in efforts to create order in the midst of threatened political and social disorder. Two major sources of differentiation in the nineteenth century were gender and class (with race acting as a third in the complicated prism of Victorian cosmography). Neither of these categories is discrete nor are they absolute or fixed. As both forms of social relationships and sources of personal identity they are constructed and reconstructed simultaneously. They are also subject to negotiation and dispute, reassessment and change. In the nineteenth century, both categories were at the centre of continual struggles to map out new world views and new constellations of relationships. Those caught up in the struggles had different interests at stake according to what they stood to gain or lose in the process of renegotiation and redefinition. In the interaction between gender and class, employment became a key area of struggle. This was because it both highlighted gaps in social and economic status and represented for those involved the chief means by which that gap might be closed.

The explanatory model used to make sense of these developments and their outcomes has relied on the use of patriarchy as an analytical tool with which to dissect different constellations of power relationships and interests in varying historical contexts. The use of this tool owes much to the body of theoretical work generated by Heidi Hartmann's contention that patriarchy constitutes 'a set of social relations between men, which have a material base, and which though hierarchical, establish or create interdependence and solidarity among men and enable them to dominate women.'[1] Although representing a separate structure of relationships, patriarchy, in this model, operates in partnership with capitalism, a system of social relations through which capitalists exploit workers, in the shaping of women's experience. Thus patriarchy and capitalism are independent but interacting social structures which, according to Hartmann, reach a mutual accommodation via a system of job segregation by sex and the institution of the family wage whereby a male breadwinner is assumed to earn sufficient for a whole family's needs.[2]

There are ambiguities in Hartmann's analysis not least of which is the inconsistency surrounding her identification of what constitutes the material base of patriarchy. At times it is defined as men's control over women's labour power, at others men's control over women's sexuality and at yet others as 'all the social structures that enable men to control women's labour'.[3] Another problem lies in Hartmann's over-emphasis on processes of accommodation between patriarchy and capitalism. This tends to play down the possibility of tension, conflict and contradiction between patriarchal and capitalist interests. Associated with this is a tendency to conceptualize 'men' and 'capitalists' as separate categories belonging to two distinct systems. If gender and class interact in the construction of identity, 'men' are subject to different class experiences and 'capitalists' are influenced by their membership (usually) of the male sex. The separation of these categories is misleading and is a danger inherent in dualist approaches.[4]

This does not mean reverting to a position which defines patriarchy principally in ideological terms.[5] Nor is it necessary to resort to an acceptance of the existence of a class system which is shaped by 'the economy' and a gender system which is shaped by 'the family'.[6] I wish to argue for the possibility of economic and familial relations being continuous with one another in ever-shifting constellations and with varying potential for conflict and harmony. The particular configuration of economic and familial relations in different historical contexts constitutes the material base of patriarchy. In this conceptualization, the search for 'causes' beyond the privileges and advantages accruing to those who benefit from such arrangements becomes irrelevant.[7] This formulation offers a way of conceptualizing 'men' as members of differing class positions and 'capitalists' as being gendered. It allows for 'men' and 'capitalists' to have identities and interests shaped by both class and gender considerations. This makes it possible to explore the co-existence of differing relations within one institution *and* the tensions and conflicts between different relations. Beyond this, it also makes it conceptually possible to find tensions and conflicts within the same group of people or even within the same individual. If some 'men' are 'capitalists' too, their patriarchal interests might at times conflict with their capitalist interests and they would need to seek ways of resolving such conflicts.

It is the *distinctiveness* of the type of social relation which is at issue rather than the institutional separation of patriarchal and capitalist interests.[8] It is arguable that patriarchal interests became more distinguishable from capitalist ones during industrialization but this is not to preclude their being part of the same dynamic. In fact, it was the very intertwining of economic and familial power in the centuries preceding industrialization which provided the major impetus for the emergence of industrial capitalism. This is a thread that can be traced back even further to the rise of early capitalism itself.[9]

Women's multitude of economic activities had been founded on a household-based economy organized on a patriarchal structure of authority.[10] This authority structure enabled heads of households (through the exercise of familial/economic power relationships) to exploit the labour not only of female kin, primarily wives and daughters, but also of living-in servants, the majority of whom were female. It was this specific form of exploitation which facilitated the primitive accumulation of capital necessary for the development of a class of male capitalists.[11] The concentration of capital into male hands provided new means of control and domination over women in this class. The scope for independent female economic activity rapidly narrowed.[12] This process has been described as a 'patriarchal victory'[13] for in the transition from a feudal to a capitalist economy it secured a new base of male domination. It also highlights the way in which it was patriarchal relations which spawned the capitalist economy.

In the ensuing period of commercial growth a semi-permanent class of journeymen was also created whose access to the status of master became extremely attenuated. This produced mounting tension between journeymen and masters over entrance to a variety of trades. The main solution for journeymen was to oppose women's access to craft skills which had formerly been tightly controlled by guild regulations.[14] The spread of a market economy based increasingly on individual wage labour instead of household production fuelled male fears of competition from women and a loss of patriarchal status. This was well in evidence prior to industrialization but became intensified with the separation of home and workplace entailed in the growth of the industrial enterprise.

The predominance of women (and children) in the early factories served to accentuate the anxieties of male workers. It also increased their attempts to control women's access to paid employment and the organizations aimed at advancing the conditions and legal rights of wage labourers. Their interests in controlling women's labour coincided with the concern of a growing number of politicians and philanthropists that certain types of labour did not accord with their definition of femininity and standards of morality. Nor did such work concur with their perception of the 'domestic ideal', which by this time they were avidly seeking to establish in their own lives. This collusion of interests manifested itself predominantly in a longstanding series of efforts to enact legislation controlling women's employment.

By no means did all men from higher up the social hierarchy agree with the attempts to secure such legislation. Significant opposition came from the manufacturers who were largely dependent upon female labour in their factories. The men in parliament who supported legal reform were mostly Tory and Evangelical and were more representative of the landed aristocracy than the ascendant industrialist class. These men had patriarchal interests at stake as much as did male working-class operatives. It was the loss of the patriarchal form of familial relationships which they feared. This represented to them not only the 'natural' unit of society but also one which acted as a major mediator of harmony and order amidst the threat of social and political unrest posed by working-class organization in the form of trade unions and Chartism.

The appeal of paternalism was as strong to these men as it was to industrialists like Courtauld, Ashworth and Bright but it took a different form. For them, the state rather than individual employers should take on the duties, responsibilities and benefits of controlling and protecting women and children. Much of the debate between manufacturers and the landowning aristrocracy over 'protective' legislation was a contest for class superiority but it was fought over the issue of who should control women and what form this control should take. Since the debate was open also to the voices of working-class men it was essentially a debate among men about what to do about women and one in which women themselves were given little say. In the early stages of the discussion there was very little organized representation of women workers' opinions although expressions of female opposition to the proposed Factory Acts appeared in the 1830s in both popular publications and government reports.[15]

The basis of support for women's employment among manufacturers was connected to their own interests rather than those of women. Their interests as capitalists were expressed through their opposition to 'protective' legislation. Their interests as patriarchs were represented through the combined strategies of paternalism and a rigorously enforced vertical segregation of labour by sex so that many workplaces came themselves to represent a patriarchal family structure. In industries and trades where this pattern predominated another bond of allegiance was forged between a male aristocracy of labour and their male employers based on a mutuality of interest in sustaining higher status for men in both the labour market and the home.

In many ways, there was 'a continuity of traditional values and behaviour in changing circumstances'.[16] Whereas this continuity is usually depicted at the level of labouring families,[17] it is important to trace the ways in which such traditional values remained central to those who actually owned and controlled industrial enterprises. The employer decisions which produced patriarchal sex-segregated labour forces were rooted in a traditional form of authority which carried on being pivotal to the organization of production in circumstances frequently characterized as impersonal, rational and legalistic. By the nineteenth century an increasing wedge was driven physically and ideologically between households and work-places but the two domains were linked together via a complex web of patriarchal and capitalist interests which were the result of human agency rather than the neutral progress of technology. Certain 'strategies of survival' operated among labouring households but these were influenced by traditional divisions of sex and age and took place within circumstances structured by changing forms of power relationships controlling the livelihoods and life chances of the population. The themes of both continuity *and* change therefore have to be paramount in any exploration of the processes involved in industrialization.

These themes are present in the case study of the Courtauld silk firm. Samuel Courtauld built up a business based on the development of a mechanized and collectivized workplace within a rural community at the beginning of the nineteenth century. In doing so he made decisions about the structure of his workforce and the cultural values which should be encouraged among its members. In this position, he was influenced by both patriarchal and capitalist interests. The strategy he pursued, which was also influenced by his interpretation of the Unitarian faith, was a paternalistic one in which patriarchal and capitalist interests could be combined. Members of his workforce came from households where decisions were shaped by the employment opportunities available and the particular age and sex composition of the family. Young single women sought work wherever they could get it, much as they had always done, and continued to contribute their earnings to the household. For young women living in and around Halstead, the mainstay of employment was provided by the Courtauld mill. Because of the low wages characterizing both men's and women's work in the locality, a significant proportion of married women also held jobs in the mill, but were more likely than men to stay at home to look after dependent relatives, often combining such duties with casual work such as strawplaiting and taking in washing. The only exception to this rule was the diminishing number of households where male handloom weavers still operated their looms in the home and were often assigned the care of young children while their wives and older children worked in the mill.

The vertical segregation of the mill labour force along lines of gender ensured a patriarchal structure at the workplace. Paternalism operated to reinforce and justify such divisions and to perpetuate the traditional values influencing decision-making and authority hierarchies in the homes of the workers. In addition, paternalistic practices served to strengthen the development of a male labour elite at the expense of female workers. Male workers had more to gain from paternalism and from employment which rewarded them more highly than women in terms of both status and income. This led primarily to a collusion of interests between middle-class employers and working-class men and to expressions of protest and subterfuge on the part of women workers. There were times at which tensions between working-class women and their employers were so sharpened that disputes erupted both directly concerning conditions of work and concerning ways in which the 'domestic ideal' was being translated into their lives. Such disputes invariably involved conflict between the women and the menfolk of their own class. At times it also meant conflict between working-class women and those middle-class women whose philanthropic activities embraced the policing of female silk workers via their own interpretation and implementation of domestic ideology. At other times, tensions surrounding both gender and class were less overt.

Not all types of employment were characterized by the same strategies as found in the silk industry. The constellation of patriarchal and capitalist interests varied between different sectors of the economy, between different geographical locations and over different periods of time. In some trades like printing, patriarchal interests triumphed for a long time over capitalist ones in securing the complete exclusion of female workers. Trade unions in this context operated simultaneously to oppose the effects of capitalism and to uphold the principles of patriarchy. They represented vehicles for this kind of strategy by working-class men in many trades and industries where women's work was redefined, deskilled or diluted. Such a strategy often ran counter to that of employers who put their capitalist interests first. At the same time, it coincided with the patriarchal interests of politicians and philanthropists who sought to enshrine women's secondary place in the labour market in legislation. Control of women's labour was strongest where the challenge to patriarchal relations was perceived to be the greatest. 'Protective' legislation, for instance, was levelled at women in the more visible 'public', and therefore 'masculine', domains such as mines and factories rather than at the much vaster numbers of women employed in equally debilitating work like the sweated garment trade and domestic service. Paternalism too was much more common in situations where women, although needed in the industry, had to be kept in their place in order not to usurp or become independent of male authority. 'Protective' legislation can be seen, in fact, as a form of paternalism which represents another element in the rationalization of patriarchal relationships. As we have seen, many of the debates over 'protective' legislation were about which group of men should control women and how, with different groupings of women coming together to assert their right to decide their own destiny in the labour market.

The only areas of expansion in women's employment in the nineteenth century were in occupations based on the family model and women's subordinate and servicing role within that model. Teaching, nursing and clerical work were significant additions to domestic service in this realm and ones which blurred conventional social class categories by virtue of the escape route from unpaid home-based servicing roles which they opened up to many women with middle-class fathers. Even these jobs were perceived in some quarters as threatening to male privilege because of the self-defined bases of power present in some of them, particularly those located in all women institutions, and because of the challenge to conventional stereotypes of femininity represented by some of the women occupying such positions. Strategies of deskilling and segregation were accompanied in this instance by control in the form of ideological stereotypes of deviant sexuality.

Strategies generally shifted away from exclusion and towards more and more segregation by the end of the nineteenth century. The whole century had witnessed varying responses, from both men and women, to the 'Woman Question' in general and the relationship of women to employment in particular. Early in the century, the visibility of women and children in the mines and factories at the time when the notion of the 'angel in the house' was gaining ground in the aspirant middle class led to struggles over legislation taking the centre of the stage. Even at this time, however, women's position was being linked not just to their legal rights to employment but to the unequal power relationships embodied in the institution of marriage. Chief among those who were critical of marriage and of men's control of women's sexuality were the Owenites and some of the overlapping circles of radicals from different parts of the social spectrum with whom they were associated.

These circles spawned a more organized voice in the form of the Langham Place Circle in the mid years of the century. This focused specifically at women's rights to wider employment opportunities, so long as they enlarged the scope for the practice of women's domestic and nurturing qualities. Opposition to marriage became muted in the struggle to gain a voice in the all-male corridors of parliament and to influence male employers about the justice of their cause. It was a cause, however, which represented a meeting point betwen women of different social classes whose different motives brought them into conflict with the patriarchal interests of middle-class and working-class men who preferred to restrict women's rights to employment and property. Paradoxically, the tactics of the Langham Place Circle, by using women's perceived feminine qualities as the basis of their argument, served to reinforce male efforts to segregate and devalue women's employment. Some of the women involved in the broader struggle to widen opportunities for women, however, put the issues of marriage and sexuality firmly back on the agenda with the advent of the campaigns to reverse the Contagious Diseases Acts. Again, these campaigns revealed a number of alignments across class and gender lines which defy any easy identification of predominant social relations. Middle-class and working-class women were brought into contact of a kind not previously experienced. Their relationship to the Acts was distinctly different but this divide was openly characterized by Josephine Butler as one produced in the interests of men rather than in the interests of capital. In the face of such patriarchal control women are not without power or resources. During most of their struggles around both restrictive legislation and the Contagious Diseases Acts in the second half of the century they used the strength gained from their own culture to fight the general culture within which they lived.[19]

In both ideology and practice, there were constantly shifting meeting points and contradictions between patriarchal and capitalist interests throughout the nineteenth century. The closest meeting point of all is represented by the notion of the 'family wage' which operated to reinforce the patriarchal relations of marriage at the same time as marginalizing women's position in the labour market. It facilitated the ever-increasing shift towards unequal segregation of occupations between men and women and a growing desire among many women to settle for a secondary position in the labour market. The ideal of the 'family wage', which remains a contestable issue today, emerged as the culmination of a series of dialectical exchanges between an individual wage labour system and traditional patriarchal principles. This book has attempted to map out those exchanges and to bring to life some of the participants with their motivating interests, anxieties and aspirations.

NOTES

1 H. Hartmann, 'The unhappy marriage of Marxism and feminism: towards a more progressive union', in *Capital and Class*, no. 8, Summer 1979, p. 11.

2 H. Hartmann, 'Capitalism, patriarchy and job segregation by sex', in Z. Eisenstein (ed.), *Capitalist Patriarchy and the Case for Socialist Feminism*, Monthly Review Press, 1979.

3 H. Hartmann, 'The unhappy marriage', p. 13.

4 I. Young draws attention to some of the problems of dualist approaches in 'Beyond the unhappy marriage: a critique of the dual systems theory', in L. Sargent (ed.) *Women and Revolution: A Discussion of the Unhappy Marriage of Marxism and Feminism*, South End Press, 1981, pp. 43–69.

5 This tends to be the direction in which I. Young's analysis leads, ibid.

6 This is inherent in the approach initiated, for example, by Gayle Rubin and her concept of a 'Sex-gender system' – 'the traffic in women', in R. Reiter, *Towards an Anthropology of Women*, Monthly Review Press, 1975.

7 See J. Lown, 'Not so much a factory, more a form of patriarchy: gender and class during industrialisation', in E. Gamarnikow et al., *Gender, Class and Work*, Heinemann, 1983.

8 See S. Walby, *Patriarchy at Work*, Polity Press, 1987, p. 46.

9 See C. Middleton, 'Patriarchal exploitation and the rise of English capitalism', in Gamarnikow et al., *Gender, Class and Work*.

10 L. Tilly and J. Scott, *Women, Work and Family*, 2nd edn, Methuen, 1987.

11 Middleton, 'Patriarchal exploitation'.

12 A. Clarke, *Working Life of Women in the Seventeenth Century*, Routledge and Kegan Paul, 1982.

13 Middleton, 'Patriarchal exploitation', p. 27.

14 G. Unwin, *The Guilds and Companies of London*, 4th edn, Cass, 1963. See also C. R. Dobson, *Masters and Journeymen: A Prehistory of Industrial Relations, 1717–1800*, Croom Helm, 1980.

15 See, for example, instances cited in I. Pinchbeck, *Women Workers and the Industrial Revolution 1750–1850*, Virago, 1981, pp. 196–201.

15 J. Scott and L. Tilly, 'Women's work and the family in nineteenth century Europe', *Comparative Studies in Society and History*, 17, 1975.

17 Ibid; see also Tilly and Scott, *Women, Work and Family*.

18 This reveals how important it is not just to look at class-specific responses to paternalism as in P. Joyce, *Work, Society and Politics*, Harvester Press, 1980, but at gender-specific responses as well.

19 Gerda Lerner characterizes this feature of women's lives as a duality in which women are both 'members of the general culture and . . . partakers of woman's culture', G. Lerner, *The Creation of Patriarchy*, Oxford University Press, 1986, p. 242.

BIBLIOGRAPHY

PUBLIC RECORDS

All original manuscripts consulted at the Essex Record Office in Chelmsford or the Public Record Office in London are referred to in the notes with the abbreviation ERO or PRO, together with the full catalogue number. The complete business records of Courtaulds are deposited at the ERO under the catalogue reference D/F.

BOOKS AND PAMPHLETS

Abram, A., *Social England in the Fifteenth Century*, Routledge, 1909.

Abrams, P., *Historical Sociology*, Open Books, 1982.

Adams, C., Bartley, P., Lown, J., and Loxton C., *Under Control: Life in a Nineteenth-century Silk Factory*, Cambridge University Press, 3rd edition, 1986.

Anderson, M., *Family Structure in Nineteenth Century Lancashire*, Cambridge University Press, 1971.

Anderson, M., *Approaches to the History of the Western Family*, 1500–1914, Macmillan, 1980.

Alexander, S., *Women's Work in Nineteenth Century London: A Study of the Years 1820–1850*, Journeyman Press, 1983.

Anon., *A list of prices in those branches of the weaving manufactury called the Black Branch, and the Fancy Branch, together with the Persians, Sarsnets, Drugget Modes, Fringed and Italian Handkerchiefs, Cyprus and Draught Gauzes and Plain and Laced Nets*, 1769.

Ardener, S. (ed.), *Perceiving Women*, Malaby Press, 1975.

Ardener, S. (ed.), *Defining Females: The Nature of Women in Society*, Croom Helm, London, 1978.

Aries, P., *Centuries of Childhood*, Penguin, 1973.

Armstrong, W. A., *Stability and Change in an English County Town: A Social Study of York 1801–51*, Cambridge University Press, 1974.

Ashley, W. J., *The Early History of the English Woollen Industry*, 1887.

Ashton, T. S., *The Industrial Revolution 1760–1830*, Oxford University Press, 1948.

Ashton, T. S., 'The standard of life of workers in England, 1790–1830', in F. A. Hayek (ed.), *Capitalism and the Historians*, Routledge and Kegan Paul, 1954.

Babbage, C., *On the Economy of Machinery and Manufactures*, Charles Knight, 1832.

Badnall, R., *A View of the Silk Trade*, John Miller, 1828.

Bailey, P. C., *Leisure and Class in Victorian England: Rational Recreation and the Context for Control 1830–1885*, Routledge and Kegan Paul, 1978.

Baines, T., *Yorkshire, Past and Present*, W. Mackenzie, 1871–7.

Baker, Michael, *The Book of Braintree and Bocking*, Barracuda, 1981.

Bamberger, P., *A Pictorial History of Halstead and District*, Halstead and District Local History Society 1979.

Banks, O., *Faces of Feminism: A Study of Feminism as a Social Movement*, Basil Blackwell, 1986.

Barrett, M., *Women's Oppression Today*, Verso 1980.

Barry, K., *Female Sexual Slavery*, Avon Books, 1979.

Beechey, V., *Unequal Work*, Verso, 1987.

Berg, Maxine, *The Machinery Questions and the Making of Political Economy, 1815–1848*, Cambridge University Press, 1980.

Berg, Maxine (ed.), *Technology and Toil in Nineteenth Century Britain*, CSE Books, 1980.

Berg, M., *The Age of Manufacturers 1700–1820*, Fontana, 1985.

Best, G., *Mid-Victorian Britain, 1851–1875*, Panther 1973.

Bischoff, *A Comprehensive History of the Woollen and Worsted Manufactures*, 2 vols, Smith, Elder and Co., 1842.

Bland, L., '"Guardians of the race" or "Vampires upon the nation's health"? Female sexuality and its regulation in early twentieth century Britain', in E. Whitelegg et al. (eds), *The Changing Experience of Women*, Martin Robertson, 1982.

Booker, J., *Essex and the Industrial Revolution*, ERO Publications, no. 66, 1974.

Bowley, A., *Wages in the United Kingdom in the Nineteenth Century*, Cambridge University press, 1900.

Boyd, N., *Josephine Butler, Octavia Hill, Florence Nightingale: Three Victorian Women who Changed Their World*, Macmillan, 1982.

Braudel, F. *Capitalism and Material Life: 1400–1800*, Fontana, 1974.

Braverman, H., *Labor and Monopoly Capital*, Monthly Review Press, 1974.

Bridenthal, R. and Koonz, C. (eds), *Becoming Visible: Women in European History*, Houghton Mifflin, 1977.

Briggs, A. (ed.), *Chartist Studies*, Macmillan and Co., 1959.

Briggs, A. and Saville, J. (eds), *Essays in Labour History*, Macmillan, 1971.

Briscoe, L., *The Textile and Clothing Industries of the United Kingdom*, Manchester University Press, 1971.

British Industrial Publishing Company, *Industries of the Eastern Counties*, 1980.

Brown, A. F. J., *English History from Essex Sources 1750–1900*, ERO Publications, no. 18, 1952.

Brown, A. F. J., *Essex at Work, 1700–1815*, ERO Publications, no. 49, 1969.

Brown, A. F. J., *Essex People 1750–1900*, ERO Publications, 1972.

Brown, A. F. J., *The Chartist Movement in Essex and Suffolk*, Local History Centre Publication, University of Essex, 1979.

Brown, A. F. J., *Colchester 1815–1914*, ERO Publications, no. 74. 1980.

Brownmiller, S., *Against Our Will*, Penguin, 1975.

Bryan, B. et al., *The Heart of the Race: Black Women's Lives in Britain*, Virago, 1985.

Burke, G., 'The decline of the independent bal maiden: the impact of change in the Cornish mining industry', in A. V. John (ed.), *Unequal Opportunities: Women's Employment in England 1800–1918*, Basil Blackwell, 1986.

Burnett, John (ed.), *Useful Toil – Autobiographies of Working People from the 1820s to the 1920s*, Allen Lane, 1974.

Burstyn, J., *Victorian Education and the Ideal of Womanhood*, Croom Helm, 1980.

Butler, J., *Woman's Work and Woman's Culture*, Macmillan and Co., 1869.

Bythell, D., *The Handloom Weavers*, Cambridge University Press, 1969.

Campbell, *London Tradesmen*, 1747.

Cantor, Milton and Laurie, Bruce, *Class, Sex and the Woman Worker*, Greenwood Press, 1977.

Chaloner, W. H., 'Sir Thomas Lombe (1685–1739) and the British silk industry', in *People and Industries*, Frank Cass and Co., 1963.

Chambers, E., *Cyclopaedia: An Universal Dictionary of Arts and Sciences*, 1784 and 1827.

Chambers, J. D., *The Workshop of the World*, Oxford University Press, 1961.

Chapkis, W. and Enloe, C. (eds), *Of Common Cloth: Women in the Global Textile Industry*, Transnational Institute, 1983.

Chayanov, A. V., *The Theory of Peasant Economy*, Richard D. Irwin for the American Economist Association, Homewood, 1966.

Clapham, J. H., *The Woollen and Worsted Industries*, Methuen and Co., 1907.

Clarke, Alice, *Working Life of Women in the Seventeenth Century*, Routledge and Kegan Paul, 1982 (original edition 1919).

Claude-Mathieu, Nicole, *Ignored by Some, Denied by Others: the Social Sex Category in Sociology*, WRRC Publications, 1977.

Cobbe, F. Power, *Wife Torture in England*, 1878 (reprinted in S. Jeffreys (ed.), *The Sexuality Debates*, Routledge and Kegan Paul, 1987).

Cobbett, W., *Advice to Young Men, and Incidentally to Young Women*, published by the author, London 1829.

Cockburn, C., *Brothers: Male Dominance and Technological Change*, Pluto Press, 1983.

Cockburn, C., *Machinery of Dominance: Women, Men and Technical Know-how*, Pluto Press, 1985.

Coleman, D. C., *The Domestic System in Industry*, Historical Association Aids for Teacher series, no. 6, 1960.

Coleman, D. C., *Courtaulds: An Economic and Social History*, Clarendon Press, 1969.

Coleman, D. C., 'Textile Growth' in N. B. Harte and K. G. Ponting, *Textile History and Economic History*, Manchester, 1973.

Coleman, D. C., *Industry in Tudor and Stuart England*, Macmillan, 1975.

Coller, *People's History of Essex*, Meggy and Chalk, Chelmsford, 1861.

Collier, F., *The Family Economy of the Working Classes in the Cotton Industry, 1784–1833*, Manchester University Press, 1964.

Collier, J., Rosaldo, M. Z. and Yanagisako, S., 'Is there a family? New anthropological views', in B. Thorne and M. Yalom, *Rethinking the Family: Some Feminist Questions*, Longman, 1982.

Collyer, *Parents' Directory*, 1761.

Cooke Taylor, W., *Bentley's Handbook of Science, Literature and Art: The Handbook of Silk, Cotton and Woollen Manufacturers*, London, 1843.

Cott, N., *Bonds of Womanhood: 'Woman's Sphere' in New England, 1780–1835*, Yale University Press, 1978.

Courtauld, S. L., *The Huguenot Family of Courtauld*, vol. I (1957), vol. II (1966), vol. III (1967), privately published.

Courtauld, S. L. (ed.), *The Courtauld Family Letters 1782–1900*, 8 vols, Bowes and Bowes, 1916.

Crisp's Marriage Registers, Colchester Public Library, Local History Department.

Dale, M., *Women in the Textile Industry and Trade of Fifteenth Century England*, London, 1928.

Davidoff, L. *The Best Circles*, Croom Helm, 1973.

Davidoff, L., 'The separation of home and work? Landladies and lodgers in nineteenth and twentieth century England', in S. Burman (ed.), *Fit Work for Women*, Croom Helm, 1979.

Davidoff, L., 'Class and gender in Victorian England: the diaries of Arthur J. Munby and Hannah Cullwick', in J. Newton, M. P. Ryan and J. Walkowitz, *The Double Vision: Sex and Class in Women's History*, Routledge and Kegan Paul, 1983.

Davidoff, L., 'Mastered for life: servant and wife in Victorian and Edwardian England' in P. Thane and Anthony Sutcliffe (eds), *Essays in Social History*, Oxford University Press, 1986.

Davidoff, L. and Hall, C., *Family Fortunes: Men and Women of the English Middle Class, 1780–1850*, Hutchinson, 1987.

Davidoff, L., L'Esperance, J. and Newby, H., 'Landscape with figures: home and community in English society', in J. Mitchell and A. Oakley, *The Rights and Wrongs of Women*, Penguin, 1976.

Davies, C. (ed.), *Rewriting Nursing History*, Croom Helm, 1980.

Davies, D. P., *A new historical and descriptive view of Derbyshire from the remotest period to the present time*, Belper, S. Mason, 1811.

Davis, N. Z., *Society and Culture in Early Modern France*, Stanford University Press, 1975.

Deane, P. and Cole, W. A., *British Economic Growth, 1688–1959*, University of Cambridge, Department of Applied Economics, Monographs, no. 8, 1969

Defoe, D., *Tour through Great Britain*, vol. I, 1828, Everyman edition, 1962.

Delphy, C., 'Women in stratification studies', in H. Roberts (ed.),*Doing Feminist Research*, Routledge and Kegan Paul, 1981.

Demos, J., *A Little Commonwealth: Family Life in Plymouth Colony*, Oxford University Press, 1970.

Dobson, C. R., *Masters and Journeymen: A Prehistory of Industrial Relations 1717–1800*, Croom Helm, 1980.

Doeringer, P. B. and Piore, M. J., *Internal Labour Markets and Manpower Analysis*, Heath, 1971.

Dodd, W., *The Labouring Classes of England, especially those concerned in agriculture and manufactures; in a series of letters*, J. Putnam, 1848.

Drake, B., *Women in Trade Unions*, London, 1920, reprinted by Virago, 1984.

Dublin, T., *Women At Work: The Transformation of Work and Community in Lowell, Massachusetts, 1826–60*, Columbia University Press, 1981.

Dublin, T., (ed.), *Farm to Factory: Women's Letters 1830–1860*, Columbia University Press, 1981.

Dunlop, R. and Denman, R. D., *English Apprenticeship and Child Labour*, London, 1912.

Dyhouse, C., *The Education of Girls and Young Women in Victorian and Edwardian England*, Routledge and Kegan Paul, 1981.

Edwards, M. M. and Lloyd-Jones, R., 'N. J. Smelser and the cotton factory family: a reassessment', in N. B. Harte and K. G. Ponting, *Textile History and Economic History*, Manchester University Press, 1973.

Edwards, R., Reith, M. and Gordon, D., *Labour Market Segregation*, Heath, 1975.

Eisenstein, S., *Give Us Bread But Give Us Roses*, Routledge and Kegan Paul, 1983.

Eisenstein, Z. (ed.), *Capitalism, Patriarchy and the Case for Socialist Feminism*, Monthly Review Press, 1979.

Eisler, B. (ed.), *The Lowell Offering: Writings by New England Mill Women, 1840–1845*, Harper, 1980.

Ellis, S. Stickney, *The Wives of England – Their Relative Duties, Domestic Influence and Social Obligations*, Fisher, Son and Co., 1843; *The Daughters of England: Their Position in Society, Character and Responsibilities*, Fisher, Son and Co., 1842; *The Women of England: Their Social Duties and Domestic Habits*, Fisher, Son and Co., 1838.

Encyclopaedia Britannica, 1771, 1810, 1842 editions.

Engels, F., *The Condition of the Working Class in England in 1844*, first published London, 1892, Panther edition, 1967.

Engels, F., *Origins of the Family, Private Property and the State*, Pathfinder Press, 1972.

English, Walter, *The Textile Industry: An Account of the Early Invention of Spinning, Weaving and Knitting Machines*, Longmans, 1969.

Enloe, C., *Does Khaki Become You – The Militarisation of Women's Lives*, Pluto Press, 1983.

Evans, W. J., *Old and New Halstead*, Stationers Hall, 1886.

Fairbairn, W., *Treatise on Mills and Millwork*, vols I and II, Longmans 1864 and 65.

Ferber, M. A. and Lowry H. M., 'Women: the reserve army of the unemployed', in M. Blaxall and B. Reagan (eds), *Women and the Workplace: The Implications of Occupational Segregation*, University of Chicago Press, 1976.

Fielden, J., *The Curse of the Factory System*, 1836, 2nd edn, Cass, 1969.

Figes, E., *Patriarchal Attitudes*, Faber, 1970.

Firestone, S., *The Dialectics of Sex*, Bantam, 1972.

Fitton, R. S. and Wadsworth, A. P., *The Strutts and the Arkwrights, 1758–1830*, University of Manchester, 1958.

Flandrin, Jean-Louis, *Families in Former Times: Kinship, Household and Sexuality*, Cambridge University Press, 1979.

Foster, John, *Class Struggle and the Industrial Revolution*, Weidenfeld and Nicolson, 1974.

Foucault, M., *History of Sexuality*, vol. 1, Allen Lane, 1979.

Friedman, S., 'Heterosexuality, couples and parenthood: a "natural" cycle?', in S. Friedman and E. Sarah (eds), *On the Problem of Men*, The Women's Press, 1982.

Gamarnikow, E., 'Sexual division of labour: the case of nursing'', in A. Kuhn and A. M. Wolpe (eds), *Feminism and Materialism: Women and Modes of Production*, Routledge and Kegan Paul, 1978.

Gammage, R. G., *History of the Chartist Movement*, Merlin, 1969.

Gaskell, E., *Mary Barton*, 1848; Penguin edition, 1970.

Gaskell, E., *North and South*, 1855; Penguin edition, 1970.

Gaskell, P., *The Manufacturing Population of England*, Baldwin and Cradock, 1833.

George, M. D., *London Life in the Eighteenth Century*, Kegan Paul and Co., 1925; Penguin, 1966.

Goody, J., Thirsk, J. and Thompson, E. P. (eds), *Family and Inheritance: Rural Society in Western Europe 1200–1800*, Past and Present Publications, Cambridge, 1976.

Goubert, P., 'The French peasantry of the seventeenth century: a regional example', in T. Ashton (ed.), *Crisis in Europe 1560–1660*, 1965.

Grey, Edwin, *Cottage Life in a Hertfordshire Village*, Fisher, Knight and Co., Ltd., 1935.

Griffin, S., *Woman and Nature*, The Women's Press, 1985.

Habermas, J., 'Technology and science as ideology', in G. Esland et al. (eds), *People and Work*, Edinburgh, 1975.

Hajnal, J., 'European marriage patterns in perspective', in D. V. Glass and D. E. C. Eversley (eds), *Population in History*, Arnold, 1965.

Hall, C., 'The early formation of Victorian domestic ideology', in S. Burman (ed.), *Fit Work for Women*, Croom Helm, 1979.

Halstead Board of Guardians, *Migration Explained: With a true and particular account of the condition of a number of poor families who have removed to the great manufacturing counties*, 1836.

Hareven, T., 'Family time and industrial time: family and work in a planned corporation town, 1900–1924', in T. Hareven (ed.), *Family and Kin in Urban Communities, 1700–1930*, Croom Helm, 1977.

Hareven, T. (ed.) *Transitions: The Family and the Life Course in Historical Perspective*, Academic Press, 1978.

Hareven, T., *Family Time and Industrial Time*, Cambridge University Press, 1982.

Hareven, T., and Langenbach, R., *Amoskeag: Life and Work in an American Factory-city in New England*, Methuen, 1979.

Harris, O., 'Households as natural units', in K. Young, C. Wolkowitz and R. McCullagh, *Of Marriage and the Market*, CSE Books, 1981.

Harrison, B., *Drink and the Victorians*, Faber and Faber, 1971.

Harte, N. B., and Ponting, K. G., *Textile History and Economic History*, Manchester University Press, 1973.

Hartmann, H., 'Capitalism, patriarchy and job segregation by sex', in

Z. Eisenstein (ed.), *Capitalist Patriarchy and the Case for Socialist Feminism*, Monthly Review Press, 1979.

Heard, N., *Wool: East Anglia's Golden Fleece*, Lavenham Press, 1970.

Hewitt, Margaret, *Wives and Mothers in Victorian Industry*, Rockcliff, 1958.

Hills, A., *The Dutchmen at Halstead, 1576–1589*, Halstead and District Local History Society.

Hilton, R., *The English Peasantry in the Later Middle Ages*, Clarendon Press, 1975.

Hinde and Sons Ltd, *The Story of Norwich Silks*, 1947.

Hirst, W., *History of the Woollen Trade for the Last Sixty Years*, S. Moody, 1844.

Hobsbawm, E. J., *Labouring Men: Studies in the History of Labour*, Weidenfeld and Nicolson, 1964.

Hobsbawm, E. J. and Rudé, G., *Captain Swing*, Lawrence and Wishart, 1969.

Hobsbawm, E., 'From social history to the history of society', in M. W. Flinn and T. C. Smout, *Essays in Social History*, Oxford Univeristy Press, 1974.

Hodgkinson, A. E., *The Great Adventure*, Halstead Co-operative Society Ltd, 1960.

Holcombe, L., *Victorian Ladies at Work*, Archon Books, 1973.

Holcombe, Lee, *Wives and Property: Reform of the Married Women's Property Law in Nineteenth Century England*, University of Toronto Press, 1983.

Holt, R. V., *The Unitarian Contribution to Social Progress in England*, G. Allen and Unwin, 1938.

Houghton, W., *The Victorian Frame of Mind, 1830–1870*, Yale University Press, 1963.

Hudson, D., *Munby: Man of Two Worlds – The Life and Diaries of Arthur J. Munby 1828–1910*, John Murray, 1972.

Hunt, F., 'Opportunities lost and gained: mechanisation and women's work in the London bookbinding and printing trades', in A. V. John (ed.), *Unequal Opportunities: Women's Employment in England 1800–1918*, Basil Blackwell, 1986.

Hunt, A. (ed.), *Women and Paid Work: Issues of Equality*, Macmillan, 1987.

Hurnard, J., *The Setting Sun*, Book 3, Samuel Harris and Co., 1878.

Hutchins, B. L. and Harrison, A., *A History of Factory Legislation*, P. G. King and Son, 1903.

Hutton, W., *The History of Derby*, J. Nichols, 1791.

Innes, R. A., *The Halifax Piece Hall*, Halifax Museums Service, 1975.

Jameson, A., 'Woman's mission and woman's position', in *Memoirs and Essays illustrative of Art, Literature and Social Morals*, Wiley and Putnam, 1846.

Jameson, A., *"Sisters of Charity" and "The Communion of Labour": Two Lectures on the Social Employment of Women*, Longman, Brown, Green, Longmans and Roberts, 1859.

Jeffreys, S., ' "Free from all uninvited touch of man": women's campaigns around sexuality, 1880–1914', in L. Coveney et al., *The Sexuality Papers: Male Sexuality and the Social Control of Women*, Hutchinson, 1984.

Jeffreys, S., *The Spinster and Her Enemies: Feminism and Sexuality 1880–1930*, Pandora, 1985.

Jeffreys, S. (ed.), *The Sexuality Debates*, Routledge and Kegan Paul, 1987.

Jenson, J. et al., *Feminization of the Labour Force: Paradoxes and Promises*, Polity Press, 1988.

John, Angela, *By the Sweat of Their Brow: Women Workers at Victorian Coal Mines*, Routledge and Kegan Paul, 1980.

John, A. (ed.), *Unequal Opportunities: Women's Employment in England 1800–1918*, Basil Blackwell, 1986.

Jordanova, L., 'Natural facts: A historical perspective on science and sexuality', in C. MacCormack and M. Strathern (eds), *Nature, Culture and Gender*, Cambridge University Press, 1980.

Joyce, Patrick, *Work, Society and Politics: the Culture of the Factory in Later Victorian England*, Harvester Press, 1980.

Kay-Shuttleworth, J., *The Moral and Physical Condition of the Working Classes Employed in the Cotton Manufacture in Manchester*, J. Ridgway, 1832.

Kerr, C., *Industrialism and Industrial Man*, Heinemann, 1962.

Kitteringham, J., *Country Girls in Nineteenth Century England*, History Workshop Pamphlet, no. 11, 1973.

Kline, S., *A Manual of the Processes of Winding, Warping and Quilling of Silk and other Various Yarns from the Skein to the Loom*, J. Wiley and Sons, 1918.

Klingender, F. D., *The Condition of Clerical Labour in Britain*, Martin Lawrence, 1935.

Knight, C. *London*, vol. IV, *History and Topography*, Charles Knight, 1851.

Knight, C., *Mind Among the Spindles: A Selection from the Lowell Offering*, Jordan, Swift and Wiley, 1845.

Kussmaul, A., *Servants in Husbandry in Early Modern England*, Cambridge University Press, 1978.

Landes, D., *The Unbound Prometheus*, Cambridge University Press, 1969.

Larcom, L., *An Idyl of Work*, J. R. Osgood and Co., 1875.

Larcom, L., *A New England Girlhood*, Houghton, Mifflin and Co., 1890.

Lasch, Christopher, *Haven in a Heartless World – the Family Beseiged*, Basic Books, 1977.

Laslett, P., *The World We Have Lost*, Methuen, 1965.

Laslett, P., *Family Life and Illicit Love in Earlier Generations*, Cambridge University Press, 1977.

Laslett, P., and Harrison, J., 'Clayworth and Cogenhoe', in H. E. Bell and R. L. Ollard (eds), *Historical Essays 1600–1750 presented to David Ogg*, Adam and Charles Black, 1963.

Laslett, P. and Wall, R. (eds), *Household and Family in Past Time*, Cambridge University Press, 1972.

Lazonick, W., 'Historical origins of the sex-based division of labour under capitalism', Harvard Institute of Economic Research, 1976.

Leonard, D. and Allen, S., *Dependency and Exploitation in Work and Marriage*, 1976.

Lerner, G., *The Creation of Patriarchy*, Oxford University Press, 1986.

Levine, D., *Family Formation in an Age of Nascent Capitalism*, Academic Press, 1977.

Lewenhak, S., *Women and Trade Unions*, Ernest Benn, 1980.

Lewis, J., 'Women lost and found: the impact of feminism on history', in D. Spender (ed.), *Men's Studies Modified*, Pergamon Press, 1981.

Lewis, J., *Women in England, 1870–1950*, Wheatsheaf, 1984.

Llewellyn, C., 'Occupational mobility and the use of the comparative method', in H. Robert (ed.), *Doing Feminist Research*, Routledge and Kegan Paul, 1981.

Llewellyn Davies, M., *Maternity Letters from Working Women*, Bell, 1915.

Liddington, J. and Norris, J., *One Hand Tied Behind Us: The Rise of the Women's Suffrage Movement*, Virago, 1978.

Lockwood, D., *The Black Coated Worker*, Allen and Unwin, 1958.

Lofgren, O., 'Family and household among Scandinavian peasants', in M. Anderson (ed.), *Sociology of the Family*, Penguin, 1980 (2nd edn).

Lord, J., *Capital and Steam Power, 1750–1800*, F. Cass Co., 1966.

Loudon, J. C., *An Encyclopaedia of Agriculture*, Longman, Rees, Orme, Brown, Green and Longman, 1835.

Lown, J., 'Not so much a factory, more a form of patriarchy: Gender and class during industrialisation', E. Gamarnikow et al. (eds), *Class, Gender and Work*, Heinemann, 1983.

Lown, J. and Chenut, H. 'The patriarchal thread – a history of exploitation', in W. Chapkis and C. Enloe, *Of Common Cloth: Women in the Global Textile Industry*, Transnational Institute, 1983.

Lukes, S., *Power: A Radical View*, Macmillan, 1974.

MacCormack, C. and Strathern, M. (eds), *Nature, Culture and Gender*, Cambridge University Press, 1980.

MacFarlane, A., *The Family Life of Ralph Josselin: a seventeenth century clergyman*, Cambridge University Press, 1970.

MacFarlane, A., *The Diary of Ralph Josselin, 1616–1683*, Basil Blackwell, 1976.

MacFarlane, Alan, *The Origins of English Individualism*, Cambridge University Press, 1979.

MacFarlane, A., *Reconstructing Historical Communities*, Cambridge University Press, 1978.

MacKendrick, N., 'Home demand and economic growth: a new view of the role of women and children in the industrial revolution', in N. MacKendrick (ed.), *Historical Perspectives: Studies in English Thought and Society in Honour of J. H. Plumb*, Europa, 1974.

Mantoux, P., *The Industrial Revolution in the Eighteenth Century*, Methuen, 1964.

Marcuse, H., 'Industrialisation and capitalism in the work of Max Weber', in J. J. Shapiro (trans.), *Negations: Essays in Critical Theory*, Allen Lane, 1968.

Martin, R. and Fryer, R. H., *Redundancy and Paternalist Capitalism*, George Allen and Unwin, 1973.

Martineau, H., *Illustrations of Political Economy*, 9 vols, Routledge, Warnes and Routledge, 1859.

Martineau, H., *Society in America*, 3 vols, Saunders and Ottley, 1837.

Martineau, H., *Autobiography*, with memorials by Maria Weston Chapman, 3 vols, Smith, Elder and Co., 1877, reprinted by Virago, 1982.

Marx, K., *Capital*, volume I, Lawrence and Wishart, 1957 edition.

Matthias, P., *The First Industrial Nation*, 1964.

Merryweather, Mary, *Experience of Factory Life: Being a record of 14 years work at Mr. Courtauld's silk mill at Halstead in Essex*, 3rd edn, Emily Faithfull Publishing Co., 1862.

Middleton, C., 'Patriarchal exploitation and the rise of English capitalism', in E. Gamarnikow et al. (eds), *Gender, Class and Work*, Heinemann, 1983.

Mill, J. S., *Principles of Political Economy*, Longmans, Green, Reader and Dyer, 1848.

Mineka, F. E., *The Dissidence of Dissent, The Monthly Repository, 1806–1838*, University of North Carolina Press, 1944.

Millett, K., *Sexual Politics*, Abacus, 1970.

Mitchell, J., and Oakley, A., *The Rights and Wrongs of Women*, Penguin, 1976.

Morant, P., *History of Colchester*, 1748.

Morgan, D., *Social Theory and the Family*, Routledge, Chapman and Hall, 1975.

Morgan, D., 'Men, masculinity and the process of sociological enquiry', in H. Roberts (ed.), *Doing Feminist Research*, Routledge and Kegan Paul, 1981.

Morris, R. J., *Class and Class Consciousness in the Industrial Revolution, 1780–1850*, Humanities, 1979.

Murray, J. M., *Strong-minded Women and Other Lost Voices from Nineteenth Century England*, Penguin, 1984.

Neff, W., *Victorian Working Women: An Historical and Literary Study of Women in British Industries and Professions, 1832–1850*, Cass, 1966.

Ogburn, W., and Nimkoff, N., *Technology and the Changing Family*, University of Chicago Press, 1955.

Osterud, N. G., 'Gender divisions and the organisation of work in the Leicester hosiery industry', in A. V. John (ed.), *Unequal Opportunities: Women's Employment in England, 1800–1918*, Basil Blackwell, 1986.

Pankhurst, C., *The Great Scourge and How to End It*, E. Pankhurst, 1913.

Parkin, F., *The Social Analysis of Class Structure*, Tavistock Publications, 1974.

Pember Reeves, M., *Round About a Pound a Week*, Bell, 1913.

Phillips, M. and Tomkinson, W. S., *English Women in Life and Letters*, Oxford University Press, 1926.

Phizacklea, A., *One Way Ticket: Migration and Female Labour*, Routledge and Kegan Paul, 1983.

Picharik, V., *Harriet Martineau: the Woman and her Work, 1802–1876*, University of Michigan Press, 1980.

Pinchbeck, Ivy, *Women Workers and the Industrial Revolution*, Virago, 1981.

Porter, L., *Silk: Treatise on the Origin, Progressive Improvement and Present State of the Silk Manufacture*, London, 1831.

Power, E., *Medieval Women*, Cambridge University Press, 1975.

Radcliffe, W., *Origin of the New System of Manufacture Commonly Called Power Loom Weaving*, J. Lomax, 1828.

Razzell, P. E., and Wainwright, R. W. (eds), *The Victorian Working Class – Selections of Letters to the Morning Chronicle*, Cass, 1973.

Rees, A. (ed.) *Cyclopaedia of Arts, Sciences and Literature*, London, 1819.

Reid, M. (Mrs Hugo Reid), *A Plea for Woman: being a vindication of the importance and extent of her natural sphere of action; with remarks on recent works on the subject*, W. Tait, 1843.

Reiter, R., *Toward a Anthropology of Women*, Monthly Review Press, 1975.

Rendall, J., *The Origins of Modern Feminism: Women in Britain, France and the United States, 1780–1860*, Macmillan, 1985.

Rich, A., *Of Woman Born*, Norton, 1976.

Roberts, D., *Paternalism in Early Victorian England*, Croom Helm, 1979.

Robinson, H. H., *Loom and Spindle: Or life among the early mill girls*, T. Y. Crowell and Co., 1898.

Rosaldo, M. and Lamphere, L., *Woman, Culture and Society*, Stanford University Press, 1974.

Rosebery, Lord Archibald, *Pitt*, Macmillan, 1891.

Rubin, G., 'The Traffic in Women', in R. Reiter, *Toward an Anthropology of Women*, Monthly Review Press, 1975.

Salmon, N., *The History of Essex from the Papers of Mr Holman, etc., 1740 fol.*, J. Cooke, 1740.

Samuel, R., *Miners, Quarrymen and Saltworkers*, Routledge, Chapman and Hall, 1977.

Sargent, Lydia (ed.), *The Unhappy Marriage of Marxism and Feminism: A Debate on Class and Patriarchy*, Pluto Press, 1981.

Saul, S. B., *Technological Change: The U.S. and Britain in the Nineteenth Century*, Methuen, 1970.

Saville, J. (ed.), *Democracy and the Labour Movement*, Lawrence and Wishart, 1954.

Schober, J., *Silk and the Silk Industry*, Constable, 1939.

Seem, W. P., *Raw Silk and Throwing – A Guidebook of Practical Experience*, McGraw-Hill, 1929.

Sellers, I., *Nineteenth Century Nonconformity*, Holmes and Meier, 1977.

Sholl, S., *A Short Historical Account of the Silk Manufacture in England*, London, 1811.

Shorter, E., *The Making of the Modern Family*, Fontana, 1975.

Shrimpton, Colin, *The Landed Society and the Farming Community of Essex in the Late Eighteenth Century and Early Nineteenth Century*, Arno Press, 1977.

Singer, C. et al. (eds), *History of Technology*, vol. IV, *Industrial Revolution 1750–1850*, Oxford, 1958.

Smelser, N. J., *Social Change in the Industrial Revolution*, University of Chicago Press, 1959.

Smiles, S., *Self-Help*, John Murray, 1859.

Smiles, S., *Character*, John Murray, 1871.

Smiles, S., *Thrift*, John Murray, 1875.

Smiles, S., *Dirty*, John Murray, 1880.

Smiles, S., *Workmen's Earnings*, John Murray, 1876.

Smith, A., *Inquiry into the Nature and Causes of the Wealth of Nations*, Book I, 1776.

Smith, Bonnie G., *Ladies of the Leisure Class – the Bourgeoises of Northern France in the Nineteenth Century*, Princeton University Press, 1981.

Solly, H., *James Woodford, Carpenter and Chartist*, 2 vols, S. Low, Marston, Searle and Rivington, 1883.

Solly, H., *Working Men's Social Clubs and Educational Institutes*, Simpkin, Marshall and Co., 1904.

Solly, H., *These Eighty Years or the Story of an Unfinished Life*, 2 vols, Simpkin, Marshall and Co., 1893.

Spufford, M., *Contrasting Communities: English Villages in the Sixteenth and Seventeenth Centuries*, Cambridge University Press, 1974.

Stanley, L. (ed.), *The Diaries of Hannah Cullwick, Victorian Maidservant*, Virago, 1984.

Stanley, L., 'Feminism and Friendship: two essays on Olive Schreiner', *Studies in Sexual Politics*, no. 8, University of Manchester, December 1985.

Stinchcombe, A., *Theoretical Methods in Social History*, Academic Press, 1978.

Stone, Lawrence, *The Family, Sex and Marriage in England, 1500–1800*, Harper Row, 1980.

Strumingher, Laura A., *Women and the Making of the Working Class: Lyons 1830–1870*, Eden Press Women's Publications, 1979.

Strutt, C. R., *The Strutt Family of Terling 1650–1873*, privately printed, London, 1939.

Stuard, S. M. (ed.), *Women in Medieval Society*, University of Pennsylvania Press, 1976.

Summers, A., 'A home from home – women's philanthropic work in the nineteenth century', in S. Burnman (ed.), *Fit Work for Women*, Crook Helm, 1979.

Summers, A., *Angels and Citizens: British Women as Military Nurses, 1854–1914*, Routledge and Kegan Paul, 1988.

Taylor, B., *Eve and the New Jerusalem: Socialism and Feminism in the Nineteenth Century*, Virago, 1983.

Taylor, P. A., *Some Account of the Taylor Family*, privately published, London, 1875.

Thompson, D., *The Early Chartists*, Macmillan 1971.

Thompson, D., 'Women and nineteenth century radical politics: a lost dimension', in J. Mitchell and A. Oakley (eds), *The Rights and Wrongs of Women*, Penguin, 1976.

Thompson, E. P., *The Making of the English Working Class*, Pelican, 1968.

Thompson, W., *Appeal of one half the Human Race, Women, against the pretensions of the other half, Men, to retain them in political, and thence in civil and domestic slavery*, 1825, (reprinted by Virago, 1983).

Thorn, B., and Yalom, M. (eds), *Rethinking the Family: Some Feminist Questions*, Longman, 1982.

Tilly, L., and Scott J., *Women, Work and Family*, 2nd edn, Methuen, 1987.

Tomlinson, C. (ed.),*Cyclopaedia of Useful Arts*, Virtue and Co., 1866.

Tonna, Co., *The Wrongs of Woman*, M. W. Dodd, 1843–1844, 4 vols.

Trudgill, E., *Madonnas and Magdalens: the Origins and Development of Victorian Sexual Attitudes*, Holmes and Meier, 1976.

Trustram, M., *Marriage and the Victorian Army at Home: the regulation of soldiers' wives*, Cambridge University Press, 1982.

Uglow, J., 'Josephine Butler: from sympathy to theory', in D. Spender (ed.), *Feminist Theorists*, The Women's Press, 1983.

Unwin, G., *The Guilds and Companies of London*, 4th edn, Cass, 1963.

Ure, A., *The Philosophy of Manufacturers*, C. Knight, 1835.

Ure, A., *Dictionary of Arts, Manufactures and Mines*, Longmans and Co., 1878.

Vancouver, *General View of the Agriculture in the County of Essex*, Board of Agriculture, 1795.

Vetterling-Braggin, M. et al., *Feminism and Philosophy*, Totoyar, 1977.

Vicinus, M., *Independent Women: Work and Community for Single Women, 1850–1920*, Virago, 1985.

Walby, S., *Patriarchy at Work: Patriarchal and Capitalist Relations in Employment*, Polity Press, 1987.

Walkowitz, J., *Prostitution and Victorian Society: Women, Class and the State*, Cambridge University Press, 1980.

Ward-Jackson, C. H., *A History of Courtaulds*, Curwen Press, 1941.

Warner, F., *The Silk Industry of the U.K.*, Dranes, 1921.

WEA Eastern District, *Chartism in East Anglia*, WEA, 1951.

Weeks, J., *Sex, Politics and Society*, Longman, 1981.

Weiner, G., 'Harriet Martineau – a reassessment', in D. Spender (ed.), *Feminist Theorists*, The Women's Press, 1983.

Widdowson, F., *Going Up Into the Next Class: Women and Elementary Teacher Training, 1840–1914*, Explorations in Feminism, no. 7, WRRC, 1980.

Williams, Raymond, *The Country and the City*, Chatto and Windus, 1973.

Williams, Raymond, *Keywords: A Vocabulary of Culture and Society*, Oxford University Press, 1976.

Willmott, P. and Young, M., *Family and Kinship in East London*, Penguin, 1955.

Wilson, A., *Finding a Voice: Asian Women in Britain*, Virago, 1979.

Wrigley, E. A., *An Introduction to English Historical Demography*, Weidenfeld and Nicolson, 1966.

Wrigley, E. A., *Nineteenth Century Society: Essays in the Use of Quantitative Methods for the Study of Social Data*, Cambridge University Press, 1972.

Young, A., *Six Weeks Tour of England*, 1769.

Young, A., *A General View of the Agriculture of Essex*, 1795 and 1807.

Young, I., 'Beyond the unhappy, marriage: a critique of the dual systems theory', in L. Sargent (ed.), *Women and Revolution: A Discussion of the Unhappy Marriage of Marxism and Feminism*, South End Press, 1981.

Young, K., Wolkowitz, C., and McCullagh, R. (eds), *Of Marriage and the Market*, CSE Books, 1981.

Zimmeck, M., 'Jobs for the girls: the expansion of clerical work for women, 1850–1914', in A. V. John (ed.), *Unequal Opportunities: Women's Employment in England, 1800–1918*, Basil Blackwell, 1986, pp. 53–78.

PERIODICALS

Abram, A., 'Women traders in medieval London', *Economic Journal*, XXVI, 1916, p. 276.

Anderson, M., 'Smelser revisited: sociological history and the working class family', *Social History*, vol. 1, no. 3, October 1976.

Anderson, M., 'Review of E. M. Shorter's "The Making of the Modern Family"', *Social History*, vol. 3, no. 1, January 1978.

Bachrach, P. and Baratz, M. S. 'The two faces of power', *American Political Science Review*, 56, 1962, pp. 947–952.

Barrett, M. and McIntosh, M., 'The "Family Wage": some problems for socialists and feminists', *Capital and Class*, no. 11, 1980, pp. 51–72.

Barton, D. M., 'The course of women's wages', *Journal of the Royal Statistical Society*, July 1919, LXXX, ii, p. 508.

Beechey, V., 'Some notes on female wage labour in capitalist production', *Capital and Class*, no. 3, 1977.

Benston, M., 'The political economy of housework', *Monthly Review*, 1969.

Berg, M., 'Responses to machinery in eighteenth century England', *Bulletin of the Journal of the Society for the Study of Labour History*, no. 49, Autumn, 1984.

Berkner, L., 'Rural family organisation in Europe: a problem in comparative history', *Peasant Studies Newsletter*, 1, 1972.

Berkner, L., 'Recent research on the history of the family in Western Europe', *Journal of Marriage and the Family*, 35, 1973, pp. 395–405.

Berkner, L., 'The use and misuse of census data for the historical analysis of family structure', *Journal of Interdisciplinary History*, IV, 1975, p. 721.

Berkner, L., 'The stem family and the development cycle of the peasant household: An eighteenth century example', *American Historical Review*, 1977.

Berkner, L. K. and Shaffer, J. W., 'The joint family in the Nivernais', *Journal of Family History*, III, 1978.

Bowley, A. L., 'Wages between 1860 and 1891', *Journal of the Royal Statistical Society*, 1895.

Brighton Labour Process Group. 'The capitalist labour process', *Capital and Class*, no. 1, Spring 1977.

British Journal of Sociology, Special Issue, 'Sociology and History', XXVII, no. 3, September, 1976.

Bulmer, M., 'Sociology and history: some recent trends', *Sociology*, vol 8, 1974.

Chaytor, M., 'Household and kinship: Ryton in the late sixteenth century and early seventeenth century', *History Workshop Journal*, no. 10, Autumn 1980.

Clapham, J. H., 'The Spitalfields Acts 1773–1824', *Economic Journal*, vol. XXVI, 1916.

Claude-Mathieu, N., 'Homme-culture et femme-nature', *L'Homme*, 13, 1973.

Clawson, M. A., 'Early modern fraternalism and the patriarchal family', in *Feminist Studies*, 6(2), Summer 1980.

Coulson, M., Magas, B. and Wainwright, H., 'The housewife and her labour under capitalism – a critique', *New Left Review*, 89, 1975.

Creighton, C., 'Family, property and relations of production in Western Europe', *Economy and Society*, vol. 9, May 1980.

Crossick, G., 'The labour aristocracy and its values: a study of mid-Victorian Kentish London', *Victorian Studies*, March 1976.

Dale, Marion K., 'The London silkwomen of the fifteenth century', *Economic History Review*, vol. 4, 1932–4.

Davis, N. Z., 'The reasons of misrule: youth groups and charivaris in sixteenth century France', *Past and Present*, no. 50, February 1971.

Davis, N. Z., 'Women in the crafts in sixteenth century Lyons', *Feminist Studies*, 8 (1), Spring 1982.

Davin, A., 'Telegraphists and clerks', *Bulletin of the Journal of the Society for the Study of Labour History*, no. 26, Spring 1973, pp. 7–9.

Demos, J., 'The American family in past time', *American Scholar*, 43, 1974.

Dixon, E., 'Craftwomen in the Livre des Metiers', *Economic Journal*, V, 1895, p. 209.

Demos, J. and Bocock, S. S. (eds), 'Turning points: historical and sociological essays on the family', Supplement to *American Journal of Sociology*, 1978.

Dutton, H. I. and King J. E., 'The limits of paternalism: the cotton tyrants of North Lancashire, 1836–54', *Social History*, 7 (1), 1982.

Fairchilds, C., 'Female sexual attitudes and the rise of illegitimacy', *Journal of Interdisciplinary History*, Spring 1978.

Gallie, W. B., 'Essentially contested concepts', *Proceedings of the Aristotelian Society*, 56, 1955–6, pp. 167–98.

Gardiner, J., 'Women's domestic labour', *New Left Review*, 89, 1975.

Garnsey, E., 'Women's work and theories of class stratification', *Sociology*, 12 (2), September 1978.

Gillis J. R., 'Affective individualism and the English poor', *Journal of Interdisciplinary History*, Summer 1979.

Gittins, D., 'Inside and outside marriage', *Feminist Review*, 14, Summer 1983.

Goubert, P., 'Family and province: a contribution to the knowledge of family structures in early modern France', *Journal of Family History*, II, 1977.

Gray, R., 'Styles of life, the "labour aristocracy" and class relations in later nineteenth century Edinburgh"', *International Review of Social History*, 18, 1973.

Greg, W. R., 'Why are women redundant?', *National Review*, 14, 1862, pp. 434–60.

Hareven, Tamara K., 'The family as process: the historical study of the family life cycle', *Journal of Social History*, 7, 1974.

Hartmann, H., 'The unhappy marriage of Marxism and feminism: towards a more progressive union', *Capital and Class*, no. 8, Summer 1979.

Hartwell, R. M., 'The rising standard of living in England 1800–1850', *Economic History Review*, 2nd series, XIII, April 1961.

Hertz, G. B., 'The English silk industry in the eighteenth century', *English Historical Review*, XXIV, 1909, p. 710.

Himmelweit, S. and Mohun, S., 'Domestic labour and capital', *Cambridge Journal of Economics*, 1, 1977.

Hobsbawn, E. J., 'The British standard of living, 1790–1850', *Economic History Review*, August 1956.

Honegger, I. E., 'Looms for the silk and rayon industries: with reference to their structure and performance', *Journal of the Textile Institute*, 25, 1934, p. 116.

Hopkins, A. E., 'Strawplaiting', *Essex Countryside*, Spring 1955.

Hostettler E., 'Gourlay Steel and the sexual division of labour', *History Workshop Journal*, no. 4, Autumn, 1977.

Humphries, J., 'Class struggle and the resistance of the working class family', *Cambridge Journal of Economics*, I, (3), 1977.

Humphries, J., 'The working class family, women's liberation and class struggle: the case of nineteenth century British history', *Review of Radical Political Economy*, Autumn 1977.

Hutchins, B. L., 'Statistics of women's life and employment', *Journal of the Royal Statistical Society*, LXXII, part II, June 1909.

Jones, D., 'Women and Chartism', *History*, 68, February 1983.

Joyce, Patrick, 'The factory politics of Lancashire in the later nineteenth century', *The Historical Journal*, 18 (3), 1975.

Kelly, J., 'The doubled vision of feminist theory: a postscript to the "Women and Power" Conference, *Feminist Studies*, 5, (1), Spring 1979, pp. 221–2.

Land, Hilary, 'The family wage', *Feminist Review*, 6, 1980.

Le Mouvement Sociale, 'Paternalisme d'hier et aujourd'hui', 144, Juillet–Septembre, 1988.

Lerner G., 'Politics and Culture in Women's History: A Symposium', *Feminist Studies*, 6, 1980, pp. 52–3.

L'Esperance, Jean, 'Woman's mission to woman: Explorations in the operation of the double standard and female solidarity in nineteenth century England', *Social History – Historie Sociale*, 1979.

Lewis, J., 'The debate on sex and class', *New Left Review*, 149, January–February 1985, pp. 108–20.

Lown, J., 'Review of *Family Time and Industrial Time* by T. Hareven', *Feminist Review*, Summer 1983, 14, pp. 104–9.

Lown, J., ' "Père plutôt que maître . . . ": le paternalisme à l'usine dans l'industrie de la soie à Halstead au XIXe siècle', *Le Mouvement Social*, 144, Juillet–Septembre, 1988. pp 51–70.

MacFarlane, A., 'Review of Stone, *Family, sex and marriage in England, 1500–1800, History and Theory*, XVIII, 1979.

Marglin, S., 'What do bosses do? The origins and functions of hierarchy in capitalist production', *Review of Radical Political Economics*, 6 (2), Summer 1974.

Medick, H., 'The proto-industrial family economy: The structural function of household and family during the transition from peasant society to industrial capitalism', *Social History*, October 1976.

Mendels, F., 'Proto-industrialisation: the first phase of the process of industrialisation', *Journal of Economic History*, xxxii, 1972.

Merryweather, M.,'Cottage Habitations', *English Woman's Journal*, vol. IV, 1 October 1859.

Molyneux, M., 'Beyond the domestic labour debate', *New Left Review*, 116, 1979.

Musson, A. E., 'Review of Smelser's "Social change in the industrial revolution"', *Journal of Social History*, XX (2), 1960.

Newby, H., 'The deferential dialectic', *Comparative Studies in Sociology and History*, 17, (2), April 1975.

Oren, L., 'The welfare of women in labouring families: England 1860–1950', *Feminist Studies*, Winter 1973.

Ortner, S., 'Is female to male as nature is to culture?', in M. Rosaldo and L. Lamphere (eds), *Woman, Culture and Society*, Stanford University Press, 1974.

Parkes, B. R., 'The balance of public opinion in regard to woman's work', *English Woman's Journal*, IX, July 1862.

Phillips, A., and Taylor, B., 'Sex and skill: notes towards a feminist economics', *Feminist Review*, no. 6, 1980.

Phillips, R., 'Women and family breakdown in eighteenth century France', *Social History*, May 1976.

Pilgrim, J. E., 'The rise of the "new draperies" in Essex, *University of Birmingham Historical Journal*, no. 7, 1959.

Pleck, E. H., 'Two worlds in one: work and family', *Journal of Social History*, 10 (2), Winter 1976.

Pleck, E. H., 'Review of Shorter, "The making of the modern family"', *Canadian Newsletter of Research on Women*, 7, 1978, p. 74.

Pollard, S.,'Factory discipline in the industrial revolution', *Economic History Review*, 2nd series, XVI (2), December 1963.

Rapp, R., Ross, E. and Bridenthal, R., 'Examining family history', *Feminist Studies*, 5 (1), Spring 1979.

Richards, E., 'Women in the British economy since about 1700: an interpretation', *History*, LIX, October 1974.

Roberts, M., 'Sickles and scythes: Women's work and men's work at harvest time', *History Workshop Journal*, no. 7, Spring 1979.

Rosaldo, M. Z., 'The use and abuse of anthropology: reflections on feminism and cross-cultural understanding', *Signs*, 5 (3), Spring 1980.

Rose, R. W., 'The art of strawplaiting in Essex', *Essex Countryside*, April 1965.

Rushton, P., 'Marxism, domestic labour and the capitalist economy: a note on recent discussions', in C. Harris, 'The sociology of the family', *Cambridge Journal of Economics*, 1 (2), 1977.

Samuel, R., 'The workshop of the world: steam power and hand technology in mid-Victorian Britain', *History Workshop Journal*, no. 3, Spring 1977;

Scott, J., and Tilly, L., 'Women's work and the family in nineteenth century Europe', *Comparative Studies in Society and History*, January 1975.

Smith-Rosenberg, C., 'The female world of love and ritual: relations between women in nineteenth century America', *Signs*, 1, 1975, pp. 1–29.

Stedman Jones, G., 'From historical sociology to a theoretical history', *British Journal of Sociology*, September 1976.

Summers, A. 'Ladies and nurses in the Crimean War', *History Workshop Journal*, 16, 1983, pp. 33–56.

Sussman, G. D., 'The end of the wet-nursing business in France 1874–1914', *Journal of Family History*, 11, 1977.

Taylor, B., '"The men are as bad as their masters . . .": socialism, feminism and sexual antagonism in the London tailoring trade in the early 1830s', *Feminist Studies*, 5 (1), Spring 1979.

Thomas, Keith, 'The double standard', *Journal of the History of Ideas*, 20, 1959.

Thompson, E. P., 'Time, work-discipline and industrial capitalism', *Past and Present*, no. 38, 1967.

Thompson, E. P., '"Rough music": Le Charivari Anglais', *Annales Economies Societes Civilisation*, 27, March/April 1972.

Thompson, E. P., 'Under the same rooftree', *Time Literary Supplement*, 4th May 1973.

Thompson, E P., 'Anthropology and the discipline of historical context', *Midland History* I, 3, Spring 1973.

Thompson, E. P., 'Happy families', *Radical History Review*, Spring/Summer 1979.

Tilly, L. A., 'Individual lives and family strategies in the French proletariat', *Journal of Family History*, IV, 1979.

Tilly, L. and Scott, J., 'Women, work and the family in nineteenth century Europe', *Comparative Studies in Society and History*, 17, 1975.

Tilly, L., Scott, J. and Cohen, M., 'Women's work and European fertility patterns', *Journal of Interdisciplinary History*, VI, (3), Winter 1976.

Tomes, N., '"A Torrent of Abuse": crimes of violence between working class men and women in London, 1840–58', *Journal of Social History*, 11, 1978, pp. 323–45.

Vann, R. T., 'Review of Shorter, "The making of the modern family"', *Journal of Family History*, I, 1976.

Weinstock, M., 'Portrait of an eighteenth century Sherborne silk mill owner', *Studies in Dorset History*, 1953.

Wheaton, R., 'Family and kinship in Western Europe: the problem of the joint family household', *Journal of Interdisciplinary History*, V (4), Spring 1975.

Work and Leisure, vol, V, June 1880.

Wrigley, E. A., 'A simple model of London's importance in changing English society and economy, 1650–1750', *Past and Present*, no. 37, 1967.

Wrigley, E. A., 'Mortality in pre-industrial England: the example of Colyton, Devon, over three centuries', *Daedalus*, XCIII, (2), 1968.

CONFERENCE AND SEMINAR PAPERS

Anderson, M., 'Family, work and household in Britain, 1857–1981', Paper given at University of Essex, Social History Seminar, November 1981.

Conference of Socialist Economists, 'The labour process and class strategies', London Conference of Socialist Economics, Stage One, 1976.

Conference of Socialist Economists, 'On the political economy of women', London Conference of Socialist Economics, 1976.

Davidoff, L., 'Power as an "essentially contested concept": can it be of use to feminist historians?', International Women's History Conference, University of Maryland, November 1977.

Davidoff, L., with Hall, C., 'Marriages and enterprise: The English middle class in town and countryside 1780–1850', Anglo-American Historical Association paper, July 1982.

Friedman, S., 'The Marxist paradigm: radical feminist theorists compared', BSA Conference paper, Gender and Society, April 1982.

Gamarnikow, E., 'Women's re-entry into health care: medical reactions to the Nightingale reforms', BSA Conference paper, Gender and Society, University of Manchester, April 1982.

Gillis, J. R., 'Resort to common law marriage in England and Wales, 1700–1850', Law and Human Relations, Past and Present Socialism Conference, July 1980.

Kelly-Gadol, J., 'History and the social relations of the sexes', Barnard College Women's Centre Conference paper, 'The scholar and the feminist II: toward a new criteria of relevance', April 1975.

Rubery, J. and Wilkinson, F., 'Notes on the nature of the labour proess in the secondary sector', Low Pay and Labour Markets: Segmentation conference papers, Cambridge 1979.

Siltanen, J., and Stanworth, M., 'The politics of public man and private woman', BSA National Conference, 'Beyond the fringe: the periphery of industrial society', April 1983.

UNPUBLISHED THESES

Abendstern, M., 'Expression and Control, a study of working class leisure and gender 1918–1939: a case study of Rochdale using oral history methods', PhD thesis, University of Essex, 1986.

Burley, K. H., 'The economic development of Essex in the late seventeenth and early eighteenth centuries', PhD thesis, University of London, 1957.

Cunningham, S., 'Changes in the pattern of rural settlement in northern Essex between 1650 and 1850', MA thesis, University of Manchester, 1968.

Dale, Marion, K., 'Women in the textile industry and trade of fifteenth century England', MA thesis, University of London, 1928.

Dupree, M. 'Family structure in the Staffordshire Potteries, 1840–1880', DPhil thesis, Oxford University, 1981.

Herstein, S. R., 'Barbara Leigh Smith Bodichon (1827–1891): a mid-Victorian feminist', PhD thesis, City Uiversity of New York, 1980.

Kussmaul, A., 'Servants in husbandry in early modern England', PhD thesis, University of Toronto, 1978.

Jordan, W. M., 'The silk industry in London, 1760–1830', MA thesis, University of London, 1931.

Wilson, H. C., 'The geography of an industrial enterprise: the Essex mills of Samuel Courtauld and Co. Ltd', MA thesis, Jesus College, Cambridge, 1970.

Worzala, M. C., 'The Langham Place Circle: the beginnings of the organised women's movement in England, 1854–1870', PhD thesis, University of Wisconsin-Madison, 1982.

PARLIAMENTARY PAPERS [listed in date order]

Journals of the House of Commons, Report and appendices of tables relating to the Committee to whom the Petition of the Bailiffs, Wardens, Assistants and Commonality, of the Trade, Act and Mystery of Weavers of London, on behalf of themselves and the Silk Manufacturers of Great Britain, vol. XXX, 10 January 1765–16 September 1766, p. 212.

Census Report 1801, Population Tables and Census.

Two Reports of the Select Committee on Petitons of Ribbon Weavers of Coventry and Leek, Silk Weavers of Macclesfield and Reading, and Silk Manufacturers of Macclesfield, with evidence, 3 parts, 1818.

Evidence before Lords Committee on the Wages of Persons employed in the manufacture of Silk or of Silk mixed with other materials, 5 parts, 1823.

Return of Wages, 1830–86, LXXXIX, 1887 (C-5172).

Report of the Select Committee on the Present State of the Silk Trade and the Legislative Measures Advisable in order to Promote it, with evidence, vol. XIX, 1831–2.

Report on Manufactures, Commerce and Shipping, 1833, VI.

Reports on Handloom Weavers' Petition, 1834, X; 1835 XIII.

A Return of the Number of Power Looms used in Factories in the Manufacture of Woollen, Cotton, Silk and Linen respectively, House of Commons Acts and Papers, 1836, XLV.

Return of Mills and Factories, 1838.

Reports from Commissioners . . . on the State of the Handloom Weavers: 1839, XLIII; 1840, XX, XXIII, XXIV; 1841, X.

Children's Employment Commission, appendix A; Instructions from the Central Board of the Children's Employment Commission to the Sub-Commissioners, House of Commons, 1842, CXIV.

Hansard, 15 March 1844; 3rd series, 142, 1856.

Factory Inspectors' Reports: 1842, XXII; 1849, XXII; 1866, XXIV; 1868/9, XIV; 1871, XIV; 1888, XXVI; 1893, XVII.

Return of Total Number of Persons Employed in Silk Factories, 1847, XLVI.

Board of Trade Accounts and Papers 10, 1850, XLII, Returns of the Number of Cotton, Woollen, Worsted, Flax, and Silk Factories.

G. B. Command Papers, 1851 Census, Ages, Civil Condition . . . vol. I, 1852–3, Occupations.

G. B. Command Papers, 1861 and 1871 Census, Ages, Civil Condition . . . Census Reports: 1861; 1863; 1871; 1881; 1891.

Medical Officer Reports, 1864, vol. XXVIII.

Report on Housing, 1867.

First Report of the Commissioners on the Employment of Children, Young Persons and Women in Agriculture, 1867–8 (4068.1), XVII.

Richmond Commission on Agriculture, 1882.

Report of the Livery Companies Commission, 1884.

Wage Census: 1889, LXX (C-5807); 1890, LXVII (C-6161); 1891, LXXVIII (C-6455); 1892, LXVIII (C-6715); General Report LXXXIII, Part II of 1893 (C-6889).

Labour Commission 1894: Summary by Mr Little of the Commission on Employment of Women and Children.

Labour Department, Changes in the Rates of Wages and Hours of Labour: 1st Report 1893 (C-7567); 2nd Report 1894 (C-8075); 3rd Report 1895 (C-8374); 4th Report 1896 (C-8444); 5th Report 1897 (C-8975).

Royal Commission on Labour: Appendix on the Employment of Women 1893–4, XXXVII, i.

Royal Commission: Statistics of Employment of Women and Girls, 1894, LXXXI, ii.

NEWSPAPERS, DIRECTORIES AND JOURNALS

Chelmsford Chronicle, April–May 1772; 2 April 1784; 28 January 1881.

Chelmsford Gazette, 12 September 1823.

Daily News, 2 July 1846.

English Woman's Journal, 1859–1866.

Essex Almanac, 1889.

Essex County Standard, 27 October 1897; 18 June 1898; 15 July 1899.

Essex Herald, 30 June 1846.

Essex Independent, 12 November 1836.

Essex Review, XLVII, 1840.

Halstead Gazette, January 1860; March 1860; May 1860; September 1860; April 1861; September 1921; August 1936.

Halstead Times, April 1861, May 1861; June 1861; July 1861.

Kelly's Directories of Essex, 1855; 1862; 1866; 1870; 1874; 1878; 1882.

Mechanics Magazine, vol. I, 1823–4.

Pigot and Company, *Essex Directories*, 1827 and 1835.

Saturday Review, 19 July 1857.

The Shield, 9 May 1870.

Victoria County History of Essex, volumes I and II, 1907.

Appendix 1
Processes and Technical Terms used in Silk Manufacture

There are four main stages in the production of silk after the skeins of raw silk reach the silk throwster or manufacturer. Although the means by which each stage was effected have changed over time, the basic processes have remained the same since the beginning of the industry.

WINDING, DRAWING, THROWING AND DOUBLING

The skeins of raw silk are first subjected to a process called winding. Here the thread is simply wound off from large reels on to bobbins. Any broken threads are joined together again by hand. Simple wooden hand-operated equipment was used for this stage for many years. The process was speeded up considerably by the use of power-driven iron machinery in the nineteenth century.

After being wound on to bobbins, the silk is cleaned by being drawn through cleaning devices on a drawing engine where it is wound on to another set of bobbins ready for throwing.

Throwing is equivalent to spinning in wool and cotton manufacture, but because silk is a long and continuous thread rather than a series of short lengths, it is not spun but twisted. The precise procedure followed at this stage varies according to the type of silk yarn required. The basic throwing action consists of revolving two sets of bobbins at different speeds. The bobbin containing the silk to be thrown is attached to a spindle at the top of which is fastened a flyer. The silk passes from the bobbin through the eye of the flyer which has a rotating action, thus inserting a twist into the yarn. The amount of twist depends upon the relative speeds of the two bobbins, one feeding the silk to be thrown and the other taking it up after the flyer has twisted it.

This conversion of the silk into a single twisted thread produces yarn which is known as 'singles'. Unthrown silk is called 'dumb' and yarn in the form of a single thread taken directly from winding and cleaning without being throw is known as 'dumb singles'.   Some yarn is converted into 'tram' ready for use as the weft threads. This is produced on a 'doubling' machine which winds together on to a single bobbin two or more 'dumb singles'. And the final form in which yarn is produced is called 'organzine', which is the strongest of all types of yarn and used for the warp threads. To produce this, two or more 'dumb singles' are twisted in one direction, doubled, and then twisted again in the opposite direction like a rope.

The amount of twist in thrown silks is measured in terms of twist per inch. Ten to thirty twists per inch yields a yarn with a low throw, while thirty to seventy or more yields a high throw. Yarns with a very high twist are known as 'crapes'.

All the procedures described for this throwing stage of the operation were conducted by hand on simple machinery for many centuries. Even Thomas Lombe's mill, frequently heralded as the first factory in this country, contained completely hand-operated machinery for throwing. It was not until the nineteenth century that, first water power and later steam power (followed eventually by gas and electricity) were used to drive the machinery.

WARPING, SPOOLING AND WEAVING

Warping consists of preparing the warp for the loom. This is done by winding the prepared organzine yarn on to cylindrical rolls called beams which are placed at either end of the loom and which generally have iron heads on them for holding the ropes that guide the tension of the woven cloth. The beams were generally made of wood, whether they were being used for hand looms or power looms.

Spooling is the procedure by which tram yarn is wound from bobbins on to small wooden cylinders that are placed into spindles inside the shuttles.

The shuttles are then used by the weavers in the process of operating the looms which involves passing the shuttle back and forth across the warp threads, forming the weft, and weaving a continuous length of cloth. Handlooms were used for many centuries and continued in use throughout most of the nineteenth century, by which time, however, they were gradually being outnumbered by power looms. Different types of loom have been used for producing different types of silk fabric. In 1801, for example, the Jacquard loom was invented for the production of more elaborate designs. This loom required another attendant, apart from the weaver, usually known as a 'draw boy', who operated the mechanism holding the cards at the top of the loom which determined the pattern of the woven fabric. Looms of a fairly simple construction, based on the Hattersley loom used extensively in the North of England, were mainly used in the weaving of crape.

The basic art of weaving varies very little, however, whatever material is being produced. The main difference between looms used in silk weaving and those used in the weaving of woollen fabrics is that the latter are generally larger and heavier because of the stronger and more durable nature of the yarn.

DYEING

The stage at which dyeing takes place varies. Sometimes the yarn is dyed before it has been woven, and sometimes dyeing takes place 'in the piece' after the fabric has been removed from the loom. From the sixteenth century, various types of metallic salts were mainly used for dyeing, since they also added weight to the silk.

FINISHING

This procedure is the final stage before the fabric leaves the manufacturer and is the same for silk as in the cotton and wool trade. Here, the cloth is taken from the looms or from the dyeing room, examined for flaws, prepared, measured into lengths and pressed ready for transporting to warehouses or retailers.

One procedure that did not take place in the production of crape was degumming. This is where the gum on the raw silk is boiled off so as to produce what is known as 'soft silk'. This was for the production of fancy goods like velvets and brocades which were mainly woven on handlooms. Silk with the gum still in it was known as 'hard silk' and it was this type of silk which was used in the production of the black mourning crape in Courtauld's mills.

GLOSSARY

There follows a short glossary of some of the main terms used in the various processes involved in silk manufacture:

Beam   a cylindrical wooden roll, with an iron pin at each end, used to wind the finished warp upon.

Beaming   the operation of unwinding a finished warp off from the reel on to a beam.

Bobbin   a cylindrical piece of wood, with a head on each end, bored through to receive an iron pin, used to wind thread upon.

Boiling-off (or degumming)   the removal of the natural gum from silk goods or yarns by boiling in soap and water.

Cut   the length at which a piece of woven cloth is cut off. The most usual length of broad silk cuts is 60 yards and for ribbons, 10 yards.

Doubling machine   machine used to wind two or more ends from two or more bobbins on to one bobbin in order to make a stronger yarn.

Drawing-in (or entering)   the drawing of the warp ends individually through the eyes in the heddles of the harness on the loom.

Dyeing   the colouring of the silk including the boiling-off, weighting and colouring.

End   a term applied to any thread used in textile work, more particularly applied to a warp thread.

Hard silk   silk from which the natural gum has not been removed.

Harness   a mechanism of the loom for causing the warp threads to open in a prearranged manner, consisting of light wooden frames surrounding the warp, equipped with thread, or wire, heddles, running vertically from bottom to top within the frames, and with an eye in the centre of each heddle. There are as many frames as are required by the weave, and a heddle for each warp thread. The alternate rising and falling of the harnesses in the orderly separation of the warp threads, with the weft thread passing in the shuttle between them, creates the weave of the cloth.

Jacquard machine   a machine, named after its French inventor, for raising and lowering the harness threads in a loom, each thread having its individual heddle. It enables figured patterns of a large size to be made as opposed to the very small patterns produced on the ordinary harness loom.

Journeyman/woman   craftsworker who had work put out to him/her by a master in the craft or trade and was responsible for producing the finished piece of work and returning it to the master for an agreed wage.

Organzine   silk specially twisted for use as warp threads. Sixteen turns in one direction and fourteen in the other is the usual amount.

Piece   a length of goods (see Cut).

Plug-winding the winding of tram yarn on to tapered wooden cylinders (usually called spools or sometimes quills) which fit on to spindles in the shuttle ready for making the weft on the loom.

Punching the process of making holes in the cards which determined the pattern of the fabric produced in Jacquard looms.

Reed a series of flat metal blades, or thin wires, arranged like the teeth of a comb, and held in place at both top and bottom, used to keep the ends separate and in their proper places while warping and weaving. The main function is to beat the weft threads into the cloth.

Reeding (or sleying) the operation of putting the warp ends through the reed in their designated order.

Reel a cylindrical frame upon which warps are wound. There is also a reel used for winding skeins from the cocoons.

Shuttle a wooden, steel-tipped, carrier for the weft yarn, used on the loom to shoot the weft threads into the cloth.

Soft silk thrown silk yarn from which the gum has been boiled off, undyed or dyed.

Throwing the combining and twisting of raw silk threads in various ways.

Tram raw silk threads doubled together and twisted, usually about two to five turns per inch, used for the weft threads.

Twisting the uniting of the threads of a new warp to those of one woven out, by twisting the threads together. Also applied to the putting in of the second-time twist in throwing.

Warp the threads running lengthwise in the cloth.

Warping the process of making a warp.

Waste cuttings, pickings, damaged yarn, etc., produced during the various processes of textile manufacture.

Waster a worker whose task it was to collect the waste silk produced during the preparatory processes of silk production and wind it on to bobbins.

Weft (or filling) the threads running crosswise in the cloth.

Winding the process of transferring yarn from skeins on to bobbins.

Appendix 2
Note on Measurements and Currency

MEASURES OF LENGTH

Cloth was formerly measured by the ell (45 inches) or the yard (36 inches). One metre equals 39 inches.

CURRENCY VALUES

The pound sterling prior to decimalization in 1971 was divided into shillings and pence. There were 12 pence (d) in one shilling (s or /-) and 20 shillings in one pound (£). Thus, for example, 22/6d equals one pound, two shillings and six pence. One shilling equals 5 new pence (p) in decimal currency.

Index

Index by Isobel McLean